'I read Satadru Sen's brilliant study of Benoy Kumar Sarkar with keen interest and great benefit. Sen explores the writings and activities of an immensely difficult political thinker. He develops a sensitive and rich critique of a cosmopolitan, modernist right-wing nationalist whose nationalism incorporated multiple layers: Bengali, Indian and anti-British, cohabiting with Western nationalisms and the world. Sen disentangles each strand and unearths the many layers in his discourse with admirable suppleness and precision. He writes with immense lucidity about extremely complex themes. An excellent book.'

Sumit Sarkar, Professor of History (retired), University of Delhi

'A bold and stimulating piece of intellectual history. Sen is restoring one of the most fascinating, if neglected, figures of modern Indian history to current academic debates on Indian nationalism and its multifaceted global entanglements. Sen shows how the Bengali intellectual provided intriguing alternatives to the better-known political discourses of his time, occupying an interstitial space between staunch anti-Westernism and a deep admiration for Euro-American technocratic modernity.'

Harald Fischer-Tiné, Professor of Modern Global History, ETH Zürich

'Satadru Sen succeeds brilliantly in explaining Sarkar's complex views and in situating them in their historical and cultural contexts. This is not only a major work on an important but partly-forgotten figure, but a valuable effort to broaden and complicate the history of Indian nationalism.'

Chandak Sengoopta, Professor of History, University of London

'Here, at last, is a book on the enigmatic Benoy Kumar Sarkar with which it is well worth arguing. Sarkar emerges from Satadru Sen's engaging account not as a giant cardboard cut-out figure, but as a complex thinker of nevertheless gigantic proportions.'

Benjamin Zachariah, University of Heidelberg

Benoy Kumar Sarkar

This book explores the life and times of the pioneering Indian sociologist Benoy Kumar Sarkar. It locates him simultaneously in the intellectual history of India and the political history of the world in the twentieth century. It focuses on the development and implications of Sarkar's thinking on race, gender, governance and nationhood in a changing context.

A penetrating portrait of Sarkar and his age, this book will be of great interest to scholars and researchers of modern Indian history, sociology and politics.

Satadru Sen is Associate Professor of South Asian History at the City University of New York. He is the author of *Savagery and Colonialism in the Indian Ocean: Power, Pleasure and the Andaman Islanders* (2010), and other works on the history of discipline and race in modern India.

Pathfinders

Series Editor: **Dilip M. Menon**
Professor of History and Mellon Chair in Indian Studies, University of the Witwatersrand, Johannesburg

This series explores the intellectual history of South Asia through the lives and ideas of significant individuals within a historical context. These 'pathfinders' are seen to represent a break with existing traditions, canons and inherited histories. In fact, even the idea of South Asia with its constituent regions and linguistic and religious divisions may be thrown into crisis as we explore the idea of territory as generated by thought. It is not cartographic limits that determine thinking but the imagining of elective affinities across space, time and borders. These thinkers are necessarily cosmopolitan and engage with a miscegenation of ideas that recasts existing notions of schools of thinking, of the archive for a history of ideas and indeed of the very notion of national and regional limits to intellectual activity. The books in this series try to think beyond the limited frameworks of colonialism and nationalism for the modern period and more generally of histories of societies that are told through the prism of the state, its institutions and ideologies. These slim volumes written by leading scholars are intended for the intelligent layperson and expert alike, and written in an accessible, lively and authoritative prose. Through telling the lives of celebrated names and lesser-known ones in context, this series will expand the repertoire of ideas and individuals that have shaped the history and culture of South Asia.

Also in the Series

Javed Majeed
Muhammad Iqbal: Islam, Aesthetics and Postcolonialism
ISBN: 978-0-415-44578-8

Lakshmi Subramanian
Veena Dhanammal: The Making of a Legend
ISBN: 978-0-415-44611-2

Kris Manjapra
M. N. Roy: Marxism and Colonial Cosmopolitanism
ISBN: 978-0-415-44603-7

Savithri Preetha Nair
Raja Serfoji II: Science, Medicine and Enlightenment in Tanjore
ISBN: 978-0-415-53504-5

Brian A. Hatcher
Vidyasagar: The Life and After-life of an Eminent Indian
ISBN: 978-0-415-73630-5

Harald Fischer-Tiné
Shyamji Krishnavarma: Sanskrit, Sociology and Anti-Imperialism
ISBN: 978-0-415-44554-2

Benoy Kumar Sarkar
Restoring the nation to the world

Satadru Sen

NEW DELHI LONDON NEW YORK

First published 2015
by Routledge
1 Jai Singh Road, New Delhi 110001, India

by Routledge
2 Park Square, Milton Park, Abingdon, Oxon OX14 4RN

and by Routledge
711 Third Avenue, New York, NY 10017

Routledge is an imprint of the Taylor & Francis Group, an informa business

© 2015 Satadru Sen

The right of Satadru Sen to be identified as author of this work has been asserted in accordance with sections 77 and 78 of the Copyright, Designs and Patents Act 1988.

All rights reserved. No part of this book may be reprinted or reproduced or utilised in any form or by any electronic, mechanical, or other means, now known or hereafter invented, including photocopying and recording, or in any information storage or retrieval system, without permission in writing from the publishers.

Trademark notice: Product or corporate names may be trademarks or registered trademarks, and are used only for identification and explanation without intent to infringe.

British Library Cataloguing-in-Publication Data
A catalogue record for this book is available from the British Library

Library of Congress Cataloging-in-Publication Data
A catalog record has been requested for this book.

ISBN: 978-1-138-82250-4 (pbk)
ISBN: 978-1-315-68494-9 (ebk)

Typeset in Gentium Basic
by ApexCovantage, LLC

For Leila Noor, the late-afternoon light

Contents

Acknowledgements   xi

   Introduction   1
1   An Indian Race   49
2   Wars of the Emasculated   95
3   A Romance of the State   132
   Conclusion   183

Selected Bibliography   189
Index   203

Acknowledgements

I am indebted to the following colleagues and friends who read drafts of the manuscript, entertained my questions and ruminations, loaned me books and papers, and in all cases provided feedback, advice and encouragement: Ian Petrie, Julia Sneeringer, Harald Fischer-Tiné, Benjamin Zachariah, Sumit Sarkar, Chandak Sengoopta, Dina Siddiqi, Peter Connolly-Smith, Bholanath Bandyopadhyay, and of course, Dilip Menon. I am thankful also to Amanda, Mira and Leila for accepting gracefully the absences and diversions that went into the writing of this book, at a particularly important time in their lives.

Introduction

This book is not a biography of Benoy Kumar Sarkar. Biographies of Sarkar—perhaps the most prominent Indian social scientist of the period before independence—already exist.[1] It is, rather, an attempt to examine him as a man from a particular moment in the history of modern India and the modern world, when the certainties of liberalism and empire were confronted by their own bastard offspring: anticolonial agitation, runaway competition, world wars, fascism, revolution in Russia, the devolution of British power in India, and eventually, partitioned sovereignty. Sarkar did not simply 'reflect' his moment. He was a notoriously contrarian thinker who was, in critical ways, 'out of step' with the nationalist mainstream of contemporary India. For that very reason, however, Sarkar gives us glimpses into alternative possibilities of thinking and being: not alternative modernities in S.N. Eisenstadt's sense of the expression,[2] but fluid, strategic and tactical postures of modern citizenship that have been partially lost after 1947. He is a reminder of the contested nature of the liberal imaginary of the state and the Romantic imaginary of nationhood in India in the crucial decades before independence, when the condition of freedom was both imminent and elusive.[3] Sarkar gives us Indias that might have been, as well as the India that came to be.

By way of biography, it should suffice to note that Sarkar emerged from the district town of Malda and swadeshi-era Bengal, with its agendas of mass mobilisation and economic self-sufficiency, its Hindu-inflected rhetoric of militant nationhood, and its politics of frustration with peasants, Muslims and Moderates.[4] In 1901, he entered Calcutta University as a precocious 13-year-old. After the partition of 1905, he plunged into National Education, which sought simultaneously to replace and replicate colonial agendas of transformation by creating an autonomous pedagogical structure that was 'racially appropriate' but not racist: excavating the place of India in the ancient world, and generating the vocational, technological and moral bases of an industrial-capitalist future.[5] A much-travelled man, he lectured and published in German, Italian and French in addition to English and Bengali, spoke some Czech, experimented with new methods of teaching Sanskrit, and left many admiring colleagues when he died in Washington in 1949.[6] Sarkar developed quickly into a prolific writer on Indian nationhood, culture and history. He also became a 'China expert' and a theorist of Pan-Asian solidarity,[7] and while this was undergirded by what Prasenjit Duara has characterised as a search for alternatives to the European/Christian bases of 'civilisation', it neither rejected the Enlightenment nor invested in 'Asian spirituality'.[8] In a contentious intellectual and ideological setting that included Bhudeb Mukhopadhyay and Bankim, Gandhi and Savarkar, Sarkar articulated a concept of the Indian people that drew from cosmopolitan as well as Völkisch imperatives, seeking to negotiate Darwin and Gobineau on the one hand and Manu and the Mughals on the other, with Nietzsche and Mill mediating, as it were. The tensions within and around those boundaries of Indianness are still with us.

The implications, however, are not narrowly Indian. They touch upon a wider problem of producing postcolonial subjectivity (in others). Musing recently on the difficulty of reconciling identity and individuality, Kwame Appiah called for a liberal universalism based upon two related mentalities, both of which must be acquired. One is an awareness of the historically determined nature of cultural difference. The other is a recognition of the narrative—including history—and its internal logic as a shared characteristic of humanity: people can grasp each other's stories. Sarkar, who desired both individuality and identity, would have agreed. The milk begins to curdle with the logistics of the grasping. Appiah quotes Michael Ignatieff: 'Human rights is the only universally available moral vernacular that validate the claims of women and children against the oppression they experience in patriarchal and tribal societies'.[9] The elision of other vernaculars reflects Ignatieff's neo-conservative turn, and Appiah's approval points towards a *necessity* of violence embedded within liberal-pedagogical experiments. Two forms of liberalism can be derived from *On Liberty*, Appiah reminds us: one that envisions the state ensuring only nonencroachment upon the freedoms of others and another that gives the state a pedagogical role in helping individuals realise their identities.[10] In the state emerging from the colony, the latter vision predominated, and Sarkar articulated the nature of the 'help'. The state must teach an efficiency that *made* the individual and the collective, and Indians had far to go: '31 Bengalis = 1 German', he calculated ruefully in 1929.[11]

Sarkar's work has not escaped the attention of historians of modern India. He makes tantalising appearances in recent work on Pan-Asianism by Harald Fischer-Tiné and Pankaj Mishra, in Benjamin Zachariah's writings on fascism, and Andrew Sartori's remarks on 'Bengali Germanism'.[12] Bholanath Bandyopadhyay, Giuseppe Flora and Manu Goswami have made more sustained studies. Bandyopadhyay's study is largely expository, and Flora's dissertation exhaustive but theoretically undercooked. Curiously pre-Said, pre-Foucault and pre-Subalternist, unconcerned with race or gender, Flora's study deals with Sarkar's work on its own terms without fully taking the terms apart, oversimplifying Sarkar's status as an anti-Western indigenist.[13] Goswami is more perceptive, arguing that colonial internationalisms like Sarkar's should not be trapped within national narratives that culminate in sovereign states.[14] The problem with Goswami's analysis is an excessive separation between Sarkar's world and its local utility, which is precisely that culmination. Although he recognised both internal and external constraints on national sovereignty,[15] the militarised nation-state and not a radically reordered world was the keystone of Sarkar's postcolonial Utopia.[16] Within those limits, however, he was able to reimagine political Selves and Others in ways that both maintained and destabilised the meanings of community in the modern world.

Sarkar matters not because his scholarship has stood 'the test of time': much of it is dated. That, of course, is where its value lies. Sarkar represents a moment in the intellectual history of Indian modernity when three broad cultural and political projects came together for many—but not all—nationalists. One was the project of opposing, rather than reinforcing, Orientalist narratives of difference. For a man steeped in the social sciences, Sarkar was highly sensitive to the tendency of modern scholarship to humiliate the objects of its attention, and of his kinship with the humiliated. The intellectual self that he asserted amplified an accusation of thwarted racial equality, and the Romantic nationalist's sense of being denied his place in the sun.[17] The second was the imperative of restoring the nation to the world. India had become isolated from world-history, Sarkar perceived, and imperialism had reinforced that ghettoisation with its orders of politics and knowledge.[18] The task of the nationalist male was to break out of the ghetto, which both reflected and exacerbated his emasculation. The third, and most basic, was a transformation at the level of the individual, to produce the Indian as a fundamentally new creature, precisely aware of his location in the historical world and capable of responding to that world with reasoned, calibrated and selfless violence. These considerations shaped Sarkar's vision of the kind of state that was most conducive to racial dignity, imbuing it with an obsessive militarism and an acceptance of coercion that frequently overrode other concerns, such as rights, legality and anti-colonialism itself. Only when there is a clear threat to nation, state and society will I accept infringements upon the rights of the individual, Sarkar insisted during the suppression of the Quit India Movement, but the 'threat' was built into his vision of Indian freedom.[19] The pursuit of racial equality and democracy became a 'right-wing' project not entirely compatible with the pursuit of justice. When we look closely at Sarkar, we glimpse this vision of justice in its 'naturalness' and its contrivances.

The chapters in this volume examine Sarkar's overlapping engagements with the idea of race, the idea of Japan, and the idea of the state. These ideas were not adrift in some ether of intellectual history, but mired in everyday experiences of domination and defiance. Rather than recapitulate each chapter individually in this introduction, it is more useful to survey the wider conflicts in which Sarkar's particular fights are imbedded: the tension between national and international identities, the politics of knowledge and difference, the uses of history in articulating the purposeful political community and the Bengali predicament in India.

The Patriot's World

By the end of the Great War, Sarkar's thinking contained a noticeable tension between nationalism and 'internationalism'. He would rail against a global 'albinocracy', but insist that he was a member of a global, mobile and horizontal community of scholars and experts who would 'liberate' the social sciences from the clutches of nationalists.[20] He could be downright sacrilegious: soon after returning to India in 1925 after a decade in Europe, America and East Asia, he declared that Indian nationhood was fictional and unity unimportant.[21] What mattered, he said, was independence, and multiple independent Indian states would be acceptable. The remarks were not well-received by the patriotic: Sarkar seemed to be denying the basic assumptions of Congress-led nationalist agitation and echoing the colonial discourse of Indian unfitness for freedom.[22] Closely related to this perception was the anxiety generated by Sarkar's cosmopolitan enthusiasms, which, even more than those of Rabindranath Tagore, seemed to conflict with his national loyalties.[23] He had evidently been 'decultured' or exiled from his authentic self, as Ashis Nandy might say.[24] (Fear of the 'rootless cosmopolitan' is not felt by nationalists alone.)

Sarkar was unrepentant: cultural authenticity was a trap, he represented a new vanguard that he called 'Young India', and his critics were obsolete.[25] He was, moreover, not remotely hostile to Indian unity. He had long been willing to straddle civilisational, geographic, racial and state-centric ideals of nationhood, pursuing parity between 'India' and 'Europe'.[26] It allowed him to avoid a wholesale concession of the 'unreal' nature of nations even as he insisted that the precise relationship between the nation and the state necessarily depended upon historical realities. Sarkar vacillated continuously between realism and romance: between a Machiavellian inclination to see politics as inherently amoral and an irrepressible *ressentiment*, in which the perception of having been wronged generates an essentially whole community of grievance.[27] Machiavelli and Nietzsche both undergirded his Indianness. Unified nation-states on the European model, he argued from the mid-1920s onward, needed a level of institutional strength and military power that India simply did not possess. Under the circumstances, unity was unrealistic.[28] Rather than wait a century or more for that reality to change, Sarkar accepted multiple autonomous states, and argued simultaneously for the consolidation and centralisation of a limited number of institutions.[29] He was not so much accepting the colonialist accusation of unfitness as circumventing it by reversing the order of precedence between the nation and the state: unity could come later as an outcome of the pedagogical work of the state. Moreover, his vision—influenced by Renan and Mancini—of a nationhood that expands and recedes, consolidates and fragments, across a geography that is itself demarcated by national will, distinguished between an 'ideal' (unified statehood across the national geography) and a 'residual' (fragmented or atrophied states that retain a residue of the full potential).[30] The nationalist's task was to convert the residue into the ideal.

That vision, obviously, is very much within the mainstream of Indian nationalism: it is a variant of the process by which 'the soul of a nation, long suppressed, finds utterance'.[31] Sarkar and Nehru both insisted upon an extant nation, but also emphasised nation-building as a task. Sarkar's emphasis, however, was more naked than Nehru's. The Indian nation, he believed, was too underdeveloped to be a serious historical agent. The state would have to play that role, and here too weakness cast its shadow, eroding the possibility of unity. We are left with a vision of several weak states that overlap the weak nation. It reflects the tendency of even the biggest Indian jingoists of the late-colonial era to underestimate the Indian potential for 'development'—i.e., independence itself—and to overcompensate. They could not see beyond the colonial horizon, but could fantasise about it, and the fantasies drifted in the direction of coercive governance. Sarkar's self-representation as a 'realist' is relevant here: the bigger the jingo, the greater the 'realism' or sense of weakness. It was inevitably the more militant nationalists, like Sarkar's occasional collaborator Taraknath Das (who also imagined a modest Indian confederation[32]), who obsessively pursued foreign allies.[33]

That 'realism' and its implications are inseparable from a pessimism about the change in circumstances that independence might bring, and how large a change was historically necessary. For the veteran of National Education, rapid industrialisation—being the key to prosperity and power—was basic to justice. With his eye on Germany, Sarkar wanted a re-socialisation of the Indian working class, so that the working man might join the ranks of society's 'creative individuals' instead of remaining a mere labourer. Simultaneously, he argued, industrialists must themselves become technocrats, attuned to the role of technology in world-history. Only then could they function as 'Titans'. The worker, the industrialist and the white-collar professional would then be joined together by the individuality of the workshop, in what Sarkar called 'mistrification' and the basis of democracy.[34] The idea that the 'respectable' should become habituated to manual labour, and that the habit would amount to national regeneration, has an Indian-nationalist pedigree going back to 1882, when Bhudeb Mukhopadhyay exhorted Bengali patriarchs to acquire the tools, skills and mentality of do-it-yourself home-repair.[35] It subsequently became attached to agendas of independence and social justice in swadeshi-era experiments like Satish Chandra Mukherjee's attempt to have industrial workers teach their trades to *bhadralok* youth.[36] (It also has roots in the America of Henry Ford and Booker T. Washington, which was a part of Sarkar's formative soil.[37]) It has a parallel pedigree in the early Gandhi, but whereas Gandhi's vision of labour threatened to dissolve respectability as a concept, Sarkar's did not. For Sarkar, the Czech shoemakers Tomas and Jan Bata, who insisted that executives be able to make shoes (and whose factory in Batanagar Sarkar inaugurated in 1934[38]), best represented Titanic individuality, and Batanagar was a model of the Indian future: the classes were distinct but harmonious, held together by the enlightened managerial state.

The problem was that rapid industrialisation and mistrification were fantasies for the long term.[39] Sarkar envisioned half a million *mistries* in Bengal alone.[40] But when he listed his Titans of industry in 1949, he did not include a single Indian, although he did include Bata.[41] The effective (mistrified) population of India was tiny, he wrote in 1932: much smaller than Britain's.[42] In 1944–45, the situation had only slightly improved. He was proud of his role in the creation of the engineering college at Jadavpur, and imagined hundreds of technical and vocational schools that, in conjunction with the factory floor, would produce a nation of technician-entrepreneurs where there were only lawyers. Yet in Bengal, there were barely a hundred engineering graduates that he could point to.[43] That indicates the nature of his circumspection about the Indian future: the paucity of individuals who recognised and valued the transformational potential of the historical moment was not going to be made up quickly. Significant cultural changes had to precede industrialisation.[44] Like many contemporary colonial officials, Sarkar understood 'development' not just as economics but as a moral transformation.[45] The didactic-pedagogical state could help the process along, but it could not bypass it. Just as importantly, independence could not wait for the fruits of education. The Western experience was itself proof that literacy is not a prerequisite for self-government, Sarkar insisted, and the decolonised native would lift the 'burden' of education more energetically than the white man.[46] But whereas independence need not wait for education and unity, unity would have to wait until culture had learned its lessons.

Like Orwell, who (in 1941) demanded immediate Dominion status for India but also believed that in the age of tanks and bombers, 'backward, agricultural countries like India . . . can be no more independent than can a cat or a dog', Sarkar imagined that India would remain a peasant society, if not a Balkanised backwater, for the foreseeable future.[47] India would continue to rely on Anglo-American military power for its survival. Britain remained a geopolitical genius and senior ally: a curious conviction in an anti-colonial polemicist, but unsurprising in a colonised intellectual facing the end of the colony. Nirad Chaudhuri was only a more extreme case.[48] Sarkar in the 1940s virtually grovelled before London, singing praises and swearing eternal fealty even after the fall of Singapore.[49] From within his existentially adversarial relationship with Britain, he could not see or acknowledge that his adversary might be anything less than formidable and permanent. Sarkar therefore imagined continuity: a new trusteeship in which nationalists would emphasise institution-building and the acquisition of foreign knowledge within a state of limited sovereignty, but without the poisonous racial-economic handicaps that made cosmopolitanism impossible in the colony.[50] In this regard, his heroic imagination capsized at a critical moment. More than Nehru, who also envisioned the 'engineering nation,' Sarkar remained a man of the colony, fantasising about grand achievements but allowing only for small ones. But he was not far removed from Bose, who could not imagine unqualified independence either. In their imagination, there would always be a hegemon—whether it was Britain, America or Japan—and independence would be a process of continuous subterfuge: client states trying to maximise their autonomy in a world of empires.[51]

Sarkar's understanding of a new trusteeship, however, was located within a vision of international relations that reflected his longstanding conviction that nations realised themselves through 'manly give-and-take with other nations'.[52] The cosmopolitan Young-Indian nationhood he postulated in the interwar period was pragmatic and unconcerned with authenticity; it sought to incorporate whatever was useful from anywhere in the world, even if that world was mainly Western.[53] Western youth were its allies, as were Chinese and Japanese youth.[54] Eclecticism—which Sarkar identified as a refusal to be bound by any one authority—became a form of not only counter-conquest (going anywhere, assessing everything, assimilating anything) but also freedom, democracy and 'pluralism'. Sarkar aligned this cosmopolitanism explicitly with individualism and individual rights.[55] In this, he was close to Rabindranath in a certain mode,[56] except that Sarkar wanted to bind expansive freedom to a single national purpose and particular nation-states. The position would have been familiar and agreeable to Nehru: it was, essentially, a late-colonial liberal-nationalist posture.

Articulating the international scope of Young India after the Great War, Sarkar revealed two competing notions of isolation and contact.[57] There was an imperial discourse of cosmopolitanism, in which empire facilitated contact across places, races and cultures, and overzealous nationalism and independence represented ghettoisation. The Congress Moderates before 1907 and a section of the Indian princes epitomised the Indian acceptance of that discourse.[58] By the 1920s, the channel was moribund. Sarkar was able to suggest that empire was an impediment to the worldly man, whereas national identification promised the racial justice on which cosmopolitanism could proceed. Moreover, engagement with the world was essential to self-awareness, providing an external perspective unavailable to the insulated. Tilak's metaphor of the *kupamanduk* or frog-in-a-well perfectly fit Sarkar's own perspective that nationhood could not be realised from the inside alone: the nationalist must know what India looks like from New York, Tokyo and Berlin.[59] *Hote chao swadeshi, toh agey hao bideshi* ('If you want to be Indian, first become a foreigner'), he quipped after his return from his first spell overseas.[60] Colonialism was nothing if not an external perspective, of course, but it was tainted by racism and the loss of agency. There was thus a circular relationship between national self-awareness and what Sarkar called world-grasping: the self-aware would grasp the world, and in the process, become more self-aware.

That self-awareness was the key to what Sarkar called *vishwashakti* or the force of history in the world.[61] Indian academic and literary journals were 'organs of *vishwashakti*', he wrote in 1922, indicating not only his desire for a world open to Indian engagement, but also his investment in an India that initiated and controlled the organs of engagement.[62] He complained, however, that modern Indian scholarship was not as good as the European and American, and it was especially impoverished in its understanding of the West.[63] It was not enough for Indians to read foreign journals in order to access the knowledge of the world, which would have been the typical colonial arrangement of knowledge and race. *Vishwashakti* was not only a resource 'out there' to be accessed by the nation, but was generated in the process of accessing, through the proliferation of texts and institutions. Once tapped, it took the nation more deeply into the world, bringing about a 'Greater India'.

The nation thus fed on the world as it grew. While Sarkar's conceptualisation of this growth was generally benign, it was shot through with late-nineteenth-century European and American imperial rhetoric—a discourse of 'conquest' and 'virility'—and a thick seam of *ressentiment* that kept out other Euro-American discourses: the suspicion that aggression is uncivilised, Heinrich Heine's sardonic observation that when Germans submitted to their princes to fight Napoleon, 'we conquered our [own] freedom', or the cartoonish absurdity that clung to Theodore Roosevelt.[64] For the colonised nationalist, the alternative to virility and conquest would have been impotence and insularity. Sarkar's paeans to Greater India tended to conclude with threats of war: narratives of culture and knowledge became prescriptions of statecraft and Realpolitik.[65]

Sarkar borrowed the term 'Greater India' from his friend, the historian Radhakumud Mookerji, but made it his own.[66] He was not the only one; as Susan Bayly and others have noted, 'Greater India' in its various meanings—some derived from French Orientalism—was popular with a wide spectrum of Indian nationalists in this period, from Savarkar to Nehru.[67] Sarkar's 'Greater India' was not just a political project of expansion (of the nation in the world) or even of control (of its internal components), but a wider project of 'discovery'. Its language of discovery was similar to Nehru's 'discovery' of India, but it was the other side of the coin: whereas Nehru discovered India's 'greatness', Sarkar discovered the ordinariness of the West. Mediocrity was as ubiquitous and universal as greatness.[68] The demystified and prosaic, more than flowery formulations of greatness, was thus the stuff of the cosmopolitanism of the nationalist, and the key to a newer, more capacious and ubiquitous sense of self.

For national elites able and willing to extend themselves internationally, Sarkar indicated in a call for expanded Indo-French contact, the operative words were camaraderie and partnership.[69] Ironically, comradeship was intended to facilitate competition (the most extreme form of which was war) between nations, reflecting critical inconsistencies in Sarkar's cosmopolitanism: camaraderie across race exists, it does not; we are equal, we are not. The vacillation marked his notion of a 'science-world'.[70] On the one hand, the science-world was an international haven of expertise. On the other, it was a structure of exclusion, rendered fraudulent by its primary 'superstition', which was race. It allowed whites to steal colonial knowledge and retreat into the insularity of the albinocracy.[71] More infuriatingly, it compelled the colonised-nationalist intellectual to choose between transcending the restrictions and resentments of nationality, and wearing national uniform out of need and responsibility. There was ultimately no choice: scholars-abroad must be India's diplomats, alive to the national interest, Sarkar insisted after his first stint overseas.[72] They must chase the thieves all the way to the metropole. When they come home, they must not hold themselves apart or show delusions of grandeur. Sensitive to Indian criticism of the arrogant foreign-returned, he conceded that Indians often saw little of the societies they visited, and demanded that they try harder to leave the shells they carried with them.[73] For those who represented weak nations, the world was an asset and a compensation that could not be eschewed.

Rebel Knowledge

Sarkar's predicament as a colonial intellectual who must declare his membership in the science-world and simultaneously protest his exclusion was centred on his awareness of great differences of power when it came to the production and consumption of knowledge. Every aspect of his political project—the articulation of race and nationhood, the infatuation with 'militarism', the relentless pursuit of the state—was influenced by that awareness: his was a rebellion of knowledge, sometimes brash, sometimes defensive. Early in his career, Sarkar called for a far-reaching remaking of the West, beginning with education. Education is a science, he declared in 1913, and must be based on the principles of 'Freedom, Race-tradition, and Modernity'.[74] Otherwise, 'the world will witness the rise of an abnormal and degenerate society'. He soon lost interest in race-specific education, and adjusted his polemic accordingly: Western pedagogy was unscientific and degenerative *because* it was infected by the superstitions of racial essence, compromising the ability of white scholars to deploy universal yardsticks of progress.[75] That awareness must undergird the global field of sociology; the colonial academy under native control could be a site of genuine exchange.[76] Smugly superior Europe was self-provincialised: marooned from the world. The Orient was the victim of Europe's dereliction, its old partner in progress, and the coming agent of its repair.[77]

This was liberal revenge on Macaulay and Mill: Sarkar referred cuttingly to the need for new 'manners and morals' in European pedagogy.[78] It was also at least partly the confrontational pleasure of throwing a well-worn but powerful vocabulary ('superstition', 'science', 'civic sense') back at Europe.[79] At university, Sarkar had accepted the idea of a spiritually superior, materially impoverished India.[80] But between 1911 and 1914, his study of 'old' texts like the *Sukraniti* (possibly a nineteenth-century forgery[81]) convinced him of a resolutely political, secular and social-scientific Indian past that was as universal as the human brain itself, and that had been ignored by Orientalist scholarship.[82] (If the *Sukraniti* is a forgery, it too is a response to that perception of neglect.) The Great War and world-travel did the rest. In China in 1916, Sarkar concluded that discourses of difference had confined him to a margin; refuting them was crucially important to repositioning himself authoritatively.[83] To be similar was to be comparable and at least potentially equal.[84] By war's end, he rejected the dominant nationalist tendency to highlight the civilisational superiority of India over Europe.[85] The terms of that superiority—usually moral or 'spiritual'—were racist,[86] closely related to the Orientalist insistence on Indian passivity and fatalism, and directly opposed to his own search for rejuvenation and heroic agency.

The discourses of ancient ('dead') India and 'spiritual' India became, for Sarkar, both discrete and connected. The former was academic, born directly from Orientalist scholarship. The latter was popular and new, born within the realm of Western art and contemporary phenomena like the beginnings of the guru industry. The East is not the guru of the West, he insisted.[87] Not surprisingly, he remained ambivalent about Rabindranath and even Vivekananda. He could not reject them: they were central to any construction of 'Young India'. Sarkar described Rabindranath as a 'great youth' when the latter was 67, and Vivekananda as a seminal icon of courage coupled with organisational genius.[88] He retained close ties with the Ramakrishna Mission, regarding the monks as men of action akin to Jesuits.[89] But he recoiled from their *effective* reinforcement of spiritual India, and from Rabindranath's brand of cosmopolitanism, which, with its post-swadeshi critique of nationalism, was different from his own.[90] He recoiled also from Rabindranath's criticism of American modernity, which remained a vital source of inspiration for Sarkar.[91] (India needed a sensibility more prosaic and material than Rabindranath's, he suggested mischievously.[92])

Yet for a nationalist to disavow difference entirely is to invite insurmountable difficulties, even when race and nation are rescued from similarity by a new emphasis on political purpose. Anti-colonial nationalism, obviously, needs both difference and similarity.[93] Sarkar, accordingly, recast the European intellectual establishment itself as the push-board of difference. Only Oriental scholars working autonomously of white supervision knew the Orient, he argued, even (and especially) when they utilised modern systems of knowledge. A double conquest was thus demarcated as the *existential project* of resurgent Indian nationhood: an outward-directed conquest of Western knowledge and its institutions, and an inward-directed conquest of the cultural—and human—raw material of the East.[94] These would produce the institutions, culture and citizenry of the nation-state, snatched from the colony and liberated into the world.

Sarkar's emphasis on similarity is typical of the insurgent in a particular mode. It marks a liberalism that is partially distinct from the Eurocentric universalism of the Mills: Europe remains the template of the universe, but it has no monopoly on the universe. Moreover,

Europe itself becomes unstable, open for debate. Sarkar's insistence on 'pluralism' in the arts and sciences was a technique of disaggregation: it broke up the monoliths of race and culture. In that sense, it was potentially counterproductive for a nationalist. But the monolithic vision is inseparable from hierarchy, and, in the age of empire, inferiority. Disaggregation was thus necessary for the assertion of equality, and not only because it eroded Western claims to knowledge of the non-West. Disaggregation created space: room for progress, counterpoints, similarities, counterflows of knowledge and influence, and new experts like Sarkar himself. Fittingly, the 'mentality' that Sarkar claimed for the insurgent/resurgent Orient paralleled the European: it was also sceptical, it was also an Aufklärung, it could be described as 'Sturm und Drang' on the very first page of *The Futurism of Young Asia*.[95]

Sarkar perceived a double problem with Western knowledge of Asia: the West, on the one hand, did not know enough (and did not want to know, being uninterested in what it had marginalised), and on the other, it knew much that was wrong. The impact of race on knowledge was twofold. There was a proliferation of bad knowledge (the production of difference, tied to empire), and also a laziness in which classification—the identification of difference—became an end in itself and the culmination of intellectual inquiry. A further effect of the latter was the objectification and mummification of the 'flesh and blood'. Also, the volume and spread of knowledge was vitally important to Sarkar, because diffusion produced a political attitude in the public: an inclination towards either equality or inequality. Yet if diffusion came at the expense of the teaching of similarity, then the result would always be inequality. Accordingly, Sarkar wanted a double democratisation of Western knowledge of the Orient: a horizontal democratisation (diffusion) in which that knowledge was widely taught and learned, and a vertical democratisation (elimination of racial hierarchy) in which knowledge became prosaic, organised under the same headings and taught with the same techniques as European subjects.

For Sarkar, the democratisation of esoteric knowledge promised to liberate the Orient from the musty confines of academic Orientalism, creating a popular awareness of Asia in Europe that was valuable in itself.[96] Without that awareness, the new networks of 'informed contact' that colonial intellectuals craved would remain elusive. But mass culture—which encircles popular culture as well as new disciplines of scientific inquiry, which after Darwin and Freud were not fully distinct from popular culture—also threatened to stifle the Orient with even more powerful new discourses, such as those of abnormality and the specimen, which amplified difference to unprecedented levels. A destabilisation of the wider knowledge industry was evidently required, which might take advantage of the shake-up of white authority in the Tsushima Straits, Curzon's Bengal and Flemish trenches. In Sarkar's emerging treatment of Orientalist tropes, therefore, the oversexed Oriental became the oversexed European, the Oriental despot became the Occidental despot, the tyrannical Indian husband became the white patriarch, and it was Europeans who were hopelessly divided against each other.[97] In these reversals, he borrowed the counter-discourses of the colony: sexually undisciplined Europeans, women's rights within the family, the connection between civilisation and democracy.[98] He remained willing to acknowledge that his methodology and generalisations about the warts of European history might be flawed. But more important was to demonstrate, by exposing his counter-knowledge to charges of error, that Orientalist knowledge was also suspect:

> [My] interpretation ... may be easily condemned on the simple ground that one must not generalize about millenniums of Occidental civilization from the single verses of a single poet. But this very truism disappears from the consciousness of Eur-American 'scientists' while they apply their brains to the interpretation of what they call the heart or soul or spirit of the Orient. The injustice of this method is probably the greatest of all factors that have contributed to the rupture of fellow-feeling between the East and the West. And the futurists of Young Asia have their permanent fountain of inspiration in the intellectual pain and ill-treatment they have been accustomed to get from Eur-America.[99]

In this scorched-earth approach to discourse, what mattered more than the content of knowledge was the political value of knowledge in a race war marked by 'pain and ill-treatment'. The inconsistency reflected the nihilism of a colonial-cosmopolitan intellectual enterprise that could not find its way out of the colony and exploded. But it was also an attempt to utilise the rubble as ammunition.

When Sarkar cited European social scientists like Havelock Ellis and Vilfredo Pareto in his counter-narrative of Europe, he widened a gap between the primitive white masses and an intellectual vanguard to which he could relate as an equal, and to which he rightfully belonged.[100] The gap between the 'aristocracy of intellect' and the 'half-fed masses' is universal, he argued in 1921–22.[101] Visible differences between societies indicated different locations on a common chronological trajectory; the lag of the Oriental was of recent vintage.[102] Sarkar was not entirely hostile to the idea of 'natural' differences between human populations. He allowed that immigrants to America had distinct racial characteristics in their countries of origin ('under natural conditions').[103] But natural conditions were relatively unimportant. In spite of the resemblance to Social Darwinist enthusiasts of 'natural' conflict, Sarkar was a philosopher of the artificial: what mattered was the ability of the modern state to manage conflict scientifically. That ability was a liberating force, making it possible to rearrange race (through assimilation and amalgamation[104]) and articulate more just forms of nationhood. But justice was not just about scientific-administrative capability. It was affected by political will, which could be perverse and irrational. The American example was both promising and infuriating: it demonstrated the exhilarating possibilities of social engineering, as well as the gross injustice of white supremacy.

Justice then simultaneously required the denial of essence and its management as the 'live' substance of politics and culture. When Sarkar wrote about classical Indian culture, he reserved the classical as a sphere in which cosmopolitan elites studied themselves even as they studied each other. The folk level was for a different kind of cosmopolitan bonding, in which intellectuals across racial lines clarified their distinctions from the objects of their study.[105] Within the racial community, however, the folk bled into the classical, generated startling possibilities of novelty. Sarkar, for instance, included the legend of Chand Sadagar in an essay on classical Hindu culture.[106] It marks a slippage not fully covered by Sartori's framing of culture in Bengal, which is indifferent to the fractures and instabilities within the norm identified, and unengaged with the politics and payoffs of those instabilities.[107] For modern, nationalist *bhadralok* engaged in outlining culture, the folk and the Volk (ethnically homogenised masses that constitute the national Self) were not the same people *yet*, but may have been so in the past. It was part of the nationalist intellectual's task to (re)convert the folk into the Volk, partly by appropriating folk traditions for national culture, and partly by highlighting the folk elements that had survived within the elite discourse of who-we-are. The subaltern remained an iconic figure for the elite native in search of an alternative self, and a way of dealing with the 'gift' of European thought, which could neither be rejected nor fully owned.[108]

Sarkar could dismiss the idea of a distinct Indian art, and practically in the same breath, reject the Western ability to evaluate what must, by default, indeed be 'Indian art'.[109] By making art into a resolutely autonomous field of individual and racial self-expression, independent of history and other disciplines of inquiry, Sarkar posited it as independence itself.[110] We see this not only in his dismissal of Abanindranath Tagore as a painter who had overdone indigenousness to the point of exoticising himself,[111] but also in an earlier clash with 'Agastya' (Ordhendu Coomar Gangoly), a critic who had attacked Phanindra Nath Bose's sculpture as un-Indian and derivative of Europe.[112] Sarkar issued a withering defence of Bose. Creativity must not be crippled by provincial anxieties about authenticity; nationally identified art was the active assimilation of culture by nationally identified borrowers. The argument spiralled into a furious exchange of letters in multiple journals, drawing in the old Maniktola bomber Barin Ghosh, the Russian émigré Stella Kramrisch (already an academic expert on Indian art) and Pramathanath Chaudhuri (editor of the radical literary journal *Sabuj Patra* and close associate of Rabindranath). Agastya nastily referred to Sarkar as 'the learned ex-nationalist', a 'Europo-American', and a 'Franco-Bengalee' whose foreign exposure had disqualified him 'from recognizing and developing his own national and racial genius'.[113] Ghosh, England-born-and-raised like his brother Aurobindo, insisted that Sarkar was both a philistine and a traitor.[114] Pramathanath—suave, witty, avowedly cosmopolitan as well as nationalist—was relatively sympathetic to Sarkar. A sharp reader of colonial prose, he speculated that Agastya was white.[115] Clearly, for the self-identified Indians, the priority was to demarcate a sphere of creativity and analysis where the instruments of inquiry and judgment were free of white authority and Indian mimicry, but authority and mimicry were open to very different interpretations.

If 'Indian art' was decolonised and simultaneously de-exoticised, Western culture became fully accessible to cosmopolitan Indians. Sarkar's account of Goethe's reception of Kalidasa—which, he wrote, was like discovering America or Neptune—only appears to contradict his thesis of similarity and non-exoticism.[116] He was suggesting that Goethe's wonder came not from a discovery of the alien, but from the discovery of the familiar in an alien place: not so much like the wonder of the New World in Stephen Greenblatt's conceptualisation,[117] as like the wonder of West Asian travellers in medieval India.[118] That recognition of the Self in the Other, Sarkar argued, is fundamentally liberating. He was engaged as usual in a double movement: by highlighting Goethe's recognition of kinship with Kalidasa, he was 'grasping'

Germany for Asian cosmopolitans. National competition crept into the world-without-boundaries: 'the *schöne Weiblichkeit* which [Schiller] failed to discover in the Greek classics he found at last in the Hindu drama'.[119] Virility sometimes took unusual forms.

What 'virile' knowledge accomplished, moreover, was the Orientalising of Europe through reversals of gendered gaze and speech.[120] Here we have another echo of Bhudeb, who preceded Sarkar in treating Europe and white racism as objects of sociological study. But for Bhudeb, whose sense of normalcy and justice was rooted in religion, scientific discourse was a corrosive and distasteful necessity in colonial society; he was, in that sense, a reluctant sociologist.[121] Sarkar admired Bhudeb's approach but lacked his hesitations.[122] His ardent endorsement of social science was an assertion of agency-in-evaluation.[123] It was, at one level, a game of racial-intellectual 'gotcha': the use of Western knowledge to cut the bottom out of Western assertions of superiority, without questioning the terms of superiority and inferiority or the structures of the knowledge. His invocation of modern disciplines of knowledge has a ritualistic quality that is typical of Indian scholars of the period as they sought to establish a competing authority within modernity, out-modernsing Europeans.[124] The Oriental was the better Orientalist, as well as an Occidentalist. The compulsive use of European references indicates a racial-political-academic insecurity: the native scholar needed those references to be credible in the world.

At another level, however, Sarkar's approach was thoroughly subversive. By naming the names of European culture, some of it quite arcane, he demonstrated a fait accompli of transgression: he had already gone where natives were not supposed to go, like a servant who has gone into the master's bedroom and seen too much. He was not an 'isolated' man awaiting Columbus and Goethe; he had already broken out. That knowledge gave Sarkar considerable control over a basic dynamic of self-representation. When he acerbically pointed out that Napoleon was not trying to represent French civilisation in the Arc de Triomphe, he spoke from an understanding that in Orientalist discourse, the Oriental cannot help representing himself racially in everything he does: he is trapped entirely within race.[125] The European, on the other hand, can choose to behave either racially or race-neutrally, and thus has access to the universal. Sarkar claimed the same access for the Oriental, and the same agency of being able to choose to either display or not display a racial posture. This was a basic part of the appeal of similarity and cosmopolitanism for nationalists in the colonised world.

That freedom was closely tied to the pursuit of the independent state. Culture spread into a space cleared and defined by statecraft: without the state, it neither moved nor mattered.[126] Race (the conscious community with a shared political purpose) informed the boundaries of the state. Within this race, the cosmopolitan intellectual was a live— and thus insurgent—accumulator-producer of knowledge. Sarkar's condemnation of Orientalism for being obsessed with India's 'dead' past was a way of saying 'we are not dead'. With its immediate echo of Derozio, 'Young India' was a statement of being engaged in the production of modern modes of *living*.[127] The dead past was not without value, but that value was limited to the provision of raw materials for Sarkar's political positions. This left open the question of what knowledge system, if not the European, could form the basis of Asian inquiries without inviting charges of mimicry.[128] But if modern knowledges and disciplines were identified as universal rather than European, then the problem could be bypassed, transforming borrowing and mimicry into 'grasping' and 'conquest'.[129] (The Japanese, Sarkar believed, had done this most literally.[130]) The nationalist, engaged in universal but autonomous intellectual work determined (but not limited) by national interest, could cross national boundaries without betraying himself.

There is here a wistful echo of Kipling: Sarkar too imagined remote caravanserais where strong men or intrepid scholars came face to face, eliminating the discoverer/discovered dichotomy.[131] The equal facility of movement-across-space was thus also an equal facility for movement-across-race, or suspensions and violations of race. But while Sarkar was clear that the privileging of skin colour as a motive for political domination was new in history, he saw colour as being *literally* rather than *symbolically* important, and was uncertain how this importance had come about. He saw the colour-fetish as duplicity and false consciousness, the newest in a long chain of excuses for enslavement and ghettoisation. It remained to be answered who was making the excuse: who was wearing the white mask? Sarkar provided an answer when he touched on the idea of 'might': power itself puts on disguises, and now it wears white skin.[132] In the early 1920s, he still believed that an alteration of the direction of political expansion could make whiteness irrelevant, or rather, insignificant.

Sarkar utilised the suggestion in a stinging critique of French Orientalism: because France was reliant on French experts for its knowledge of India, that knowledge was flawed and incomplete.[133] But the success of Orientalism was also an Indian failure to represent itself. Indeed, in explaining this failure, Sarkar conceded much of the Orientalist narrative of Indian passivity. The intensity of the self-condemnation, or rather, the separation of the self from its immediate society, is startling even by the standards of nationalist angst. While Sarkar's intervention was aimed at setting the chronological and historical limits of the damaged self, there is nevertheless something pathetic about his fabrication of questions that 'the French' (and Germans, and Russians) were posing to 'the Indians'. It indicates an unspeakable awareness of how little thought Europeans actually gave to India. By inventing questions, Sarkar compensated for that lack, and placed India at the centre of European concerns. Establishing conversations was one way of being connected to the world, particularly when the conversation was in the head of the colonised.

History as *Vishwashakti*

Sarkar's nationhood was primarily political: to be a nationalist was to know what political side one was on, and to look out for the interests of that side in the current historical situation. Unlike the confining nature of the community of essence, the very artifice of nationhood was liberating and conducive to engagement and accommodation with other nationally organised culture makers. In this cosmopolitanism of competition, Young India was not only more scientific than the contemporary Western establishment, it was also more radical. That radicalism was not so much a coherent ideology as a flexible commitment to racial justice in international politics, and an assertion of potency: to be an agent in world-history, to *want* to be an agent in world-history (by first having a conception of a world of history), and to expand-and-conquer the political community's field of vision, movement and action. The scope of the political community was not fixed but not inconsistent either: it went from Bengal in Sarkar's earliest years, through Asia in the period enveloping the Great War, to India in the 1940s, although all three concepts were present at all times. He wove in and out of all three nationalisms that Eric Hobsbawm identified: enthusiasm for the liberal, multi-ethnic nation-state, autonomy-seeking 'minority' patriotism and right-wing reaction against the second type.[134]

As Dilip Menon and Janaki Bakhle have noted, colonial cosmopolitanisms are not only 'honest' in the visibility of their local roots (as opposed to the 'universalist' cosmopolitanism of metropolitan elites), they can be highly utilitarian in their outlook on the metropole: the world is there for the locality to utilise.[135] In Sarkar's case, it is not enough to ascribe the nakedness of national ties to a concept of rooted cosmopolitanism unless the relationship between the root and the branch is carefully worked out.[136] That relationship is imbedded in a particular understanding of world-history, or history as a unified force that moves the world, and moves *in* the world, in the direction of 'progress'.[137] To be a cosmopolitan, for Sarkar, was to cultivate one's place alongside other subjects and objects of world-history. The crisis of the modern era was that a large part of the world, including India, had fallen out of world-history. Sarkar remained uncertain about what had caused this fall. He generally described colonialism as a result rather than the cause, refusing to countenance theories of economic decline or 'drain' under British rule.[138] He was, however, clear that colonial rule had reinforced India's isolation from the world by detaching it from the collaborative circles that produced knowledge and power, relegating it to a backwater. Nationhood withered and died unless it remained engaged in the global arcs of progress and historiography; to restore this engagement, the nationalist would have to embark upon world-conquest, in Sarkar's Vivekananda-derived phrasing.[139] It was through conquest that European 'machine-mindedness' would be rendered universal and accessible. We glimpse here the slightly unstable meaning of Sarkar's notion of *vishwashakti*, which might be translated either as 'world-power' or as 'world-spirit'. It can suggest the re-immersion of the colonised nation in the spirit of the modern world, but it also suggests the demonstration by the nation of the modalities of power in the modern world.[140]

Not surprisingly, history—which might yield up the truth about the present—became a vital battleground for Sarkar. We find in his writings a sharp ambivalence about the utility of history. On the one hand, he posits a sharp discontinuity between the Indian past and the present: the latter is radically new and hence free, snatched from Europe in the colonial experience. 'Vedic democracy' is not the root of the democracy of Young India; it is a disconnected ancestor.[141] Likewise, when Sarkar discusses Vedic womanhood, he—like other colonial-Indian apologists for the status of Hindu women[142]—explicitly notes the similarity between the ancient and the modern, but he holds back from articulating a lineage.[143] On the other hand, the past remains directly relevant to the present. From the Great War to the eve of Indian independence, his discussions of the ancient world celebrate transfers and absorptions of knowledge, articulating a pre-historical past in which all human culture developed together as well as a historical past in which divergent cultures were able to learn from each other. That narrative places the East on par with the West, recovering a world-history that includes Asia as a full participant.[144] Thus, India may have missed the bus of modernity, but it had contributed to the design of the bus and had a national claim on Newton, Darwin and Hegel. The narrative functions, as such, as a critique of the racist present when collegiality across race has become impossible, distorting knowledge as well as humanity and culture.

Just as importantly, the past is a mirror. Modern India, and with it the modern world, are relentlessly projected onto ancient India. Faith in progress, desire for revolutionary change, optimism, capitalism: all are reproduced in ancient India, contradicting Orientalist tropes of changelessness, passivity and fatalism. That 'ancient modernity' is then reflected back into the present as a language of bureaucracy and governmentality: 'Department of Education', 'Ministry of War', 'eugenics', 'psychology', 'race'. Sarkar recognised that a past that could be described in that language was a vital source of confidence in the present, and that 'loss of nerve' was a fundamental problem of colonised nationhood. The very process of recovering the past, carried out in autonomous institutions located in India and run by Indians, would simultaneously generate nerve and knowledge. That combination—self-identified, institutionalised, assertive and competitive—would be nothing less than the realisation of the nation-state and the future.

Claiming the ancient past as a new national-historical discourse allowed Sarkar to challenge the Macaulayan narrative without conceding that he was working from within it. Even the suggestion of decline or negative progress left open the possibility of politics and regeneration. When did Indian decline begin? What should be regenerated? Sarkar identified the apex of the Indian past as the period beginning with the rise of Magadh and extending into Harsha's kingdom: i.e., the periods when strong states can be identified and Islam is yet to arrive.[145] This is uncontroversial within the framework of Orientalist and Indian-nationalist history. Yet challenging the Orientalist periodisation of the past was vital to Sarkar's articulation of a worldly new 'Indian' history and its political possibilities.[146] Hinduness was kept at a remove from Indianness: essential, but as the root, not the tree. The tree—'India'—was new, unnerved by the discontinuity between itself and its roots, and thus uneasy with itself. That discomfort, Sarkar suggested, was unwarranted, because world-history provided continuity at the level of civilised humanity. By catching up and changing, Indians fully rejoined humanity, reconnecting with their own roots and extended themselves. What appeared to be deracination was racial revival, even as race was transcended.

The nineteenth century, when the 'gap' between Europe and Asia seemed widest, remained a problem: Sarkar could insist that it was extraordinary and not a sign of Asian inferiority, but he could not fully explain it, either in terms of continuity or of discontinuity. It could, however, be accommodated within a 'long view' of history, as an unevenness that emerged in Europe but did not belong to Europe.[147] Indian historians, Sarkar believed, had failed to identify the 'Europe' in their past. The social sciences and humanities in India were afflicted by a disastrous unoriginality, insularity and timid preference for the ancient (dead) past over the turmoil of the nineteenth century. Sarkar was more appreciative of Indian historical fiction, which had compensated for the poverty of academic history.[148] Here, however, he was uncertain about how real the historicised nation was or had to be. Was the newly imagined past real or merely realistic? He acknowledged that contemporary Marathi writers were engaged in constructing a fantasy of Shivaji.[149] Such fantasies were a necessary artifice of nationhood, and Sarkar accepted them on those terms. His obsession with Marathi literature, politics and history was a typically Bengali-*bhadralok* fascination with Marathas and Rajputs: the discovery of usable martial-historical-Hindu material.[150] But even 'realistic' fantasy was unstable; the inadequacies of such nationhood produced wobbles in his polemic.

When Sarkar wrote, for instance, that it was 'generally known' that Ashoka was the Constantine of Asia, who did he think this was known by?[151] European scholars were not general enough. Sarkar presumed the existence of a submerged discourse that *should* be 'generally known': the fantasy of an alternative popular history. Decolonisation meant realising the fantasy by bringing the submerged history into the realm of general knowledge, through the competitive deployment of everyday awareness and ignorance.[152] The closer one got to the present time, the more acute the problem became. In spite of the reference to Ashoka/Constantine, Sarkar was most concerned with the *recent* history of India and the world, which contained the clues to how and why a civilisation could fall so disastrously out of step with the world that the world might not even know about it, and how it could regain its place in general knowledge. Sarkar called here for 'unsentimental', 'purely objective', 'thoroughly realistic' scholarship.[153] These needs could not be met with Romantic poetry and fiction. The failure of Indian scholars to see historiography as an agenda of national revival amounted to a failure of national will. Without that agenda or spirit, history was nothing but dry data and fossilised bones, when nations needed equally vibrant histories to meet and compete as equals. Sarkar saw in the writing of history a gregarious consciousness of others in the world. If Indian historians met that challenge, then reconnection between a regenerated India and a reformed world would become feasible.

Sarkar imagined those remakings as simultaneous, informing and facilitating each other. The opportunities, he believed, were there for the 'grasping'. The competing forces of revolution and reaction within the West had produced historical ruptures like the Great War that, by disrupting the chessboard, had made it possible for the victims of racism and colonialism to assert themselves politically. Sarkar sought a coalition of *ressentiment* that cut across race and geography, overflowing Asia. The early Soviet Union offered a way around Marx: 'backward' people, it could now be said, already possessed the tools of history.[154] America was a more intimate proposition: a place where he travelled and lectured for four years, and where his brother Dhirendra became involved in Ghadr Party activism.[155] Most pertinently, America gave Sarkar a glimpse into the processes of race-making in a modern state. Subversive as ever, he brought the history of American immigration into the same sociological frame as the histories of primitive peoples.[156] In the process, he stripped it—'it' being whiteness, modernity and America—of exceptionality. 'It' was not some climactic stage in human evolution and history, but a phase like any other, to be studied objectively by clear-eyed outsiders like Tocqueville and Sarkar. It was by looking at American immigration that Sarkar concluded that while the state could be an expression of the political aspirations of 'the race', the boundaries of the race and the state were not normatively aligned, and the content of a particular race at a given historical moment was not automatically desirable to its particular state. What modern race-science sets out to do, he suggested, is manage these incompatibilities in the interests of the state.[157] When this is done well, it also serves world-history.

These observations have serious ramifications for the quasi-fascist tendencies within Sarkar's imaginary of the Indian state. His writings on America have the usual determination to historicise racism and not take it as a given. That gives Sarkar's polemic its element of freedom: racial animosities and racist restrictions are subject to political intervention. Moreover, by emphasising that Asian exclusion in America is *similar* to racism against other groups in the past and present, he produced two universal-cosmopolitan communities: one of the victims of racism, and another—in the future—of successfully assimilated citizens. But Sarkar's understanding of the European settlement of the New World is astonishingly devoid of any acknowledgement, except in passing, of the plight of the indigenous population. (The Iroquois and Hopi entered his analysis in a desultory manner, largely via Engels and the Romantic anthropologist L.H. Morgan.[158]) The ideologue of 'conquest' accepted the hegemonic discourses of an empty land and closed frontier.[159] For a man who translated Booker T. Washington into Bengali (and eventually died in a segregated Washington DC hospital), he showed no sustained interest in slavery or Jim Crow even as he dealt with race in America.[160] Sarkar wanted to be counted in the civilised world, not to question civilisation and savagery very rigorously.[161] Civilised humanity had its boundaries. We are left, again, at the limits of the change he sought.

What Kind of State?

A limited radicalism informed Sarkar's vision of the independent state in modern India. The closer he moved towards the reality of independence, the more his writing revealed the contradictions of vanguardist democracy, in which the opportunities for freedom and justice produced by the sovereign state were also problems of coercion. Who was to be coerced? And just as importantly, what was the relationship between democracy and coercion? Sarkar was neither indifferent to democracy nor a populist as Flora has suggested.[162] But there is in his thinking an ambivalence having to do with a particular understanding of democracy. Sarkar saw democracy as the means, the process and the outcome of a transformation of the individual citizen as well as of Indian society: a mechanism of what he called 'creative disequilibrium', or the turmoil from which freedom and power flow.[163] That turmoil was the antidote to the 'decadent pessimism' that often gripped late-Victorian and Edwardian European observers of progress and democracy.[164] In

Introduction 25

India, Sarkar hoped, democracy would crack open an ossified society, sweep aside inert and obstructionist elites, and enable the emergence of a truly modern citizenry. The state is a machine and weapon, he wrote during the Round Table negotiations of the early 1930s; Indians must not only control it, but learn to operate it in the public interest.[165] That state would be literally and metaphorically a form of insurance, guaranteeing not just secure banking (a significant concern for a man with an eye on the history of modern Bengal, where bank failures had decisively shaped the middle-class predicament[166]), medical coverage and a second chance to widows, but civilisation itself.[167]

At the end of the Great War and the Non-Cooperation Movement, Sarkar used the word 'swaraj' to mean both decolonisation and democracy, suggesting their axiomatic interrelatedness.[168] He represented democracy and empire as polar opposites, but was attracted to both: whereas Radhakumud Mookerji had emphasised the survival of ancient Indian democracy at the local level in spite of the despotism of the emperor,[169] Sarkar showed a weakness for the power and prestige of the despot even when it came at the expense of democracy.[170] Nevertheless, he concluded that revolutionary self-government and republicanism were more likely in the colonial periphery than in the metropole. Unlike Europe, with its monarchies and other reactionary traditions, the colony was a tabula rasa where indigenous reaction had already been disrupted by colonial intervention. Here, new vanguards could imagine, build and educate—function as a force of creative will, in Sarkar's Nietzschean prose—with fewer compromises.[171] This vision of the decolonised state as a 'new world' and a frontier, and by implication, as the true location of freedom in world-history, was not unusual or exotic in the least. It lay at the heart of the nationalism of Nehru and his contemporary statesmen, who imagined Non-Alignment and new frontier cities—Chandigarh, Durgapur, Bokaro, Rourkela—as part of the same ideological and political project.[172]

But what was this revolutionary state that Sarkar had in mind? At the end of the Second World War, it was neither 'communist' nor 'free-market'.[173] In the activist role that Sarkar envisioned for the Indian state, and even in specific projects like the Damodar Valley Corporation, there was no real gap between him and Nehru.[174] It was and was not bourgeois democracy, and it already contained the likelihood of coercion in the name of novelty. Sarkar claimed to detest the 'bourgeoisie', but he almost completely detached the word from class. For him, 'bourgeois' was an attitude, signified by vulgarity, philistinism, timidity, self indulgence, know-nothing sloth and unmerited assumptions of superiority.[175] Without getting into the fractures of European bourgeois identity, it might be noted that such criticism is itself a bourgeois mindset; the observation that Sarkar was the quintessential bourgeois intellectual is not unfair.[176] His advocacy of mistrification is best understood as not an attack on the bourgeoisie but the longing for a *true* bourgeoisie. 'Bourgeois' dominance in politics, education, the arts and the economy was an aesthetic and moral problem, to be taken on by elites who possessed individuality, iconoclastic creativity, an affinity for *vishwashakti*, and an asceticism that was simultaneously Calvinist and renunciatory.[177] It is close to the aesthetic that Sartori has placed at the core of culture in early-twentieth-century Bengal, but Sarkar would have dismissed most of Sartori's *bhadralok* as bourgeois, indicating how conflicted the culture of identity remained in its content, membership and purposes.[178]

As a bourgeois thinker who was hostile to the available bourgeoisie, and an admirer of the folk who was not of the folk, Sarkar seemed to be suggesting a state in which coercion and transformation were free-floating principles unattached to the interests of any identifiable social class. Even as he became an apologist for the Nazis, he came to insist upon liberal democracy and the freedom of the individual: 'self-help, self-direction, individual initiative and individual creativeness' must form the basis of political action in free India, he wrote, rejecting the determinism and 'monism' of Marx and Durkheim.[179] It remained unclear, however, whether this vision of individual self-command extended beyond the vanguard that would produce democracy and development simultaneously. 'Development' was suspiciously close to what Sarkar had earlier signified with 'expansion', which left open the question of what, or who, might constitute the new frontier. Just as importantly, Sarkar could be vague about where Young India might be found. Dissatisfied with the political potential of Indian intellectuals (who were either party-bound or fickle), he remained uncertain about the extent to which the 'lion' of society—again, that telling echo of Nietzsche *and* Pareto—included the intellectual, or was autonomous of academia.[180]

Moreover, even as Sarkar posited a distinction between the nation and the national vanguard, he vacillated between different notions of 'two Indias'. His usual tendency was to suggest a conventional duality between the awake vanguard and the awakening nation. His solution to the problem of elite leadership and mass action—that by participating in local agitations subalterns become conscious of their stake in national and international issues—was compatible with contemporary Congress and Khilafatist tactics.[181] Simultaneously, however, he described a moderate, impotent and undeserving tip of the iceberg (represented by the Congress), and a radical and effective 'real opposition' represented by the men with grenades and revolvers.[182] There was an obvious complication: the bomb-throwers were a much smaller minority than the Congress-wallas and their allies. If they were nevertheless the real India, then the realness of the nation had nothing to do with demographics or political coalitions. A miniscule minority could represent nationhood even if the masses were already 'awake'. We are returned to the obsession with virility: guns represented nationhood and sovereignty better than 'speakers and writers', not to mention subalterns. The latter may or may not have affiliated themselves with the Congress, but they certainly were not with the terrorists.[183] Sarkar counted them as part of the nation, but primarily as a problem that the vanguard would resolve later.

The uncertainty within Sarkar's vanguardism was, no doubt, a tactical asset in his polemic. But it made him simultaneously enthusiastic and nervous about democracy, and ambiguous about its meaning. Italian bourgeois democracy in particular became a negative model for India: in both places, democratic institutions of governance were invariably 'plutocratic'.[184] We have here a rhetorical echo of Roosevelt and American Progressivism, emphasising chaos, corruption and correction through that odd combination of force and bureaucracy.[185] Certainly by the Second World War, Sarkar connected urban democracy to an all-round degeneracy: political, moral, social, biological. Unlike in 1913, he now found this degenerate reality both liberating (being modern and transformative) and dystopic. Like Croce, he came to see democracy as desirable.[186] But he refused to be sentimental about it, and was contemptuous of those he found sentimental: the American sociologists C.H. Cooley and E.A. Ross, and closer to home, Nehru.[187] Unlike them, Sarkar insisted that undemocratic governance could deliver social good—defined not just as prosperity and health, but as truth and justice—as effectively as democracy.[188] Votes could be purchased like any other commodity, but purchased power could be deployed for progressive purposes.[189] The individual citizen in that ambivalently democratic imagination was almost necessarily a 'minority of one', who could be either a martyr or a dictator.[190]

In either case, there would be conquest: to the end of his life, Sarkar continued to write about an impending 'conquest of the mind of the Indian masses'.[191] For the admirer of Pareto, conquest was an essential part of freedom and progress. It was also, however, a matter of unease. The unease flowed from the tension between Sarkar's liberalism and his commitment to democracy, and his modification of Pareto's theory of the circulation of elites.[192] C.A. Bayly has characterised colonial-Indian liberalism as 'the liberalism of fear', or a pessimistic ideology beset by anxieties about despotism.[193] Sarkar would not admit to such fears; the intersection of democracy and despotism was, for him, the precise location of progress. Edwardian liberalism, from which Sarkar took his most vital ideological cues, contained a morbid contradiction: the commitment to mobility was accompanied by a growing desire for order.[194] Sarkar's 'Young India' was simultaneously fighting several wars: against the coloniser, against the false elites and against the rabble.[195] This warfare was doubly democratic: it included a colonised people at the high table of the global knowledge industry, and it brought the masses into the modern nation. The folk were to be incorporated through art and scholarship: the democracy of culture was also an *order*. The masses had to be interpreted, represented and included by the vanguard; their self-representation or self-inclusion was not contemplated, although sections of the vanguard might emerge from the masses after education had done its work.[196]

Obviously, both constructions of democracy have almost insurmountable limits built into them, not least of which is the persistent importance of a knowledge elite. Sarkar increasingly came to see the state itself as the resolution of the tensions of democracy. 'It should not be regarded as a peculiar or an exceptionally regrettable feature of India that the lead will have to be given by the State', he declared in *Villages and Towns as Social Patterns*, his monumental work on the body politic in India, adding: 'My demand for étatisme and state "patriotism" in matters of public health is then adequately oriented to the moral responsibilities of the individual'.[197] The colonial state was acknowledged as having initiated an extraordinary transformation of Indian society. The effects of that transformation were both desirable and alarming, and the process needed a true elite (not the old feudal elite, not Europeans and not the pseudo-bourgeoisie) to seize the *vishwashakti* of the moment.[198] Even when the state was no longer colonial, it must continue to intervene in society, not least to ensure the continued production of 'creative individuals'. Sarkar had no patience for the politics of negotiation between formal government and informally organised communities that Partha Chatterjee calls 'political society'.[199] That was far too localised (and hence insular), and nakedly indicative of the weakness of the state. Moreover, as a liberal, he was committed to releasing the individual from murky and reactionary 'communities'.[200] But he had no doubt about what entity should be privileged in any conflict between the individual and the self-reproducing state. The state simultaneously created and neutered the individual agent, and ideological or ethical conflicts were subordinated to necessities that only the state could meet.[201]

We must now return to the question of whether Sarkar can meaningfully be considered 'right-wing', and if so, what that meaning might be. Like Pareto and Croce, he rejected Marxism as bad social science, but more than them, he acknowledged it as a moral narrative; he accepted, moreover, the centrality in history of the needs of the flesh.[202] He was anti-Soviet, but that came gradually, after Lenin's death.[203] His post-swadeshi vision of Indian economic development was premised on inflows of foreign capital,[204] but he described it as bitter medicine to be swallowed for the time being (*hajam korite hoibe*).[205] Like Indian liberals in general, he recoiled from unrestrained competition and the 'evils of modern capitalism', proposing 'capitalistic cooperation' and government regulation in the public interest that Keynes and Nehru would have found sensible.[206] The 'cultured' *bhadralok* squeamishness with the profit motive clung to him; he epitomised its connection with contemporary Western critiques of money-grubbing.[207] Well into the 1920s, he remained on good terms with the Indian communist leadership: M.N. Roy, Abani Mukherji, Virendra Chattopadhyay.[208] He admired Sidney Webb's thinking on industrial democracy, adapting it for his own visions of 'economic swaraj' through trade unionism and mistrification.[209] In the 1930s and 1940s he came out as a defender of zamindari, but it was a quixotic defence. Dismissing any absolute right to property, he insisted on the prerogative of the state to intervene in the disposal and distribution of land.[210] Moreover, he remained hopeful that with the democratisation of Indian society, a *new* landowning elite would emerge in the countryside.[211]

Sarkar was the opposite of a social conservative, imbued with an undisguised hostility to assorted defenders of the status quo in the most fundamental areas of Indian nationhood, such as the family, education, caste and gender.[212] He stood outside the 'compromised'—but ultimately dominant—colonial-Indian liberalism that, setting Mill aside, accepted the legitimacy of 'social rights'.[213] This is the first part of his departure from Bhudeb, who insisted that there was an Indianness—defined against the egalitarianism, secularism, progressivism, aggressiveness and selfish individualism of Europe—that had to be conserved even as it was reoriented to the needs of the present.[214] Sarkar dismissed such binaries. He might tenuously be considered a Hindu nationalist, which in the Indian context is the primary basis of 'right-wing' credentials, but unlike Golwalkar and Savarkar (and *like* Bhudeb[215]), he had no desire to exclude Muslims from either his nation or his state. Bayly is mistaken in insinuating otherwise.[216] Indeed, Sarkar complicates the now-conventional connections that Goswami, Joya Chatterji and others have made between swadeshi ideology, nationalist pedagogy, upper-caste-Hindu exclusiveness and a Bharat based on 'the obsessional search for authenticity, purity, and homogeneity'.[217] His Indian territory and even his Hindu nation were not that Bharat; they suggested other ways of claiming sovereign space, and equally complex projects of teaching independence, that were nevertheless produced by the swadeshi milieu and National Education, and belong within the frame of Indian nationalism.

Sarkar's location within the right stems, more than anything else, from his embrace of the state as the ultimate repository of legitimate agency in a free society. This is the second departure from the conservatism of Bhudeb's generation.[218] For Sarkar, the monopoly of the state on legitimacy and agency was inseparable from freedom itself. Here, too, caveats must be inserted. Sumit Sarkar has rightly warned against sentimentalising the 'community' as the locus of resistance to the secular-liberal state (and capital) in India.[219] Reaction is quite compatible with community, and with the related constructions of 'culture', 'civilisation', 'the people' and 'non-state agency' that Nandy has romantically designated as beleaguered domains of democracy autonomous of the state.[220] Nandy is right, however, in noting that obsession with the state is representative of a very broad section of anti-colonial nationalism.[221] It is thus not enough to label Sarkar a 'statist'; the identification must be more precise than that.[222] In seeing the decolonised state as the primary means of reform and justice, and in his suspicion of sub-national 'communities', Benoy Sarkar was again close to Nehru, and to the mainstream he was apparently at odds with. But unlike Sarkar, Nehru was also wary of the state, and sought—however inconsistently—to create mechanisms of restraint quite apart from democracy itself.[223] Sarkar showed little interest in these. It is not a coincidence that whereas Nehru recoiled from Germany and Italy in the interwar years, Sarkar became enthusiastic.

The other major dynamic that makes Sarkar 'right-wing' is the overpowering element of *ressentiment* in his thinking. Nothing gives me as much pleasure as seeing the white-skins shine my shoes, Subhas Bose wrote when he was in England preparing for the Civil Service examination.[224] For all Sarkar's cosmopolitan collegiality, that acute sense of racial humiliation and need for revenge—the desire to give whites a 'therapeutic inferiority complex'—drove his engagement with the West.[225] He acknowledged Nietzsche's vision of the sadism of slaves, but did not reject it.[226] Instead, he rearticulated it in terms of nature and wholeness: hate and violence are as human as love and peace, to be deployed with equanimity.[227] As Peter Gay noted, aggression-in-society can be neither presumed nor ignored; it is 'cultivated'.[228] The bourgeois individual is trained to experience it, and bourgeois society is organised to regulate it while producing the 'alibis'—thematics, in Gramscian parlance—that naturalise it. Controlled hatred is an artefact of 'national education', and the modern man in Sarkar was acutely sensitive to the need for institutions that would undertake the cultivation, producing the nature of the free Indian.

The decolonisation he imagined was thus a state in pursuit of a never-ending shoeshine. (The admiration of Bata was well-founded.) All Indian nationalists understood (and understand) the sentiment, which is after all part and parcel of being 'non-white' in a racialised world. But not all were driven by it; Nehru was not. That, as much as anything else, is why nobody would seriously accuse Nehru of being a fascist, the Armed Forces Special Powers Act notwithstanding. The accusation has, however, been levelled at Sarkar since the Second World War,[229] most recently by Zachariah.[230] I disagree with Zachariah, who has overlooked key aspects of Sarkar's ideology and politics: he does not account for Sarkar's liberalism and his insistence that the state is distinct from the nation. The charge of fascism functions as a blunt instrument, obliterating nuance. But I do not find the accusation frivolous. Moreover, because I am arguing that Sarkar was not so much an outlier as an alternative within Indian nationalism, I am also suggesting that his quasi-fascist tendencies have been aspects of the ideology of the independent Indian state—and more generally, of the modern state—whenever the state has confronted the dissident individual or the recalcitrant community.[231]

A Place to Begin

The end of an introduction is also a beginning, and in Sarkar's case it is useful to begin in Bengal. This must be done cautiously, avoiding Flora's tendency to cast Sarkar as a Bengali nationalist who was only incidentally Indian.[232] Even Sarkar's most Bengal-centric work, like *Naya Banglar Goda Pattan* ('Foundations of New Bengal', written between 1922 and 1932), used Bengal largely as a springboard into wider waters. For the ideological constellation that emerged from National Education, Bengali and Indian nationalisms were not a zero-sum game. Nevertheless, Sarkar's trajectory as an Indian began in the politics of Bengal, and he cultivated a nostalgia for the Pala state of the last millennium: an overflowing of Bengal resulting in something Indian.[233] Moreover, his relationship to Bengal was both a microcosmic version of his relationship to India and the world, and a foil to the latter relationships. It highlights the febrile nature of *ressentiment* nationalism in Indian political thought in the critical decades preceding 1947 and even beyond, and returns us to the historical contests over the organisation of the Indian state and identity, especially on questions of language, diversity, unity and 'assimilation'.

It is useful to see Sarkar through Brian Hatcher's lens of 'vernacularisation': the merger and translation of European, Sanskritic and folk 'speech' into a *new*, pedagogical, vernacular idiom of 'improvement'.[234] Sarkar had long praised the attention paid by younger Indian historians to India's 'living languages', suggesting that it constituted the rejuvenation of a morbid Indian race.[235] In his Bengali writings and especially his lectures and interviews, he switched back and forth between *sadhu* (formal) and *chalit* (colloquial) modes, imported copious quantities of Hindi and Urdu vocabulary, and deployed the slang of urban youth-culture, provocatively improvising a community of modern communication: a novel 'we' that has become an aborted possibility. Prior to independence, when Sarkar ruminated on the commonalities and separateness of Bengali and Sanskrit, he reflected the political and ideological concerns of a period when the relationship between Bengaliness and Indianness was still subject to considerable negotiation.[236] The pan-Indian sensibilities of the nationalist middle class were more contingent, and limited to fewer contexts, than they would later become. Indeed, the structures that would normalise the 'All-India' identity—the now-familiar alphabet soup of Indian Institutes of Technology (IITs), Indian Institutes of Management (IIMs) and

Introduction 33

institutions beginning with 'AI'—were still largely in the minds of educational visionaries like Sarkar himself. There was still such a thing as 'Bengali sociology' and 'Bengali history', or at any rate, a sociology and history of Bengal: a regionalist intellectual tradition that was not 'indigenous' to Bengal but nevertheless a semi-autonomous development within colonial culture.[237] In the immediate aftermath of independence, there was a pronounced shift. Sarkar now described Bengal much as he had described Young India two decades previously: as the reopening of a debate and a frontier. It reflected Sarkar's restlessness with the closure of the project of Indian independence, his need for new agents of heroic struggle and expansion, and his unease at the marginal place of Bengal in the post-1947 Indian polity.

Sarkar's writing in the late 1940s shows a pronounced sense of Bengali disempowerment, verging on persecution, directed against 'certain sections' of India that were 'anti-Bengali' and had supposedly collaborated with the colonial regime against Bengali militancy.[238] This was an attack on Nehru and the Congress from a disgruntled admirer of Bose, and a common strand of Bengali identity after the internal battles of the Congress in the 1930s.[239] On the eve of independence, even a Marxist like Susobhan Sarkar could articulate an almost mystical faith in Bengal's civilisational and historical mission in India.[240] Benoy Sarkar was clear: in a narrative penned just after the Indian National Army (INA) trials, the INA became the army of the Bengali nation, conquering and saving India.[241] The fact that Bose's army had few Bengali troops became a point of pride for Sarkar, because 'Field Marshal Bose' could be represented as the solitary Bengali in command of the Indian masses.[242] There is in this a familiar Pareto-derived authoritarianism, and a perverse echo of British pride in the colonial Indian Army: brave sepoys coming together under the charismatic authority of the only historically conscious individual in the unit. By adopting that posture, Sarkar extended the discourse of Bengali *ressentiment*—the self-consciousness of a community wounded in its masculinity and self-worth—beyond the colonial period. Bengal would have its revenge on ungrateful India. There is in this perspective a simultaneous sense of being wronged, victimised and triumphant: of being, like India in the world, simultaneously a centre and a backwater.[243] Bengalis, Sarkar observed with satisfaction, continued to 'create problems' for India and the world.[244] This curious praise must be understood in the context of Sarkar's faith in 'creative disequilibrium'. Neither the Indian nor the global order had been 'settled' by independence and atom bombs, he was suggesting. Bengalis—masters of *vishwashakti*—would ensure that it remained turbulent; out of that turbulence would come greater freedom, and not just for Bengal. 1947 became another 1905: a revolutionary moment.[245]

Ironically, this *ressentiment* produced not a better-defined Bengali nation or an investment in the rump state of West Bengal (let alone East Pakistan), but a curious 'formlessness'.[246] Independent India, Sarkar was saying, had undeniable boundaries which could no longer be transgressed by the advocates of Greater India. The nation-state, as Anderson noted, has the drawback of being limited.[247] But Bengal, being a mere province, remained potentially unlimited. That potential re-enabled Sarkar's expansionist fantasies: just as Indians had once overflowed any narrow definition of India, Bengalis could still overflow their corner of India and function as engineer-colonisers in a Greater Bengal sprawling across India.[248] Much as he adapted to the reality of India-after-Pakistan, Sarkar went along with the idea of West Bengal (or East Pakistan) without connecting it to any fetishised Bengali territory. He accepted the historicity of national territory. What mattered was the political reality of the present: the national ideal was not so much abandoned as adjusted to fit that reality. We see here the complexity of his nationalism, in which 'the people' were both continuous and continuously reinvented: Bengal and Bengaliness were old, just as India and Indianness were old, but also subject to repeated renewals and new historical circumstances. What endured was an identity imbedded in words (Bengali, Indian, Hindu), which—even more than land—became items to claim and contest.[249]

Indian federalism allowed Sarkar to have it both ways: he had a politically definite state, but he also retained the fluid, borderless, state of indefinite expansion. Significantly, he deployed the banyan tree as his metaphor of expansion. The tree keeps growing, moving beyond itself. That vision—better aligned with the settler colony than with the ghetto—suggests an indifference to the sensitivities and predicaments of people among whom Bengalis might settle and expand. He squirmed at the prospect of 'killing the Assamese language',[250] but added: 'Non-Bengali India has been getting acculturated to the Bengali spirit, Bengalicism and the Bengali urges for expansion'.[251] Sarkar assumed that 'they' would follow the lead of the 'dynamic' Bengalis in culture and politics. If they resented Bengalis, it was a deficit of their modernity, and Bengali colonists would face the resentment manfully.

It was not, however, a straightforwardly colonial vision. Sarkar envisioned the 'assimilation' of local minorities into the majority.[252] This meant, curiously, that he would not object to Bengalis assimilating into Hindustani society. Bengali settlers would learn Hindi; they would not only retain an inherent Bengaliness (even as they changed), but also inject that racial-cultural virus into the host community. It amounted to envisioning the relationship between Bengal and India as one of improvement, or a modified amalgamation: the diffusion of Bengal throughout India would strengthen India even if Bengali colonists dissolved partially into India in the process. Sarkar's own use of Hindi/Urdu within Bengali—in his youth, he had experimented with writing Bengali in the Nagari script—was a variant of this manoeuvre: he believed it had allowed him to befriend non-Bengali students (like Rajendra Prasad) at Presidency College, making everybody more 'Indian' even as it made him a new type of Bengali.[253]

Sarkar's support for the idea that Bengalis learn Hindi was, at one level, a delusion of compensation and conquest brought on by the apparent marginalisation of the Bengali language in the Indian Union. He was explicit: 'The cultivation of Hindi by Bengalis is a new strategy in their reconquest of Indian politics and culture'.[254] Since learning Hindi seemed unavoidable in the political environment before Potti Sriramalu's death and the Official Languages Acts, it made sense to recast it as a Bengali initiative.[255] Bilingualism could produce *Indian* unity in a process similar—but not identical—to the integration of the colonial state by British officers trained in the vernaculars. At another level, however, it was a matter-of-fact acceptance of Indian linguistic federalism: learning Hindi allowed regional elites to claim a national field of operation without losing their regional fields.

Sarkar opposed the principle of linguistic states in the emerging Indian Union. Localism must be extirpated, he warned in 1949, and minorities assimilated into the majority 'in language, morals, manners and customs' under the guidance of a Central Department of Culture.[256] But Indian unity could never be fully divorced from local urges, and the desire to eradicate localism must be understood not only in terms of the desire for a centralised nation-state, but also in terms of what federation could do for elites that emerged from the locality. Localism worked against Bengalis, who were not just a regional sub-nation but also a pan-Indian cadre. Such self-extension by learning Hindi was out of the question for the language nationalists of the South, who carried the baggage of southern identity-politics, with its anti-north, anti-Brahmin emphases.[257] Sarkar himself was fiercely opposed to the 'imposition' of Hindi as the national language; the sensibilities of the south were not alien to him.[258] What seems to have been crucial is the element of conquest: he would not accept a conquest by Hindi, whereas a conquest *of* Hindi was desirable, especially if it was 'strategic'. Languages were ideologically coded: Hindi signified a backward society; Bengali, almost as much as English and German, signified modernity. Moreover, unlike the southern languages, Bengaliness was interwoven with the hegemonic discourse of Indianness. Sarkar struggled against the terms of the relationship in order to strengthen, not weaken, the relationship. Conquest was the opposite of secessionism.

Sarkar's fantasy of Bengal-into-India is, in fact, a startlingly precise recapitulation of three decades of his thinking on race. As Peter Robb has observed, racial thinking need not be grounded in concerns of purity.[259] Biological and ethnographic indices are present in Sarkar's narrative of Bengali identity, but he is not bound by them.[260] 'Spirit' is more important, and it is fluid, open to cultural assimilations and variations of political purpose. What remains constant is its urge to flow and expand, i.e., fluidity itself. It is not, however, an infinite fluidity, since 'spirit' does not dissipate and vanish no matter how much it expands and what it incorporates. It becomes a mystical quality, of which language is an important but not irreplaceable signpost. Herder remained relevant to Sarkar, although not intact.[261] Sarkar had no qualms about conflating Young Bengal and the rest of Bengal. The latter was no different from the rest of India; they could not be said to have the 'spirit' of expansive fluidity. But they shared with the vanguard their inclusion in a historical narrative and a political destiny, which was the mystical notion of peoplehood: like the nation that Nehru awakened at midnight, they were dormant Bengalis. Bengaliness thus belonged both to the masses (in a mystical sense) and to the vanguard (in a liberal sense, and also in the Romantic sense of being conscious of a wider, mystic people).

In spite of the availability of a suitably constructed population, Sarkar refused to see post-1905 Bengal as an ethnically defined—or defining—territory.[262] Partly, this reflected his awareness that even after 1905, 'Bengal' included substantial non-Bengali-speaking areas, and many Bengalis lived elsewhere. He had, of course, been radicalised in a political movement affiliated with a specific notion of Bengali geography, its indivisibility, antiquity, divine sanction (*bidhir bandhan*), and so on. He may have outgrown that geography, but it is more likely that the creation of independent India had satisfied the need for a

Introduction 37

concrete geography and left Bengal open to experimental formulations of nationhood. Sarkar did not exclude non-Bengali-speakers from Bengaliness. They became potential Bengalis, awaiting acculturation. He refused to let an interviewer lead him into denouncing the Marwaris of Calcutta as a hostile and alien entity.[263] Race, in this formulation, could be imparted by state-directed education. This was the other side of the coin of Bengali assimilation into regional majorities anywhere in India.

Sarkar's rejection of any connection between language and territory was aligned with Nehru's own thinking on federalism in this period. Both men wanted a federalism of peoples and administrative units while steering clear of a federation of ethnic states, which is effectively the 'federal in structure but unitary in spirit' ideal of Indian constitutional discourse.[264] What is striking about Sarkar's variation is, firstly, the description of linguistic territoriality and inflexible linguistic identity as unfortunate and insignificant cultural phenomena, no different from other retrograde traditions that were to be ignored, altered or supplanted by state intervention. Second, his vision of the bureaucratic regulation of culture and identity is essentially anti-political: it cannot allow that local politics might be significant or legitimate, or that it might be necessary to accommodate local politics within a democratic state. In this, he went much further than Nehru. Sarkar's Bengali and Hindi enthusiasms were both related to his investment in a combined project of nation-building, language-building and institution-building. It was both a form of liberal self-fashioning and a form of 'nationalistic animus' (i.e., a justifiable and energising hostility), although—as usual—not the cultivation of an uncontrolled animus that would imply isolation.[265] It was an experiment in citizenship in a world of competition.

Notes

1 Bholanath Bandyopadhyay, *The Political Ideas of Benoy Kumar Sarkar*. Calcutta: K.P. Bagchi, 1984; Haridas Mukherjee, *Benoy Kumar Sarkar: A Study*. Calcutta: Dasgupta, 1953.
2 S.N. Eisenstadt, 'Multiple Modernities', *Daedalus*, Winter, 129(1), 2000, pp. 1–29.
3 C.A. Bayly, *Recovering Liberties: Indian Thought in the Age of Liberalism and Empire*. Cambridge: Cambridge University Press, 2011, pp. 1–25.
4 Sumit Sarkar, *The Swadeshi Movement in Bengal*. Delhi: Permanent Black, 2010.
5 Sarkar, *The Swadeshi Movement in Bengal*, pp. 47, 127–50; Harald Fischer-Tiné, 'National Education, Pulp Fiction and the Contradictions of Colo-

nialism,' in Harald Fischer-Tiné and Michael Mann (eds), *Colonialism as Civilizing Mission*. London: Anthem, 2004, pp. 229–47; Manu Goswami, *Producing India: From Colonial Economy to National Space*. Chicago: University of Chicago Press, 2004, pp. 248–49; Benoy Kumar Sarkar, *Naya Banglar Goda Pattan* (henceforth, *NBGP*). Calcutta: Chuckervertty, Chatterjee & Co., 1932, p. 195; Benoy Kumar Sarkar, *Comparative Pedagogics in Relation to Public Finance and National Wealth* (henceforth, *CP*). Calcutta: N.M. Ray Chowdhury & Co., 1929, pp. iii, 65.
6 Mukherjee, *Benoy Kumar Sarkar*, pp. 1–25; Giuseppe Flora, 'Benoy Kumar Sarkar: An Essay in Intellectual History', Doctoral Dissertation, Jawaharlal Nehru University, 1993, pp. 3–6.
7 Not everybody was persuaded; his critics pointed to his ignorance of Chinese and reliance on dubiously competent translators. *NBGP*, pp. 331–32.
8 Prasenjit Duara, 'The Discourse of Civilization and Pan-Asianism', *Journal of World History*, 12(1), 2001, pp. 99–130.
9 Kwame Appiah, *The Ethics of Identity*. Princeton: Princeton University Press, 2005, pp. 256–65.
10 Ibid., p. 27.
11 *CP*, p. 100.
12 Pankaj Mishra, *From the Ruins of Empire: The Intellectuals Who Remade Asia*. New York: Farrar, Straus and Giroux, 2012, pp. 3–4, 194–96; Harald Fischer-Tiné and Carolien Stolte, 'Imagining Asia in India: Nationalism and Internationalism 1905–1940', *Comparative Studies in Society and History*, 54(1), 2012, pp. 1–28; Benjamin Zachariah, 'Rethinking (the Absence of) Fascism in India, c. 1922–45', in Sugata Bose and Kris Manjapra (eds), *Cosmopolitan Thought Zones: South Asia and the Global Circulation of Ideas*. New York: Palgrave, 2010, p. 185; Andrew Sartori, in Shruti Kapila (ed.), *An Intellectual History for India*, Delhi: Cambridge University Press, 2010, pp. 80–83.
13 Flora, 'Benoy Kumar Sarkar', pp. 58, 62.
14 Manu Goswami, 'Imaginary Futures and Colonial Internationalisms', *American Historical Review*, 117(5), December 2012, pp. 1461–85.
15 Benoy Kumar Sarkar, *Creative India from Mohenjodaro to the Age of Ramakrishna-Vivekananda* (henceforth, *CI*). Lahore: Motilal Banarasidass, 1937, p. 235; *The Politics of Boundaries and Tendencies in International Relations* (henceforth, *PB*), vol. 1. Calcutta: N.M. Ray Chowdhury & Co., 1926, p. ix.
16 'Nationality . . . is the physical (territorial and human) embodiment of political freedom, maintained by military and economic strength'. *PB*, p. 21.
17 Liah Greenfeld, *Nationalism*, Cambridge: Harvard University Press, 1992, pp. 358–96; Peter Gay, *Weimar Culture: The Outsider as Insider*. New York: Harper Row, 1968, pp. 15–16.
18 Ranajit Guha, *History at the Limit of World-History*. New York: Columbia University Press, 2002, pp. 48–74.

Introduction   39

19 Benoy Kumar Sarkar, *Benoy Sarkarer Baithake*, vol. I (henceforth, *BSB-I*), ed. Haridas Mukherjee. Calcutta: Deys Publishing, 2011, p. 93.
20 *BSB-I*, p. 25; Benoy Kumar Sarkar, *Benoy Sarkarer Baithake*, vol. II (henceforth, *BSB-II*), ed. Haridas Mukherjee. Calcutta: Deys Publishing, 2011, p. 514.
21 *NBGP*, p. 206; Benoy Kumar Sarkar, *Political Philosophies since 1905* (henceforth, *PPS-1905*). Lahore: Motilal Banarsidass, 1942, pp. 40, 341–42.
22 Bandyopadhyay, *The Political Ideas of Benoy Kumar Sarkar*, pp. 47–48; Benjamin Zachariah, *Developing India*. Delhi: Oxford University Press, 2005, pp. 1–24.
23 Sumit Sarkar, *The Swadeshi Movement in Bengal*, p. 52.
24 Ashis Nandy, *The Romance of the State and the Face of Dissent in the Tropics*. Delhi: Oxford University Press, 2003, pp. 95–96, 121–31.
25 *NBGP*, pp. 178–79.
26 Benoy Kumar Sarkar, *The Futurism of Young Asia and Other Essays on the Relations between the East and the West* (henceforth, *FYA*). Berlin: Julius Springer, 1922, pp. 192–93.
27 Greenfeld, *Nationalism*, pp. 15–16; Friedrich Nietzsche, *A Nietzsche Reader*. London: Penguin, 1977, pp. 112–15.
28 *PB*, pp. 188–91.
29 *NBGP*, p. 206.
30 *FYA*, p. 192; *PPS-1905*, p. 272.
31 Jawaharlal Nehru, 'Tryst with Destiny', in Brian McArthur (ed.), *Penguin Book of Twentieth Century Speeches*. London: Penguin Viking, 1992, pp. 234–37.
32 Taraknath Das, *India in World Politics*. New York: B.W. Huebsch, 1923, pp. 170–71.
33 *PPS-1905*, p. 275.
34 Benoy Kumar Sarkar, *Dominion India in World Perspectives, Economic and Political* (henceforth, *DIWP*). Calcutta: Chuckervertty, Chatterjee & Co., 1949, pp. 42–44; *NBGP*, pp. 232–36; *BSB-I*, pp. 327–28. See also Uma Dasgupta, *Science and Modern India: An Institutional History*. Delhi: Pearson, 2011, pp. 851–82.
35 Bhudeb Mukhopadhyay, *Prabandha Samagra*. Calcutta: Charchapada, 2010, p. 85.
36 Founder of the Dawn Society (1902–6), Mukherjee mentored both Sarkar and Radhakumud Mookerji. Sumit Sarkar, *The Swadeshi Movement in Bengal*, pp. 39–52; *BSB-I*, pp. 201–2.
37 Josef Esser and Joachim Hirsch, 'The Crisis of Fordism', in Ash Amin (ed.), *Post-Fordism: A Reader*. Oxford: Blackwell, 2000, pp. 71–98.
38 Jan Baros, *The First Decade of Batanagar*. Batanagar: Club for the Graduates of Bata School (CGBS), 1945, p. 47.
39 *DIWP*, pp. 40–44.
40 *NBGP*, p. 207.

40 Introduction

41 *DIWP*, pp. 42–44.
42 *NBGP*, pp. 232–36.
43 *BSB-II*, pp. 674–79, 692–94, 798–805.
44 Benoy Kumar Sarkar, 'Economic India of Tomorrow', *Calcutta Review*, April 1944, p. 42; *BSB-I*, pp. 292–95.
45 Zachariah, *Developing India*, pp. 25–59.
46 *FYA*, pp. 204–5.
47 George Orwell, *The Lion and the Unicorn*. London: Secker & Warburg, 1962, pp. 68, 80–83. Orwell wanted India to have the right to leave the empire altogether, but believed that Indian leaders would value the right more than an unrealistic independence.
48 Satadru Sen, *Traces of Empire: India, America and Postcolonial Cultures*. Delhi: Primus, 2013, p. 84.
49 *DIWP*, pp. 143–44.
50 Benoy Kumar Sarkar, *Villages and Towns as Social Patterns* (henceforth, *VT*). Calcutta: Chuckervertty, Chatterjee & Co., 1941, pp. 566–70; *NBGP*, pp. 248–50; *BSB-II*, pp. 516, 659–61, 668–69, 714–17, 838–39.
51 *DIWP*, pp. 143–44.
52 Benoy Kumar Sarkar, *Greetings to Young India: Messages of Cultural and Social Reconstruction* (henceforth, *GYI*). Calcutta: N.M. Ray Chowdhury & Co., 1927, p. 9.
53 *FYA*, p. 169.
54 *NBGP*, pp. 183–85.
55 *FYA*, p. 169.
56 Satadru Sen, 'Anarchies of Youth: The Oaten Affair and Colonial Bengal', *Studies in History*, 23(2), 2007, pp. 206–29.
57 *FYA*, p. 303.
58 Satadru Sen, *Migrant Races: Empire, Identity and K.S. Ranjitsinhji*. Manchester: Manchester University Press, 2004, pp. 132–36.
59 *FYA*, p. 336.
60 *NBGP*, pp. 237–38.
61 Benoy Kumar Sarkar, *Vishwashakti*. Calcutta: Grihastha Prakashani, 1914; *The Science of History and the Hope of Mankind* (henceforth, *SHHM*). London: Longmans, Green & Co., 1912, pp. 55–67.
62 *FYA*, p. 305.
63 *NBGP*, pp. 357–58.
64 Peter Gay, *The Cultivation of Hatred: The Bourgeois Experience from Victoria to Freud*. New York: Norton, 1993, pp. 59, 101, 116–27.
65 *FYA*, pp. 306–7.
66 Radhakumud Mookerji, *History of Indian Shipping*. London: Longmans Green, 1912, pp. 99–129.
67 Susan Bayly, 'Imagining Greater India: French and Indic Visions of Colonialism in the Indic Mode', *Modern Asian Studies*, 38(3), 2004, pp. 703–44; Fischer-Tiné and Stolte, 'Imagining Asia in India'.

68 *FYA*, pp. 360-67.
69 Ibid., pp. 82-85.
70 Ibid., p. 18.
71 The pedagogist Andrew Bell, who outlined the 'Bell-Lancastrian system' of teaching, had borrowed a model of education that had been 'indigenous [to Madras] for centuries', Sarkar insisted. *FYA*, p. 146. Bell admitted to borrowing 'only one' native teaching method. Andrew Bell, *Mutual Tuition*. London: Roake, 1823, p. 20. On metropolitan absorption of colonial knowledge, see Ann Stoler, *Race and the Education of Desire*. Durham: Duke University Press, 1995, pp. 1-18.
72 *NBGP*, pp. 200-201.
73 Ibid., pp. 402-23.
74 Benoy Kumar Sarkar, *Introduction to the Science of Education* (henceforth, *ISE*). London: Longmans, Green and Co., 1913, pp. 54-63.
75 *NBGP*, pp. 245-47.
76 *NBGP*, pp. 288-89; *PPS-1905*, pp. 12-13.
77 *FYA*, p. 333.
78 Ibid., p. 174.
79 Ibid., pp. 171, 284.
80 *BSB-I*, pp. 193-94; 197-98.
81 Lallanji Gopal, 'The Sukraniti—A Nineteenth Century Text', *Bulletin of the School of Oriental and African Studies*, 25(1/3), 1962, pp. 524-56.
82 Benoy Kumar Sarkar, *The Positive Background of Hindu Sociology (Political)* (henceforth, *PBHS-II*). New York: AMS, 1974[1921-26], pp. 12-29.
83 Benoy Kumar Sarkar, *Chinese Religion through Hindu Eyes* (henceforth, *CRTHE*). Shanghai: Commercial Press, 1916, pp. xi-xiii.
84 *NBGP*, pp. 144-77.
85 *NBGP*, pp. 1-5; Partha Chatterjee, *Nationalist Thought and the Colonial World: A Derivative Discourse*. Minneapolis: University of Minnesota Press, 2004, pp. 1-35; Carol Breckenridge and Peter van der Veer, *Orientalism and the Postcolonial Predicament*. Philadelphia: University of Pennsylvania Press, 1993, pp. 1-22.
86 *PPS-1905*, p. 117.
87 *NBGP*, pp. 144-77.
88 *NBGP*, p. 199; *PPS-1905*, pp. 146-48, 212-19, 232-44, 267-71, 295-99; *BSB-I*, pp. 43-47, 178-79; see also Andrew Sartori, 'Beyond Culture-Contact and Colonial Discourse', *Modern Intellectual History*, 4(1), 2007, pp. 77-93.
89 *BSB-I*, pp. 10, 125-28, 147-48, 165-69.
90 *FYA*, pp. 152-54; *BSB-I*, pp. 73-75, 156. 'What you call a patriot, that I am not', Rabindranath would declare. Rabindranath Tagore, *Char Adhyay*. Calcutta: Vishwabharati Press, 1938, p. 63.
91 *The New York Times*, 'American Idealism Constantly in Evidence Here, Says Hindu Scholar', 11 March 1917.

92 *BSB-I*, p. 156; *BSB-II*, pp. 490-92.
93 Chatterjee, *Nationalist Thought and the Colonial World*, pp. 1-35.
94 *NBGP*, pp. 291-98, 342-44.
95 *FYA*, p. 1.
96 Ibid., pp. 157-64.
97 Ibid., pp. 4-6.
98 Tanika Sarkar, *Hindu Wife, Hindu Nation: Community, Religion, and Cultural Nationalism*. Bloomington: Indiana University Press, 2001, pp. 23-52; Geraldine Forbes, *Women in Modern India*. Cambridge: Cambridge University Press, 1996, pp. 10-31.
99 *FYA*, p. 6.
100 He derived his understanding of the vanguard primarily from Pareto. *PBHS-II*, p. 34.
101 *PBHS-II*, pp. i, 34; *FYA*, pp. 12-15.
102 *FYA*, p. 124.
103 Ibid., pp. 54-55.
104 On amalgamation, see Harold Miller, *Race Conflict in New Zealand*. Auckland: Blackwood & Paul, 1966, pp. xxv-xxvii, 159-60.
105 *FYA*, p. 115.
106 Ibid., pp. 109-10.
107 Andrew Sartori, *Bengal in Global Concept History*. Chicago: University of Chicago Press, 2008, pp. 1-24, 109-35.
108 Dipesh Chakrabarty, *Provincializing Europe: Postcolonial Thought and Historical Difference*. Princeton: Princeton University Press, 2000, p. 6.
109 *FYA*, pp. 116-17, 139-43; see also Tapati Guha-Thakurta, *The Making of a New 'Indian' Art: Artists, Aesthetics and Nationalism in Bengal 1850-1930*. Cambridge: Cambridge University Press, 1992, pp. 185-225.
110 Guha-Thakurta, *Making of a New 'Indian' Art*, pp. 124-25.
111 *BSB-II*, pp. 821-22; Guha-Thakurta, *Making of a New 'Indian' Art*; Partha Mitter, *Art and Nationalism in Colonial India, 1850-1922*. Cambridge: Cambridge University Press, 1994, pp. 272-94, 340-74.
112 Bose was a sculptor and art historian who wrote about 'Hindu colonies' in Southeast Asia. His outlook on the world was not far removed from that of Sarkar and Radhakumud Mookerji. See Phanindranath Bose, *The Indian Colony of Siam*. Lahore: Punjab Sanskrit Book Depot, 1927. Benoy Kumar Sarkar, *Aesthetics of Young India* (henceforth, *AYI*). Calcutta: Kar, Majumder, 1927, pp. 2-3; *FYA*, p. 116; *Rupam* (January 1922); *Bijoli* (May-July 1922, nos 28-30).
113 *AYI*, pp. 71-74.
114 Ibid., 95-99.
115 Ibid., p. 104.
116 *FYA*, pp. 147-48.
117 Stephen Greenblatt, *Marvelous Possessions: The Wonder of the New World*. Chicago: University of Chicago Press, 1991, pp. 1-25.

118 Carl Ernst, 'Admiring the Works of the Ancients', in David Gilmartin and Bruce Lawrence (eds), *Beyond Turk and Hindu: Rethinking Religious Identities in Islamicate South Asia*. Delhi: India Research Press, 2002, pp. 98–120.
119 *FYA*, p. 148.
120 Ibid., 54–55.
121 Mukhopadhyay, *Prabandha Samagra*, pp. 16–70, 107–25; Tapan Raychaudhuri, *Europe Reconsidered: Perceptions of the West in Nineteenth-Century Bengal*. Delhi: Oxford University Press, 2002, pp. 59, 76.
122 *BSB-II*, pp. 525–27.
123 *FYA*, pp. 303–4.
124 *FYA*, pp. 12–15; Satadru Sen, *Colonial Childhoods: The Juvenile Periphery of India 1850–1945*. London: Anthem, 2005, pp. 13–33.
125 *FYA*, p. 124.
126 Ibid., pp. 184–85.
127 Rosinka Chaudhuri, 'Three Poets in Search of History', in Michael Dodson and Brian Hatcher (eds), *Trans-Colonial Modernities in South Asia*. London: Routledge, 2012, pp. 189–207.
128 Homi Bhabha, *The Location of Culture*. New York: Routledge, 1994, p. 121.
129 *FYA*, p. 18.
130 *NBGP*, pp. 238–41.
131 *FYA*, p. 99.
132 Ibid., p. 66.
133 Ibid., pp. 82–85, 98–99, 166–67.
134 Eric Hobsbawn, *The Age of Empire*. New York: Vintage, 1989, p. 90.
135 Dilip Menon, 'A Local Cosmopolitanism: "Kesari" Balakrishna Pillai and the Invention of Europe for a Modern Kerala', in Sugata Bose and Kris Manjapra (eds), *Cosmopolitan Thought Zones: South Asia and the Global Circulation of Ideas*. New York: Palgrave, 2010, p. 131; Janaki Bakhle, 'Putting Global Intellectual History in Its Place', in Samuel Moyn and Andrew Sartori (eds), *Global Intellectual History*. New York: Columbia University Press, 2008, pp. 233–34.
136 Kwame Appiah, *Cosmopolitanism*. London: Norton, 2006, pp. xi–xxi.
137 Guha, *History at the Limit of World-History* pp. 6–23; Georg Hegel, *The Philosophy of History*. New York: Dover, 1956, pp. 4–10.
138 *NBGP*, pp. 225–26.
139 *PPS-1905*, pp. 115, 232–46.
140 *SHHM*, pp. 55–67.
141 Benoy Kumar Sarkar, *The Political Institutions and Theories of the Hindus* (henceforth, *PITH*). Leipzig: Verlag, 1922, pp. 54–62.
142 Uma Chakrabarty, 'Whatever Happened to the Vedic Dasi?' in Kumkum Sangari and Sudesh Vaid (eds), *Recasting Women: Essays in Colonial History*. New Brunswick: Rutgers University Press, 1990, pp. 27–87.
143 *FYA*, pp. 263–71.

44   Introduction

144 Ibid., pp. 92–93.
145 Ibid., pp. 14–15, 250–52.
146 *PPS-1905*, pp. 129–30.
147 *FYA*, pp. 279–84.
148 Ibid., pp. 308–14, 327–29, 331–32.
149 Ibid., pp. 31718.
150 Indira Chowdhuri-Sengupta, 'The Effeminate and the Masculine', in Peter Robb (ed.), *The Concept of Race in South Asia*. Delhi: Oxford University Press, 1995, pp. 282–303.
151 *FYA*, pp. 274–76.
152 Sen, *Traces of Empire*, p. 165.
153 *FYA*, p. 330.
154 *FYA*, pp. 30–31; *DIWP*, pp. 99–101.
155 Flora, 'Benoy Kumar Sarkar', p. 65. On the Ghadr Party, see Malini Sood, 'Expatriate Nationalism and Ethnic Radicalism: The Ghadar Party in North America, 1910–1920'. PhD Dissertation, State University of New York (SUNY) Stony Brook, 1995.
156 *FYA*, p. 48.
157 Ibid., pp. 48–66.
158 *PBHS-II*, pp. 20–21; *NBGP*, pp. 337–40.
159 See Richard Drinnon, *Facing West: The Metaphysics of Indian Hating and Empire Building*. New York: Schocken, 1990, pp. 460–64.
160 *FYA*, pp. 48–66; *BSB-I*, pp. 295–97.
161 *PPS-1905*, pp. 17–18; *NBGP*, pp. 361–62.
162 Flora, 'Benoy Kumar Sarkar', p. 399.
163 Benoy Kumar Sarkar, 'Sociology of Creative Disequilibrium in Education', *Calcutta Review*, July 1940, pp. 529–37.
164 Gay, *The Cultivation of Hatred*, pp. 53–54; Hobsbawm, *The Age of Empire*, p. 83.
165 *NBGP*, pp. 262–63.
166 Tithi Bhattacharya, *Sentinels of Culture: Class, Education and the Colonial Intellectual in Bengal 1848-85*. Delhi: Oxford University Press, 2005, pp. 29, 47–48.
167 Bank security was the measure of the rule of law in a given society, Sarkar wrote, commenting on the collapse of the Bengal National Bank and the Alliance Bank. *NBGP*, pp. 265–72.
168 *FYA*, p. 30.
169 Radhakumud Mookerji, *Local Government in Ancient India*. Charleston: Nabu, 2012, pp. 3–4.
170 *PITH*, pp. 54–62.
171 *FYA*, pp. 205–6.
172 Benjamin Zachariah, *Nehru*. New York: Routledge, 2004, pp. 154–60 ; Sen, *Traces of Empire*, pp. 37, 79.
173 By 1949, when Sarkar was openly anti-Soviet, he was also critical of Ludwig Erhard's prescriptions for the rebuilding of Germany, favouring a

Introduction   45

more 'socialistic' approach. *DIWP*, pp. 41–42; Hannah Schissler (ed.), *The Miracle Years: A Cultural History of West Germany 1949-1968*. Princeton: Princeton University Press, 2001, pp. 100, 189.
174 *DIWP*, pp. 43, 67.
175 *VT*, pp. 239–47; *BSB-II*, pp. 558–59, 593–95, 600–601.
176 Gay, *The Cultivation of Hatred*, 97; Hobsbawm, *The Age of Empire*, 165–91; Amal Kumar Mukhopadhyay, 'Benoy Kumar Sarkar: The Theoretical Foundation of Indian Capitalism', in Amal Kumar Mukhopadhyay (ed.), *The Bengali Intellectual Tradition*. Calcutta: K.P. Bagchi, 1979, p. 228.
177 Even more than Vivekananda, the model of this worldly asceticism was Satish Chandra Mukherjee. *BSB-I*, pp. 176–78, 193–94.
178 Sartori, *Bengal in Global Concept History*, pp. 68–108, 136–75.
179 Sarkar, 'Sociology of Creative Disequilibrium in Education'; *NBGP*, p. 353; *BSB-I*, p. 80; *BSB-II*, pp. 489, 557.
180 *VT*, pp. 239–47.
181 *FYA*, pp. 352–56; Gail Minault, *The Khilafat Movement: Religious Symbolism and Political Mobilization in India*. New York: Columbia University Press, 1982, pp. 111–66; Shahid Amin, 'Gandhi as Mahatma', in Ranajit Guha and Gayatri Spivak (eds), *Selected Subaltern Studies*. Oxford: Oxford University Press, 1988, pp. 288–350.
182 *FYA*, p. 344.
183 Sumit Sarkar, *The Swadeshi Movement in Bengal*, pp. 26–77.
184 *VT*, pp. 132–35.
185 Gay, *The Cultivation of Hatred*, p. 123.
186 On Croce and democracy, see H.S. Hughes, *Consciousness and Society: The Reorientation of European Social Thought 1890-1930*. New York: Vintage, 1977, pp. 215–22.
187 *VT*, p. 226.
188 Ibid.
189 *NBGP*, pp. 253–55.
190 *VT*, p. 93.
191 *DIWP*, p. 120.
192 Like Pareto, who accepted Marx's notion of a class struggle but saw it as primarily a conflict between manipulative elites, Sarkar insisted that apparently disadvantaged classes possessed their own 'lions', chafing for access to power. But unlike Pareto, who preserved his attachment to the Italian aristocracy, Sarkar argued that in modern India, the history-making vanguard was independent of all extant classes: It could come from any part of the race. See Hughes, *Consciousness and Society*, pp. 78–82.
193 C.A. Bayly, *Recovering Liberties*, pp. 5–6.
194 Hobsbawm, *The Age of Empire*, pp. 10, 188–89.
195 *FYA*, p. 350.
196 Ibid., pp. 322–23.

197 VT, pp. 465–66.
198 Ibid., pp. 97–98.
199 Partha Chatterjee, *The Politics of the Governed*. New York: Columbia University Press, 2004, pp. 27–51.
200 VT, pp. 136–60.
201 Ibid., pp. 465–66.
202 PPS-1905, pp. 48–49, 324; Hughes, *Consciousness and Society*, pp. 67–89; Flora, 'Benoy Kumar Sarkar', pp. 97–98; NBGP, p. 350.
203 FYA, pp. 24, 31; PPS-1905, p. 324.
204 BSB-II, pp. 517–18.
205 NBGP, pp. 208–12.
206 Benoy Kumar Sarkar, *Scheme for Economic Development in India* (henceforth, SEDI). Calcutta: Oriental Library, 1926, pp. 5–7; PBHS-II, pp. 57, 96; Hobsbawm, *The Age of Empire*, p. 40; C.A. Bayly, *Recovering Liberties*, pp. 1–25.
207 Sartori, *Bengal in Global Concept History*, pp. 1–24.
208 Flora, 'Benoy Kumar Sarkar', p. 10.
209 NBGP, pp. 10–11, 104–25.
210 Ibid., pp. 68–103, 84–88, 148–49.
211 Flora, 'Benoy Kumar Sarkar', pp. 393n95, 393n97.
212 Partha Chatterjee, *The Nation and Its Fragments: Colonial and Postcolonial Histories*. Princeton: Princeton University Press, 1993, pp. 116–57.
213 C.A. Bayly, *Recovering Liberties*, pp. 15–24.
214 Bhudeb Mukhopadhyay, *Samajik Prabandha*. Calcutta: Paschimbanga Pustak Parishad, 1981, pp. 1–6.
215 Ibid., pp. 9–15.
216 C.A. Bayly, *Recovering Liberties*, p. 282.
217 Goswami, 'Imaginary Futures and Colonial Internationalisms', pp. 167, 180, 207–8, 242–76; Joya Chatterji, *Bengal Divided: Hindu Communalism and Partition, 1932-1947*. Cambridge: Cambridge University Press, 2002, pp. 150–90.
218 Ashis Nandy is incorrect when he describes Bhudeb as an early advocate of an independent Indian nation-state. Nandy, *The Romance of the State*, p. 19n4.
219 Sumit Sarkar, *Writing Social History*. Delhi: Oxford University Press, 1999, pp. 96–103.
220 Nandy, *The Romance of the State*, p. 15–33.
221 Nandy, *The Romance of the State*, p. 5; Ronald Inden, *Imagining India*. Bloomington: Indiana University Press, 2001, pp. 188–97.
222 Andrew Sartori, 'Beyond Culture-Contact and Colonial Discourse: "Germanism" in Colonial Bengal', in Shruti Kapila (ed.), *An Intellectual History for India*. Delhi: Cambridge University Press, 2010, pp. 80–83.
223 Zachariah, *Nehru*, pp. 180–213.
224 Leonard Gordon, *Brothers Against the Raj: A Biography of Indian Nationalists Sarat and Subhas Chandra Bose*. New York: Columbia University Press, 1990, p. 57.

Introduction   47

225   PPS-1905, pp. 150, 315–18.
226   Ibid., pp. 314–16.
227   VT, pp. 510–11; PPS-1905, pp. 285, 315.
228   Gay, The Cultivation of Hatred, pp. 3–7, 34.
229   Flora, 'Benoy Kumar Sarkar', p. 9.
230   Zachariah, 'Rethinking (the Absence of) Fascism in India'.
231   Partha Chatterjee, Wages of Freedom: Fifty Years of the Indian Nation-State. Delhi: Oxford University Press, 1998, pp. 5–17.
232   Flora, 'Benoy Kumar Sarkar', pp. 454–65.
233   CRTHE, p. 249.
234   Brian Hatcher, Idioms of Improvement: Vidyasagar and Cultural Encounter in Bengal. Delhi: Oxford University Press, 1996, pp. 7–19.
235   FYA, p. 298.
236   VT, pp. 189–91; Chatterji, pp. 259–65.
237   PB, pp. 187–89.
238   DIWP, pp. 112–20.
239   Gordon, Brothers Against the Raj, pp. 374–440.
240   Susobhan Sarkar, On the Bengal Renaissance. Calcutta: Papyrus, 1985, pp. 70–71.
241   DIWP, pp. 110–11.
242   Ibid., pp. 112–20.
243   PPS-1905, pp. 108, 132–34.
244   DIWP, pp. 112–13.
245   BSB-I, pp. 192, 200.
246   DIWP, p. 107.
247   Benedict Anderson, Imagined Communities. London: Verso, 1993, p. 7.
248   BSB-II, pp. 695–99.
249   DIWP, pp. 154–57.
250   PPS-1905, p. 42.
251   DIWP, pp. 112–13.
252   Ibid., pp. 112–20.
253   BSB-I, pp. 185–87.
254   DIWP, p. 113.
255   Sumathi Ramaswamy, Passions of the Tongue: Language Devotion in Tamil India 1891–1970. Berkeley: University of California Press, 1997, pp. 168–78.
256   DIWP, pp. 155–56.
257   Ramaswamy, Passions of the Tongue, pp. 168–78.
258   DIWP, pp. 112–20.
259   Peter Robb (ed.), The Concept of Race in South Asia. Delhi: Oxford University Press, 1995, p. 3.
260   DIWP, p. 108.
261   By the Great War, Sarkar had decided that Herder could not accommodate Indian linguistic diversity. BSB-I, pp. 80–81; PB, pp. 8–9; Johann Herder,

Reflections on the Philosophy of the History of Mankind. Chicago: University of Chicago Press, 1968, pp. 3–78.
262 *DIWP*, pp. 112–20.
263 *BSB-II*, pp. 679–84.
264 Granville Austin, *The Indian Constitution: Cornerstone of a Nation*. Oxford: Clarendon, 1966, pp. 186–216.
265 *FYA*, p. 326.

1
An Indian Race

For Indian nationalists in the colony, an elemental concern was to demonstrate that there was an Indian nation, in the face of colonial discourses of a non-people who would fly apart, fly at each other's throats, and reveal their essential barbarism in the absence of European control.[1] This consideration only intensified in the decade of the Great War, when new nation-states and quasi-state entities emerged in Europe and the Levant, generating a flood of discourse about the content and entitlements of nationhood. Racial coherence was central to this discourse.[2] The narrative was deeply Eurocentric and has remained so, as the primordialism of a scholar like Anthony Smith suggests: only Europeans possess the ethnic roots of nationhood.[3] For Sarkar and his contemporaries, being able to talk about an 'Indian race' became crucial to their claims to nation and state, not least because it might resolve or contain the visible fractures of class, caste, religion and original fantasy.[4] Sarkar posited no naturally occurring racial essence. He insisted quite early that whereas Hellenic, Germanic and Vedic governance was premised on ethnicity, mature Indian statecraft rested on geography.[5] Increasingly, however, he came to see the production of race as an important function of state and geography.

Imagining an 'Indian race' was not a straightforward task for an intellectual who regarded the denial of difference as a basic mission of his historical cohort. What was needed, evidently, was a reformulation of race. Yet Sarkar never attempted a concise, consistent definition of race. This was not so much a strategic vagueness as the reflection of a historical location: the modern native's attempt to appropriate the inherent discipline of the racialised community while destabilising its hierarchies. In this trajectory, race became first and foremost a matter of political purpose, including but not limited to citizenship. The idea that an Indian race might undergird citizenship has a broadly dispersed imperial pedigree: Peter Robb has suggested that it emerged in Gandhi's South Africa; Javed Majeed has linked it to pan-Islamic ferment.[6] Sarkar went further. Like Fanon, he saw race as inseparable from an anti-colonial reading of history: injustice, oppression and resistance were at its heart.[7] But unlike Fanon, Sarkar looked for histories and processes that were considerably deeper than colonialism. He sometimes used the word 'race' to suggest a shared genealogy, but he also used it to mean a population with shifting biological and cultural content, held together by shared but changing historical predicaments and destinies. Destiny could be, for some, a matter of self-consciousness; for others, it was a condition, like an unknown disease. Accordingly, 'race' in Sarkar's usage was sometimes interchangeable with the modern European understanding of 'nation', which in the interwar period was itself in a state of flux.[8] At other times it was the prehistory of the nation, signifying primordial populations that remained relevant to the modern not only as Romantic selves but also as the raw material of governmentality. Whereas he concentrated on culture in the earlier part of his career, he became increasingly focused on biology later on, keeping pace with the more sinister developments in European politics.

Sarkar's attempt to revise the relationship between history, populations and self-conscious communities represented, as usual, a collection of historically supplied possibilities, many of which were aborted by political circumstances. In seeing race as a history of converging bodies, and history as a text of racial entropy, he derived substantially from Arthur de Gobineau.[9] He shared neither Gobineau's crude hierarchies nor his fear of miscegenation, but he understood that nineteenth-century racism had been boosted by the social and biological science of the twentieth.[10] He could not ignore this science; he was attracted to it. The presence of the scientific body at the heart of society, politics and policy was the hallmark of modernity and, indeed, of a desirable racial identity. It thus became important to claim race as an authentic legacy of the Indian past: 'Hindu literature on anatomy and physiology as well as eugenics and embryology has been voluminous', Sarkar declared in *The Sociology of Races*.[11] Such references were an attempt to indigenise the biological understanding of race as a sign of power: by recognising race as important, studying it and writing about it, Indians had historically indicated their awareness of the connection between knowledge of embodied populations and competitiveness in the world.

Sarkar's objective was to revive that awareness in the present time as part of a regeneration of the race itself. The physicality of race—the mobilisation of blood, backbone, muscle and nerve—was needed to counter the discourse of 'spiritual India':

During the nineteenth century . . . the people of India were divorced perforce from the vitalizing interests and responsibilities in every field of work. They had necessarily to fall back upon the super-sensual, the nonmaterial, the 'spiritual'. But what is the spiritual worth that is not grounded in the 'physical basis of life', the economic and the political? It can be nothing better than a nerveless fancy, a backboneless mysticism, an imbecile subjectivism, or an idle speculation.[12]

Such apparently blasphemous condemnation is well within the scope of nationalist discourse after Bankim.[13] Because Sarkar wanted to destabilise the racial body by highlighting its historical nature, he could agree occasionally with the colonial narrative of disembodied India: the crisis of the Indian race was the moment of its reinvention.

When the Great War cast its shadow on the white certainties of empire, Sarkar became convinced that a new Indian race was emerging in his lifetime. He did not see the novelty itself as new: the 'truth' of race was that it was constantly remixed and reformulated. That quality was an element of the cosmopolitan, historical identity that Sarkar sought. At the same time, fluidity and hybridity carried the threat of degeneration and racial death. Degeneracy became the substance of race: in the colony, Sarkar implied, everybody was a degenerate, and even the vanguard was promising precisely because they were a new hybrid. This is a different formulation of race than what we typically see in 'racism', where there is a clear distinction between pure/healthy and impure/degenerate populations. For Sarkar, purity was a mirage and health was elusive. What mattered was the ability to adapt to history: to respond intelligently to one's mongrel nature. In the twentieth century, racial emergence had to be managed according to hierarchies consistent with the modern nation-state, through modern methods, modern men and the modern state. It had, in other words, to be brought into alignment with national purpose.

That nationalised concern with racial health can be located alongside and in competition with parallel, contemporary projects of upper-class, often female-led activism in colonial India, which were themselves part of a global field of modern social work.[14] It also overlapped the reformisms championed by Gandhi,[15] the Ramakrishna Mission,[16] and most importantly, the Hindu right. With the last, Sarkar shared the conviction that the nationalist project must define the boundaries and contingencies of an Indian Volk by working out credible, politically viable relationships between the terms 'Hindu', 'Muslim' and 'Indian'. By the Minto-Morley era, the discourse of the 'external loyalties' of the

Muslim had been reinforced by recent politics,[17] resulting in a phobia—subsequently articulated by Savarkar—of a political entity that was within the state but without the Volk. This dystopic perception of Muslims informed the Hindu-nationalist desire for a different kind of state, and simultaneously, a different kind of racial Self: one that was self-aware *as a race* and could assert its majoritarian prerogatives. The Arya Samaji leader Swami Shraddhanand, for example, was obsessed with the statistics of population, and the author in 1926 of a book reassuringly titled *Hindu Sangathan: Saviour of the Dying Race*. Religion in such texts was almost entirely a shorthand for race.[18]

Despite the interest in extinction and salvage, racial thinking in Hindu nationalism is not entirely derivative of European racism. Some of the roots are imbedded closer to home, in late-nineteenth-century discontent and mobilisation beyond the demographics of Congress moderation. For instance, while Dayanand Saraswati's notion of a 'great people' is not fully racialised, it is nevertheless proto-racial, because his insistence on territoriality infuses his 'people' with the insularity of race.[19] Likewise, Dayanand's emphasis on a meritocracy of *varna* reinforces the idea of a 'Vedic race': it erodes the notion of caste society as a collection of hereditary and pure collectives, but brings it into alignment with liberal ideas of the community that liberates the individual even as it contains him, that is distinctive in this regard, and that values common blood within the larger community.[20] Common blood, however, complicated the problem of exclusion when it came to outlier communities. M.S. Golwalkar could emphasise common origin and write of race as constituting the 'body' of the nation, but even his idea of race was not entirely biological.[21] To be politically meaningful, race as a purely biological entity was not enough; it might as well be dead. It was the biology–culture–state combination that mattered, and the precise formula was contentious.

Race thus marks a tension within Hindutva, and within Indian nationalism generally. It is rarely as explicit as it is in European discourse, but is present, at least as a trace, in the view of Muslims as 'Turks' and *mlechchas*, in shifting outlooks on aboriginal populations and caste, and in the vocabulary of 'Aryan' India. On these issues, Sarkar was accommodating and inclusive, but as usual, inconsistent. His use of the term 'Hindu' does not fit any of the three historical usages Sumit Sarkar has identified: a vague pre-modern gesture, a nineteenth-century consolidation, and the anti-Muslim platform of the 1920s.[22] It

An Indian Race 53

was new, experimental and adaptable. On the one hand, he used the word broadly to mean 'Indian', including Muslims and assorted others within the category. On the other hand, Hindu and Muslim remained separate categories, and 'India' became a new concept—and state—within which they could be either merged or gathered and managed. Sarkar came to favour gathering and management over merging. His apparent indifference to 'national unity' (and emphasis on the state over the nation) was an attempt to bypass the difficulties of asserting a 'merged' Indianness. The state would not only substitute for the nation as the agent of history, it would produce the nation through its educative processes of race-management, extending what Dilip Menon has called 'a pedagogy of the national'.[23]

Sarkar's vacillation on whether the 'Hindu race' was coterminous with the 'Indian nation' is not merely an untidiness. The inclusion of Muslims within either was a part of his project of rejecting the dichotomy of the worldly West and the unworldly East. Neither Hindus nor Indians were wrapped up in religion; their priorities and affiliations were as prosaic and secular as those of Europeans. The vocabulary of race lent his polemic flexibility as well as boundaries, reflecting his understanding that political purpose and the contours of the purposeful community could not be the same in all contexts, and that the nation/state would have to be larger than its politically 'alive' constituencies but not too much larger. It is a reflection of the limits and hesitations within the liberal Hindu who wants to be simultaneously cosmopolitan and nationally identified. It illuminates, moreover, the evolving statist imaginary of the race-nation-Volk-state alignment in a 'diverse' country in which diversity is politically mobilised. As Pakistan became a fait accompli, Sarkar's vision of the Indian state moved from a pedagogy of mutual transformation to one of assimilation. Making the race fit for its political circumstances had long been a central function of the governance he advocated, but who was to be remade? Sarkar's understanding of justice was never indifferent to the plight of the individual; nor did it shy away entirely from acknowledging the rights of communities. But when he imagined race-making as regeneration and assimilation, he also imagined the production of individuals as wards of the state and the overhauling of communities. Ultimately, Sarkar's attempt to outline an Indian race illustrates the difficulties of imagining 'racial justice'—i.e., the combination of race and justice—within the liberal project of nation-building.

Degenerate Nationhood

Sarkar lived at the tail end of the period when the racialised human body was both most alive and dying everywhere.[24] This body was, of course, a creature of empire. The science as well as the popular understanding of race was focused on the measurable and imageable truths of biology, as ethnographers, photographers and doctors fanned out around the world, supported by criminologists, psychologists and historians.[25] Precisely because they were tied to modern political formations, these bodies were also caught up in far-reaching anxieties about competition and survival in the modern world.[26] The triumphant white body of the coloniser was shadowed by the dying bodies of natives and savages, which in turn were shadowed by the spectre of white decline. Men with rifles, steamships and soap were unquestionably masterful, but no sustainable assurance could be derived from the status of a 'master race' when British military recruiters were confronted by tubercular weaklings at the outset of the Boer War, or even when Australian and Andamanese aborigines were perceived to be dying of a 'demoralisation' brought about by contact with civilisation.[27] These anxieties are too well-documented to require detailed elaboration. It should suffice to note that in the discursive arc containing Gobineau, Risley, Baden Powell, evolutionist anthropology, eugenics, demography, and eventually the extermination of the European Untermenschen, modernity was a threat to racialised existence as well as its salvation.

Sarkar echoed these anxieties at several levels. For a native insurgent against empire, white unease produced a vindictive satisfaction: the albinocracy was a temporary phase, not the climax of history. At the same time, the apparent decimation of indigenes could not fail to alarm him, since it was difficult to deny his own location on the losing side of history. The alarm required him to modulate the modern native's relationship to the indigenous. Moreover, his investment in modernity and its political, social and cultural institutions, such as the democratic state and industrial capitalism, left him with anxieties that were similar to those of the European elites. Indeed, he was invested in this similarity, because it was only by sharing the dilemmas of the modern that he could demonstrate his own modernity. When he wrote about revolutionary terrorism in Bengal, he saw obvious parallels between Bengali alarm about the inadequacies of the rebel body, and German Romanticism with its cult of the gymnasium.[28] In each case, Sarkar suggested, national regeneration and physical regeneration were intertwined: the nation became rooted in the unstable (male) body.

To live in the modern world was to engage continuously with the degeneracy that existed in others as a fact, and in oneself as a potential. His understanding of race was increasingly biological, but it was not a primordial biology surfacing in the form of the nation. Rather, a newly biological nation came to constitute the race as a site of governance.

Sarkar engaged, therefore, in a political relocation of the native body. The decolonised native would occupy an inherently seditious racial location, where he would adopt but also abuse the predicament of contemporary whiteness, nudging it further into decline while retaining its strategies of recuperation and survival. For Sarkar, whiteness was both real and contrived. It was real in the sense that it represented an undeniable political advantage and a powerful discipline of investigation and governance, and contrived in the sense that it was fraudulent: an ass masquerading as a sacred cow. In either case, he wanted to appropriate its utility. Anti-colonial polemics of justice required reminding whites of their mongrel nature, and of the injustice tied up with an unproblematised—and hence false—whiteness. The colonised and coloured races were, in that sense, more 'real' than whites: they shared a common problem of white racism. American whiteness was a political fabrication *and* an ethical problem, he pointed out.[29] Germany was 'a land of heterogeneous peoples'.[30]

Quite early in his career, Sarkar showed a sharp awareness of the fluidity of race in history. Miscegenation was the norm, not an aberration: 'The whole epoch beginning with [Alexander's] accession to the Greek throne [was] one in which race-boundaries were being obliterated and the sense of universal humanity generated'.[31] He did not assign this fluidity an unambiguous value. When people whose boundaries were being 'obliterated' were insensitive to the change, change constituted racial death. But when change was initiated or rationally managed by the group itself, it could constitute a positive evolution. A progressive race sought to understand and manipulate its own degeneration, regenerating itself in the process. Whites, Sarkar eventually suggested, were a particular sort of degenerate race, which had not understood its historical nature and entered an uncontrolled decline in the pursuit of empire. The 'glorification of the imperial-colonial pattern' by Europeans and Americans (and Japanese), he wrote, 'is but an index to their insensibility to the calamity that is fast approaching them'.[32]

Sarkar identified the calamity with empire itself: the definitive sign of contemporary whiteness became the cause and symptom of racial damage in the coloniser, and the end of a historical trajectory.[33]

Colonialism had infected Europe with men and women who were incapable of relating normally to others. A long quote from 1922 is warranted here:

> Superiority-complex, as obtaining in the master-mentality described by Nietzsche, is no less a mark of neurosis than the inferiority-complex prevailing in the slave mentality.
> The 'inter-mental' processes that constitute social relations . . . do not exist or function in a normal, i.e., healthy manner in the imperial-colonial ecology. Rulers behave as non-social or anti-social animals vis-à-vis the ruled. This non-sociality or anti-sociality sticks to the psyche. They carry it along with them in their behaviours with all races who are their political-imperial equals or rivals. It becomes psychologically impossible for them to associate with members of other ruling races. Nervousness seizes them whenever they have to orientate themselves as men to men with persons who do not belong to their own race. The pathological obsession by the atmosphere of subject races becomes an essential part of their nervous system.
> Individual pathology sets in as soon as the rulers land in the colonies. A little parcel weighing not more than half a pound is not carried by the men and women of the empire-holders from the store even to the car that is waiting at the door.
> This little item points . . . as much to the commencement of the physical deterioration as to that of the positively anti-human, inhuman and immoral attitudes of life. The process of acculturation to physical lethargy and moral degradation goes on for a somewhat lengthy period in every individual man or woman. The *sociologie colonial* is . . . but the sociology of men and women addicted to humanly undesirable habits of life. It is these men and women, who, on returning home in Eur-America or Japan, furnish the backbone and 'social climate' as well as the intellectual and moral perspectives of democracy, freedom and socialism.[34]

Foreshadowing Fanon and Nandy but approaching from the right, Sarkar turns imperialism into a psychological condition.[35] He borrows the investigative tools of whiteness but reverses the direction of diagnosis, which is also the process of race-making.

Such diagnoses had an established pedigree. In the polemic of colonialism as a force that destroys democratic habits and institutions, there is a clear echo of the abolitionist rhetoric of the effects of slavery on slave-owning societies.[36] Sarkar noted that the damage extended into the white body itself, rendering the race regressive rather than progressive in its evolution: 'Imperialism has almost invariably spelt physical degeneracy'.[37] He devastatingly co-opted the white discourse of the evaporation of whiteness in the tropics.[38] Nietzsche was deployed again, but ambiguously, to pathologise a comfort-loving master race that had substituted games for warfare.[39] Also, Sarkar made a clear connection between degeneracy and provinciality: the colonial laager, more than the Britain itself, became a model of insularity. In one stroke, he not only stripped away the 'worldly' status of the imperial races and their colonial pets, he also suggested—somewhat like Hannah Arendt—that colonialism returns to the metropole as a cancer.[40]

Sarkar's attack on imperial whiteness utilised the discourses of addiction and habituality, further subverting the politics of science, culture and governance.[41] His historical moment was marked on the one hand by a Western tendency to blame white drug use on the 'addictive' Orient,[42] and on the other by the opposition—derived from Hegel—between (Western) reason and (Oriental) habit.[43] Sarkar noted the damage done by colonial drug policies in India and China, not only conjuring up images of white Britain poisoning the body of an Asian race (constituted, as usual, by degeneration), but also casting whites in the double role of pushers and addicts.[44] The coloniser became an effete, trembling counterpart of the inmate of the clinic, no more capable of freedom, moral choice and democratic politics than were other institutionalised patients. Far from carrying the white man's burden, the white man *was* the burden. But crucially, the concept of a burden was left intact, for newer and wiser races to take up. Whiteness was a cautionary tale: an arrogant race destroying itself through inept responses to its own (enviable) modernity and dominance.

Sarkar thus posited a complex relationship between race and history. It is not surprising that his views on an Indian racial 'condition' would be tied to the colonial city and 'municipal democracy'. These phenomena were not only white intrusions into India, they were also Indian responses and initiatives. In each sense, the city was a revolutionary space, where older structures and boundaries (such as the joint family and caste restrictions) had proved inadequate, and new migrations and aspirations generated unpredictable melting-pots of democracy-in-society.[45] Sarkar, like Nandy, recognised a connection between migration, uprooting and novelty in modern India, but he refused to see it as pathological.[46] He was influenced here by Pitirim Sorokin's vision of 'rurbanisation', or the interpenetration and mutual disruption of the city and the village.[47] The disruption was biological, social and moral: the twentieth-century metropolis produced the emerging Indian race either as degenerates or as regenerates, depending on how it was managed by the state and the vanguard.

Discussing the Montagu-Chelmsford reforms and the Government of India Act of 1935, Sarkar described the unsettling possibilities of the colonial city:

> Under these conditions the members of the alleged higher castes find themselves at a discount in interhuman relations and those of the non-higher at a premium. The economic elevation of the lower has thus been cooperating with the economic degradation of the higher in order to establish a factual equality between the two. The birth considerations are tending to melt away in the pattern of economic discriminations by which the state favours the lower as against the higher. In this general *milieu* interdining has become universal. Nay, women of the so-called higher castes may tend, although not yet in great numbers, to seek mates from among the gainfully employed persons of the alleged lower castes.[48]

This narrative of a disrupted society is more indebted to contemporary Europe than to treatises of Kaliyuga. Sarkar borrowed from the circulation-of-elites theories of Pareto and Corrado Gini, both of whom had been uneasy about democratic developments in Europe. Pareto had argued that Europe's old aristocracy was dying out on account of its own 'physical, intellectual and moral degeneracy', and that the new elites would come from the inferior classes.[49] Similarly, Gini—who befriended Sarkar in 1929—had pointed to falling birthrates among northern-Europeans as signs of an unfolding revolution. The racial elite would have to save itself by incorporating the 'energy' of Europe's margins.[50] In India, Sarkar argued, the dynamic was different: here, it was intervention by the colonial state on behalf of the lower orders that had disrupted the influence of the old native elites.[51] Sarkar had none of Pareto's fondness for the aristocracy, but he nevertheless saw the breakdown of elite monopolies in India as the precipitation of a crisis that constituted a racial condition.

The alarm within this vision is evident in the attention Sarkar paid to sex as a sign and ingredient of race, especially in the last decade of his life. His views on 'loose' women and delinquent youth, concern with birthrates and eugenics, advocacy of love and divorce, and interest in the legislation of marriage and reproduction indicate that he—along with a diverse group of dyarchy-era social scientists, social workers and legislators—believed that in modern India, the rules and products of race/sex were undergoing a radical transformation.[52] The economist Radhakamal Mookerji, Sarkar's colleague from National Education, also read sexual data as a text of demographic crisis, and in 1909, U.N. Mukherji had merged the fear of fertile Muslims with a guilty narrative of caste injustice to suggest that Hindus were a 'dying race'.[53] Sarkar did not share their specific fears,[54] but it is hard to miss the nervousness in his narrative of the impact of colonial initiatives in affirmative action. On the one hand, as an opponent of obsolete forms of community, he accepted the initiatives, arguing that caste was normatively subject to political intervention.[55] On the other hand, he belonged to the section of society that perceived a threat to its privileges and codes: not only were the unfit infiltrating the enclaves of power, they were coming for 'our' women. (Or even worse, our women were going to them.) The women could not be stopped, nor could the low-caste be disbarred from public positions: that would be contrary to Sarkar's conviction that new elites could be found in the margins of society, and his explicit rejection of caste-discrimination.[56] The situation therefore required careful regulation—and observation—by those qualified to make informed decisions about society and modernity.

The particular interventions that Sarkar sought in the sexual behaviour of his compatriots—like encouraging widows to marry and have children—were by and large liberal, and occasionally radical. They fell within a colonial-reformist trajectory that can be traced back to Vidyasagar,[57] and that in Sarkar's own time included Shraddhanand, who urged that raped women be considered virgins, eligible to marry.[58] Sarkar, who believed Indian and European (especially German!) women had similar moral qualities and similar needs for greater freedom, was certainly more liberal than Shraddhanand, who continued to fetishise the chastity of Hindu widows.[59] He also deviated sharply from the 'conservative reformism' of Bhudeb Mukhopadhyay, who, while supporting a form of companionate marriage, had also urged that widows be educated to think of widowhood as a noble vow, utilising the Indian woman's 'natural' propensity for *bhakti*.[60] Bhudeb, typically of his late-nineteenth-century moment, had sought to articulate a conjugal modernity *contained* by the 'Indian family'.[61] Sarkar demurred; neither the patriarchal family nor national peculiarity was a legitimate instrument of containment.

For Sarkar, the re-education of women was a vital complement to the mistrification of men: even domesticity must be dynamic, not static. But he shared Shraddhanand's nervousness about women's sexual agency and its connection with racial death. Sarkar was not arguing for racial purity; quite the opposite. Miscegenation was a rebel discourse of worldliness, corrosive of the Orientalist edifice of 'unchanging India'. Mongrels have been central to imaginaries of a new India, from Savarkar envisioning 'a dear little Bengali sister in-law' and a hybrid-Hindu family, to polyglot convergences of engineers on the Nehruvian frontier.[62] But the 'impurity' or hybridity that Sarkar saw in the city, which he described as 'parianisation' or the reversal of Aryanisation, brought him within the orbit of Spengler and civilisational decline even as it brought him to a liberating democratisation of culture.[63] He wrote:

> The democratization of the Hindu social pattern, the parianization of the Aryan, [and] the conquests of the so-called higher classes by the alleged lower and inferior constitute a very dominant feature of the interhuman relations in Bengal (nay, All-India) through the ages.[64]

The acceleration of democracy, hybridity and decline in colonial India was thus a cause of alarm as well as excitement, and a reason for compensating strategies of management.

As a Bengali and a migrant from the mofussil, Sarkar regarded Calcutta as a particularly active site of miscegenation. War-induced migrations and the expanded employment of women outside the home (which Sarkar supported) had intensified the crisis.[65] Noting the influx of non-Bengali men into Calcutta, Sarkar wrote on 'Non-Bengali Elements in the Bengali Biotype':

> Many alleged Bengali children are likely to have non-Bengali fathers. Race-mixture, *varna-samkara* (blood fusion) or miscegenation is . . . to be taken as a social reality, along with adultery and prostitution, in international Calcutta.[66]

The sex that Sarkar imagines features 'foreign' men and Bengali women, and not Bengali men with non-Bengali women, indicating an anxiety associated with disrupted sexual gain in a racialised patriarchy.[67] It is not that he was unaware of the other kind of sexual contact, involving Bengali men and 'foreign' women. When fathers were Indian/Bengali, miscegenation was not only 'interesting'—an experiment and opportunity for scientific observation—but also a form of cosmopolitanism and conquest: an insertion of the Self into the world and the incorporation of that world into the Self.[68] The children of these unions were a new type of Indian/Bengali, desirable adjustments in the historical evolution of the race.[69]

Sarkar had, after all, married an Austrian, and his daughter Indira was a racial asset, not an embarrassment. With its explicit subversion of Risley (who, Sarkar suggested, had failed to consider the sexual initiative of the Bengali man and misread the racial symptoms of Bengaliness[70]) and its rejection of purity, his was a project of decolonising race and the disciplines surrounding race, especially anthropology. But it remained colonial—and racist—in its assumptions about the signs of race, superiority and inferiority. Sarkar sounded a discernible note of distaste for Anglo-Indians and other 'mulattoes', implying—like P.C. Mahalanobis, who also chased people with callipers—that their main worth was that of the specimen.[71] Hindus and Muslims who had some 'European blood', however, were not beyond the pale of a healthy Indian race. Racial destabilisation was thus desirable only under the right conditions: the mongrel Self had to be qualified by the class, gender and affiliations of the parents. When fathers were 'foreign' or parents subaltern, mongrels became objects of governmentality.

Sarkar's anxiety about the proliferation of the wrong sort of Indian was firmly within an anti-Malthusian discourse of national power in which population indicated the health of a globally competitive peoplehood, and the shrinking middle-class family was decadent.[72] Every Indian couple should have 10 children, he suggested in 1944, assuming that three or four would die young.[73] Like Gandhi but for substantially different reasons, he rejected contraception.[74] It placed him alongside Gini on the edge of a fascism that was inseparable from concerns of racial health, plenitude and extinction. Urban sexuality was closely tied to disease and crime, both metaphorical and actual. The discussion of housing in *Villages and Towns* identifies the family itself as a diseased site. Controlling this ubiquitously diseased population was an essential function of urban administration, Sarkar suggested, making governance inseparable from the early-twentieth-century obsession with 'sanitation'.[75] The language remained simultaneously social-scientific, governmental, moral, medical and individualising ('over-crowding psyche', 'sin-vice-crime-awareness').[76] Domestic architecture was a problem of 'housing-immorality'.[77] There is in this concern a strong echo of American Progressivism and its characteristic mixture of medical activism, voyeurism and panic: a fastidiousness at odds with Sarkar's avowed love of 'pluralism' and creative chaos, which reminds us that Sarkar's investment in chaos was balanced by an investment in order. As in Progressivism, the outlook reflected an older platform of ecclesiastical activism[78] and a preference for government action over voluntarism. 'Sanitary-moral reform has happened in the West only when Western states have put money and bureaucratic effort into such projects of reform', Sarkar observed.[79]

For Sarkar, 'morality' was shorthand for a normativity that merged hygiene and privacy. In the absence of privacy, understood as an architecture and a mentality, sex overflowed its normal containers and became abnormal, unhygienic and racially damaging. Privacy did not mean invisibility: on the contrary, it included an assumption that as a creation of the modern state, the 'private' would remain accessible to the state. Openness to power is, in fact, a basic aspect of modern privacy. Without that openness, secrecy becomes an incubator of deviance. As in his broader vision of the city, Sarkar responded to the urban home with enthusiasm and alarm, and with the scientist's desire to 'detect' interesting phenomena and specimens. The specimens produced by the city needed 'sociation', which was a dual process of education/objectification. On the one hand, it meant *teaching* those that did not fit the mould of the docile citizen; on the other, it meant studying them. This too was National Education.

'Sociating' intervention in race was both liberating and coercive. Sarkar's formulation of criminality—in which the poor serve as a model but are not the only criminals—highlights this duality, which drew him into the Foucauldian terrain of delinquency. What mattered was not so much crime, as tendencies and inclinations that could be described either as 'sins and immoralities' or as sociations, and that were connectible to degeneracy on the one hand and regeneration on the other.[80] Sarkar emphasised both heredity and environment in his vision of the criminal, pointing to the defective individual as well as the warped population. The liberation of the former required the repression of the latter. The dynamic not only linked criminality and public health, it established a scientific triangle of crime, public health and racial degeneracy and made it over to the vanguardist state.

If a portion of the race was infected by criminality (no small concern in a colony dotted with 'criminal tribes'[81]), then public health might supply the remedy. We find, here, Sarkar debating his contemporary sociologists K.N. Rizvi and Narendranath Sen-Gupta. All three downplayed inheritance in juvenile criminality, but to different degrees: Rizvi was the most dismissive, whereas Sen-Gupta and Sarkar sought to conserve a biological foundation in the form of an inclination, i.e., delinquency itself.[82] All emphasised the environment, suggesting an academic consensus of sorts on the appropriate relationship between the nation-state and the national population. Broadly speaking, they highlighted the apparent need for coercive interventions ranging from child-removal, through expert/police surveillance of families and neighbourhoods, to the very ideas of social work and state welfare. Race was not set aside, but diffused through the environment as well as the individual body, and policed and salvaged at both sites. In the process, the individual deviant was partially set free from the inevitability of crime (in an *Awaara*-like negation of inherited criminality[83]), but the community came under greater state control. At the same time, the individual was not let loose, but retained in a state of delinquent individuality that warranted continued detention and study.

Such individuality is far removed from the political realities of Indian nationalism, which has generally relied upon the mobilisation and agency of communities. The Indian state, then as now, lacked the coercive power, the political will and the ideological commitment to deal with its citizens consistently as individuals. But the state-of-communities approach to nationhood has also been a matter of great frustration to Indian liberals, and what we see in Sarkar's idea of a degenerate race that is produced and maintained by the state is a generically modern alternative tailored to 'Indian conditions'. It was not entirely coherent, but coherence was not the priority. Sarkar was attempting a 'pluralistic' synthesis of what he himself knew to be mutually opposed discourses: eugenics (with its emphasis on letting the sick die) and public health (with its emphasis on prevention and salvage). Between the 'old school' of eugenics represented by Galton and Pearson, which saw public health as a counterproductive waste of resources, and the 'new school' represented by Mendel and the Dutch botanist Hugo DeVries, he preferred the latter, because whereas a strict, unimaginative eugenics could only sustain a 'Brahmanocracy in race relations', the more sophisticated eugenicist understood that 'the existing poorer, inferior, and lower orders,—the non-Brahmans—the poor and the pariah—may contain some desirable units which deserve perpetuation and justify their claim for survival'.[84] Colonial-nationalist eugenics complicated what Daniel Pick has described as a relationship of anxiety between mass political participation and the spectre of degeneracy.[85] Sarkar had no interest in preserving an ossified caste-Hindu elite. The pariah, the folk, the Muslim, the aborigine, and even the criminal were more productive and more conducive to the state-guided evolution of a new Indian population.

The Folk Nation

By emphasising degeneracy and regeneration, Sarkar had articulated a vision of race-as-population. Population, however, is a generic concept, based on the universality of delinquency, criminality and sexual deviance, and the universal relevance of governmentality. It offers no ready answers to what makes a particular race Indian. Geography is not enough, since Sarkar had gone out of his way to stress the similar predicaments of the human body in Calcutta, Berlin and Shanghai. One solution was to highlight the 'deep history' of the population by pointing to the indigenous roots of governmentality, articulating a romance of national culture (that might be excavated by the vanguard), and revisiting the political functions of racial identity. An Indian race and its component races could be demonstrated to exist, and as having existed historically, under the surface of universality. Such a fetish of 'authentic' culture can be characterised as nativism: Flora situates Sarkar's ethnological interests within a swadeshi desire to find 'traditional' explanations for tradition.[86] That would, however, be misleading. When Sarkar wrote *The Folk Element in Hindu Culture* in 1914–15, he was already searching for universal categories for the indigenous. Moreover, his interest in culture was not identical to the quest that Sartori has outlined for late-colonial Bengal. Sartori argues that in concept and content, 'Bengali culture' was a reaction (in both senses of the word) to the political impasse of liberal nationalism.[87] Both he and Joya Chatterji have emphasised the Hindu/Vedantic, authoritarian and anti-Muslim core of this culture.[88] Sarkar was not untouched by those considerations, but he was not a believer (he dismissed Vedantic monism as rubbish[89]), not least because his investment in a democratic culture of 'parianisation' and 'pluralism' coexisted with his investment in state authority. He represents a way of thinking about race that is undoubtedly elitist but also eclectic and inclusive, determined to look beyond—and below—the colony to find the postcolonial nation. It retains the shadow of Vidyasagar, who saw in Santals an alternative, desirable civilisation.[90]

We need, at this point, to recall Sarkar's enduring Romanticism: that yearning for something intimate and essential lost in history. His construction of early India reflects a particular conception of wholeness,[91] an embodied spirituality or moral physicality dismissed by a colonialism that cast Indians as either all-body or all-spirit. This was, to some extent, the wholeness of the *grihastha*: 'not the super-sensual or extra-mundane universe [but] a sphere in which men and women get married, build homes, acquire wealth and cultivate heroism'.[92] The Indian *grihastha*, however, had to be married to the European. Here, Sarkar made a direct intervention in the discourse of race. Culture itself became the stuff of bodies. Indian girls of the 'respectable' classes must learn to dance, he insisted; freedom must be a physical joy.[93] The discovery of a profane, pro-sex Indian culture—facilitating the insistence that 'there is no Oriental love, there is no Occidental love'[94]—and the unrestrained, uncertainly civilised Indian body became a critique of Europe, a regeneration and the revival of the optimism that enables politics and history.

It was this investment in physicality, among other things, that took Sarkar beyond the urban culture of Brahmo-influenced *bhadrata* and its stifling restraints, to the rustic world of folk and tribal culture.[95] He praised Rajanikanta Sen, the collector of folk music, for having 'given a fresh lease of life to the traditional folk-melodies by exploiting them as a medium for modern emotions'.[96] Sarkar's remarks show, first, his outlook on folk culture: it was necessarily part of the nation, but it was also an externally located asset that had to be identified and nationalised. The folk element had value only when it was brought into the service of 'modern emotions'. Its value to the folk themselves was less important than the value of the folk to the Völkischly inclined. Second, in spite of Sarkar's focus on the circulation of elites in the colonial city, he was conscious of his location within a 'Hindu race' that had itself seen centuries of internal 'circulation', and in which the classical/Aryan elements had constantly been infiltrated and mongrelised by the marginal, aboriginal and non-Hindu.[97] Ideals of purity and hybridity, equality and superiority, coexisted within this construction of Hinduness. Sarkar embraced the mongrel aspect of his Hindu identity, and it was a jittery celebration, secure only as long as the right sort of Hindus were in charge of the boundaries of the community. The 'right sort', however, could come from unexpected places, such as the margins of the folk world. They were both agents and objects of sociation, and as such, both a part of and apart from the modern Self.

Sarkar's involvement with folk culture unfolded over several years. In the early 1910s, he became increasingly interested in the collection of folklore and folk music, as these were understood by the *bhadralok*. Here, he was well within the project of constructing and expanding Bengaliness by giving the metropolis its cultural hinterland, in which Calcutta-based intellectuals like the Tagores were already engaged.[98] Deeply rooted in swadeshi politics, the enterprise reimagined rural Bengal as a Romantic and extra-colonial world.[99] But the Tagores did not work alone; they and their peers were often supporters and patrons of obscure enthusiasts based in mofussil towns. These men were marginal in more ways than one, but for that reason they were positioned to function as intermediaries of racial identity on the frontier between modern Bengaliness and something primordial.

Sarkar's long collaboration with Haridas Palit should be seen in this context.[100] As Sumit Sarkar has noted, Palit came from a poor, Namasudra background, which he advertised even as he advertised his rise to respectability as a landlord, professional, educator (active in National Education and the creation of rural night schools) and politician.[101] His origins on the margin of Bengali society became an asset in the formulation of his subsequent social status, giving him access to knowledge that the born-respectable did not have. Whereas Benoy Sarkar had left Malda for Calcutta and beyond, Palit had remained on this inner frontier of Bengal, facilitating an inward-directed cosmopolitanism. Like many contemporary collectors of folk culture, he cultivated a reputation as a wanderer in places dislocated in time, a man uniquely in touch with the illiterate and the tribal. 'For . . . twenty long years', he told Sarkar, 'my sole enjoyment was confined to tracing the rivers and traversing the woods, . . . listening to legends and stories from the lips of illiterate villagers and collecting the varied materials of history'.[102] He began working with Sarkar (and the Mookerji brothers) as early as 1911, in the Malda Literary Research Department. He introduced Sarkar—who had just discovered Herder[103]—to his specific interests, such as the Gambhira and Gajan festivals of rural and small-town life; these quickly became Sarkar's own areas of investigation. Sarkar became the next level of collection and mediation, presenting Palit to an outer world of scholarship and race-making.

Rituals like the Gambhira and Gajan appealed to Sarkar for multiple, layered reasons. They were rural, nocturnal, Dionysian, hidden, lost, glimpses of the past in the present, and glimpses of a true or alternative racial Self, political community and form of knowledge.

An Indian Race 67

Significantly, Sarkar and Palit (each in his own way) were both located outside the educational-institutional framework of the colonial state. Neither was detached from the world of modern, European knowledge: Palit's description of his work is indistinguishable from Romantic-European narratives of 'collection' and folk-making. But their construction of an Indian Volk was an anti-colonial, counter-institutional project, conducted by people whose provinciality and marginality to the colonial order placed them at the centre of the Volk-nation.[104] Writing down the obscure ritual and intellectual lives of unremarkable people in backwaters like Malda, finding it 'dazzling'[105] and interpreting it as 'history', was the recovery of nation and race outside colonial curricular preoccupations and imaginaries of peoplehood. Indians could be posited to be neither Hindu nor Muslim, but something both newer and older.[106]

Because the primitive precedes modern identities and politically frozen boundaries, the folk could secrete an ancient worldliness, pointing towards the mingled prehistory of races. At this level, rural Indians, ancient Egyptians and contemporary Muslims could find common ground: Sarkar was eager to identify links between Shiva festivals in provincial Bengal, the worship of Osiris, and Egyptian Id celebrations.[107] What had been locked into a hinterland could prove to be a means of 'travelling'. Similarly, the folk produced new links between Indians of various types:

> One or other of the forms of this cult [of Shiva] have commanded for centuries, and do still command, the devotion of thousands of men and women in all parts of India among the Kashmiris, Punjabis, Rajputs, Marathas, Southerners, Andhras and Bengalees. In spite of the rigidity and inflexibility of customs and social life brought about by codification of laws in recent times, and notwithstanding the narrow provincial spirit of the modern educated Indians, due to the growth of habits and sentiments in watertight administrative compartments, the soul of India is really one.[108]

By seeing a national 'soul' in the folk, Sarkar echoed Herder, but they were not on the same page. Sarkar's folk were more diverse than Herder's, and diversity more valuable within a unified national project.[109] At the Gambhira, Sarkar wrote, the observant ethnologist would find not only peasants and tribal people, but also Bengalis dressed as 'Santhals and other aboriginal tribes', dancing with a decidedly *abhadra* lack of restraint, their bodies pierced by burning arrowheads.[110] Sarkar's Gambhira was thus overtly physical, and an occasion of racial confusion and rearticulation, provocatively fusing the civilised/*bhadra* and uncivilised/*abhadra* worlds. Alert to simultaneous processes of peasant-making and Hindu-making—i.e., culture-making and race-making—on the aboriginal frontier of 'settled' Bengal, Sarkar pointed out songs about Shiva becoming a cultivator.[111]

In the process, Sarkar interrupted overlapping debates in the anthropology of race. W.H.R. Rivers, whose work on the Todas had become a major influence within British anthropology and guided Radcliffe-Browne's study of the Andamanese, had seen the 'tribal' as distinct from the wider society; Marcel Mauss had already rejected the separation.[112] Sarkar aligned himself with Mauss, but for reasons, of his own. His obvious interest in the Dionysian is reminiscent of Frazer, and like the work of Morgan, informed by an unspoken desire to merge with the primitive.[113] But whereas Frazer's desire was a decadent hallucination akin to Conrad's Africa,[114] and Morgan's vision of the American Indian contained a rejection of capitalist modernity,[115] Sarkar's interest in the primitive was also recuperative: he was the native in search of wholeness. Not surprisingly, he focused on elements that had been ejected or marginalised by colonisers and modern Indians. This was the deliberate searching out of 'impurities' as the new substance of race in the colony. There were multiple folk, and each folk was historically hybrid. The folk in its varieties and convergences provided a way of getting around the political compartments of the present time, facilitating rather than impeding the project of 'national unity'.

Much of Sarkar's thinking on the racial history of Hindus developed before and during the Great War. He debated P.T. Srinivas Iyenger and C.V. Vaidya on the foundational questions of ethnographic nationalism in India: the reality of an Aryan race, its origins, and its relationship to non-Aryans. As Romila Thapar and others have pointed out, the 'Aryan question' has informed the inheritance of identity and legitimate power in India since the later nineteenth century: whereas Jyotiba Phule, Dravidian nationalists and Dalit activists read the 'Aryan invader' as a text of Brahmin/settler-colonial malfeasance, Tilak, Dayanand Saraswati, Theosophists, and Hindutva ideologues regarded Aryans as not only a gratifying link between Indianness and whiteness, but also guarantors of an Indian nationhood premised on upper-caste-Hindu hegemony.[116] The academic discourse was more uneven: Iyenger was dismissive of an Aryan race with foreign origins, seeing the Arya–Anarya distinction as merely a difference of 'cult'.[117] Vaidya, on the other hand, embraced the 'invasion' theory, positing clear ethnic and political lines between Aryan settlers and Dasyu aborigines.[118] Sarkar was receptive to Vaidya, but inserted caveats.[119] Aryans were themselves 'impure', he insisted.[120] The idea of distinct peoples converging in a common geography and history—a 'melting-pot' model—suited Sarkar's disinterest in genealogical purity. He agreed that Dasyus were distinct from Aryans, but did not fetishise Aryans as the exclusive insider-race in India. There were multiple insiders, Aryan and aboriginal/non-Aryan, and he wanted them all as his ancestors. That anthropological diversity was a discovery—or at least the claim—of unexplored nooks and crannies of ancestry and origin, exciting to a man invested in a *world* of exploration.

Sarkar's explicitly quasi-American melting-pot reflected his insistence upon the political—and hence unfixed—nature of Indian society, and a preference for the universality of race over the peculiarity of caste. Like many colonial administrator-scientists, he saw caste as being more ethnographic than ritual.[121] Moreover, unlike M.S. Golwalkar, Sarkar accepted an Indian history in which racial interpenetration and inter-caste marriage was the norm.[122] This fluidity was desirable, because it indicated the operation of political power—the ebb and flow of armies and warrior clans—without which Bengal/India would be reduced to unworldly impotence and irrelevance. The compulsively miscegenating, historically alive folk could be mined for the masculinity and militarism the elites desperately wanted, especially if its deepest racial origins were unearthed.[123] Ancient 'wild tribes' like the Kirata had supplemented 'the Army [as] Militia or National volunteers', Sarkar explained.[124] The capital letters mattered: the margins had to produce not only a racial root, but also an alternative bedrock of the modern, racially inclusive Indian state.[125] The anti-colonial basis of this state is clear in Sarkar's references to colonial proscriptions of folk culture, such as the ban on hook-swinging.[126] He foreshadowed Dirks by positing his own ethnographic state, but his agenda was different from that of Dirks's ethnographer-administrators.[127] Whereas the latter constructed a menagerie to possess, manage and enjoy, Sarkar was proposing a counter-state *of* the menagerie, in which primitive rituals demonstrated the repossession of the state by the racialised.

As usual, the racial qualities that Sarkar desired were also dangerous. The 'militarism' of the folk could be a basis of criminality:

'It was they who were occasionally found to commit dacoities'.[128] What made the state viable was precisely what the state had to manage constantly through punishment and education. Folk festivals function in Sarkar's narrative as an ancient National Education, complementing Shastric literature on 'polity, warfare, town-planning, administrative machinery and financial management, arts and crafts, sex, hygiene, sanitation, eugenics, etc.'.[129] The cleanliness of the poor and rural also formed a part of Gandhi's polemic,[130] although Madan Mohan Malaviya probably spoke for most elite nationalists when he insisted that reformers should 'teach [the masses] to be clean'.[131] But the project of creating a unified Hindu Volk was a racial cleansing in more than one sense of the term. For Sarkar, the inclusion of the folk among the clean diffused the knowledge of modern civic life throughout the body politic. Crucially, we find that education had taken on a democratic appearance: it was not just a top-down process of the urban elite teaching the rabble, but of the rabble teaching themselves, and even teaching the elites a lesson or two, although the lessons appear to be borrowed from modern textbooks. Indian democracy was nothing less than the secret history of the folk. ('The Pala dynasty owed its political legitimacy to the "election" by the Folk, and it was the Folk that dominated the age in matters of faith.' [132]) The folk were diverse but unifying, not only egalitarian, but also equipped with mechanisms of reconciliation and education that could remedy the divides of 'community' and restore to all Indians a wholeness damaged or denied by colonialism:

> The Sannyasis of the Gajan and the Gambhira are recruited from different castes, but so long as they go through the round of these festivities they observe no caste rules . . . They work together for the common good, and thus reveal the fact that the idea of a collective life governs them. Even the distinction of Hindus and Mohammedans is sunk in this institution.[133]

Education was thus not merely something that happens in formal sites of what Sarkar called *anushilan* or disciplined practice (in an oblique reference to swadeshi politics), but a diffused process of sociation. The state must normatively take the lead, but even folk festivals could be a form of sociation. In the Bengali context, moreover, education not only produced culture, it was culture itself.[134] We see in Sarkar the extension of that essentially *bhadralok* understanding of education to the folk, as the *bhadralok* sought not so much to join the folk as to appropriate them in a movement that was both strategic and nostalgic. The pedagogy of the folk generated the self-governing political community, in which the moral and the political came together in recognisably modern processes of surveillance and the 'publication' of 'annual reports' during festivals. 'The hidden offences and secret vices of individuals are exposed by them, and thus very valuable services are rendered to morals', Sarkar observed approvingly.[135] Typically, the individual was invoked and policed in the same gesture. As a quasi-state, the folk provided Sarkar with a way—and a site—of reconciling the individual and the community within the purposeful organisation, and offered a solution to the problem of racial health:

> The Gambhira has been a reformer of social defects and evils. People learn from it an earnestness and a capacity to work in a body for their common good. The truth that although independent in their individual affairs, the members of a society are but parts of the same unit, is well taught through their joint work for the Gambhira.
> The Gambhira festivals equip the people with the strength of unity . . . Further, to regulate this strength and energy, heroes grow up among themselves, each of whom voluntarily takes upon himself the responsibility of a department. Under each leader, again, there are several lieutenants, who avail themselves of his guidance and thus learn how to work in a methodical way. The Gambhira will thus be found to be a healthy organization.[136]

Sarkar was driving at connections that were both obvious and unseen. Signs of submerged Indian states, folk festivals revealed the existence of hidden indigenous elites who could be a point of recognition and inspiration for colonised urbanites:

> The title of Mandala and the system of management by the Mandala are still in vogue among the Podas and similar low-class people in the villages of Gopalanagar, Chetla, Taliganj, etc., in the Twenty-Four Parganas. And, as in the Gambhiras of Malda, . . . the Mandala is found to exercise a considerable sway.[137]

These local elites were not only natural objects of sociation and incorporation into the new national vanguard, they were already engaged in processes of sociation. References to the Twenty-Four Parganas and Taliganj placed the folk not in some far-away place, but on the edge of the colonial metropolis. Describing the worship of Mangala-Chandi in this proximal margin of civilisation, Sarkar wrote:

> The worship of Mangala-Chandi has obtained in Bengal for a [very] long time. She has been the guardian angel of Bengalee homes, and every householder installs a pitcher filled with water as her representative ... The singing of her songs is indispensable, especially in marriages.[138]

Folk traditions thus connected the *bhadralok* world with the peasant world, the peasant world with the tribal world, the present with the distant past. These bridges made possible the racial community, reducing the gap between those who value culture and those who constitute culture. Just as importantly, it established the private interior of the home, as opposed to the public altar of the temple, as the secret location of folk tradition: at heart, therefore, the *bhadralok* and the vanguard are also part of the folk.[139] Sarkar was not saying that folk rituals constituted modern statecraft, or that villagers were the 'real' modern Indians. Rustics in a particular mode were *like* modern citizens, or a useful shadow of the modern citizen. Sarkar was invested in their primitiveness, which was analogous to the primitiveness of the European folk. (Europe was too useful to ignore.) As a tongue-in-cheek reference to the Welsh as the *mlechcha* of the English indicates, Sarkar knew he was dealing in ascribed identities and utilities.[140] He did not seriously imagine that these could be seized by marginal groups and made into insurgent national identities. But the Indian folk was a thrilling glimpse of the modern in the primitive and the primitive in the modern, akin to seeing a ghost.

As in any Romantic project of recovering the folk, that ghostly element was reinforced by an anxiety—both sharp and decadent—that folk life was being destroyed by a vulgar modernity that could not be disavowed. But awareness of that death could be racially invigorating. Sarkar quoted the poet Baradacharan Mitra as saying that 'We should, all of us, do our best to see that ancient festivities ... like the Gambhira do not die out'.[141] Gas and kerosene lighting had infiltrated the Gambhira, Sarkar noted wryly, and Ravi Varma was replacing older styles of decoration to make the proceedings 'look grand and glorious ... in the eyes of modernists'.[142] It was by becoming aware of such losses that modern Indians could realise their race as a new political truth. Sarkar's attention to the details of lighting and decoration, and the conversion of obscure festivals into rituals of tourism, indicate an internalisation and also an aesthetic mobilisation of racial death. As in the notion of degeneration, race in colonial India was most real, and most useful to the anti-colonial nation, when it could be shown to be disintegrating.

Muslims

For a man who came of age politically during the Swadeshi movement in Bengal, the question of Indian peoplehood necessarily included a 'Muslim question', which is also, of course, a 'Hindu question'. Sarkar's tendency to use 'Indian' and 'Hindu' interchangeably as civilisational adjectives well into the 1920s can suggest a desire to exclude Muslims from the people with whom he identified himself. It is, however, inadequate to ascribe his vocabulary to 'Hindu nationalism'.[143] Sarkar's position on Muslims in India evolved, moving from a partial ascription of alienness, through a period when the desire for an organically integrated Indian race coexisted with visions of partnership, to a bitterness that came from the failure of partnership. The desire for integration persisted, but it migrated from the Romantic to the liberal domain. The trajectory is more representative of Indian secularism—or secularisms—than of the ideology generally understood as Hindutva. It reveals, first of all, the opportunities for accommodation afforded by Sarkar's ability to maintain a tactical slipperiness in his conceptualisation of race, nation and state: up to a point, these could be converged or disconnected in accordance with the shifting political environment, allowing outliers to be included in the community of justice (which is what anti-colonial assertions of race boiled down to). But it also indicates the difficulty of breaking free from the historiographical quicksand where the anti-colonial nationalist must necessarily begin, and the limits of liberalism in supplying a solution (justice) where Romantic visions of unity had failed.

Beginning with Bankim's reactionary turn in the mid-1880s, through the emergence of the Anushilan constituency after 1905, and intensifying after the Communal Award of 1932, the most dominant constructions of Bengaliness were upper-caste-Hindu and openly anti-Muslim.[144] This was not a Bengal-specific phenomenon; we can identify similar patterns across India.[145] Moreover, with the rise of revolutionary terrorism in Bengal, Maharashtra and Punjab, the articulation of the Hindu Volk and its pertinent exclusions became an interregional discourse, shaped by movements of right-wing revolutionaries within and without India, not to mention congregations of the incarcerated in places like the Andamans.[146] Sarkar, for instance, was aware (and casually admiring) of Savarkar even before the latter wrote *Hindutva*,[147] and it is not difficult to identify the overlaps between the Indian/Hindu races that each man visualised.[148] It is the divergences, however, that are more interesting, indicating Sarkar's status as a problem child of Indian nationalism.

'All Hindus claim to have in their veins the blood of the mighty race incorporated with and descended from the Vedic fathers', Savarkar wrote in *Hindutva*.[149] By this token, Indian Muslims were *potentially* racial brethren. Savarkar's Hindu race was also accommodating of aborigines, who, he wrote, gave Aryans the place-names that were absorbed into Aryan landscapes and languages.[150] Savarkar's understanding of race was thus apparently open, within the limits of a geography that supplied the immediately obvious boundaries. But other vitally important limits came from history. Adivasis, who had no history, could be incorporated, but Muslims—the historical enemy—were a problem in spite of blood. The willingness to 'claim' blood mattered more than blood itself. Savarkar thus made a tactical separation between race and Volk: whereas race remained essentially ahistorical, the Volk was historicised, cleaned up and nationalised. To enter the latter, even members of the former would have to pass the *punyabhumi* test.[151]

Christophe Jaffrelot has, I think, overemphasised the openness generated by Savarkar's emphasis on a national geography, comparing it with the exclusionary genealogical preoccupations of Golwalkar.[152] Golwalkar was not indifferent to geography: it was the location of the state, without which the race would have no destiny and the colonised man would remain incomplete.[153] Savarkar, for his part, was not indifferent to blood, and history was only contingently an integrating dynamic. He and Golwalkar both articulated variations of European settler-colonialism in their understanding of race, territory and history: both men saw the Hindu race emerging from the Aryan conquest of an aboriginal India. But while Golwalkar argued that the new setting did not significantly change the content of the race, Savarkar insisted that the race was fleshed out by isolation and history, and rendered as a Volk or nation. The tribalism of the Aryans led them to forget their common racial identity, he wrote, but this amnesia was a necessary step on the road to nationhood, because it allowed them to assimilate non-Aryans. The problem was resolved through the charismatic leader (*chakravartin*) and the imperial state (Rama's conquest of the south), which, Savarkar suggested, completed the circle, reconciling nationhood with racial destiny. The Hindu-nationalist politics of Savarkar's own historical moment became a re-enactment of this old circular movement after the race has been disrupted (by its own complacency and Muslim invaders), drawing the forgetful fragments together into a new (second) Hindu nation.[154]

Like Savarkar, Sarkar tended to be dismissive of Indian nationhood: until the 1930s, it was the Hindu nation that was real. Also like Savarkar, Sarkar in his earlier writings spelled 'Hindust(h)an' with an extra 'h' that obscured any Urdu/Farsi roots,[155] and resorted occasionally to the language of the *punyabhumi* or sacred homeland.[156] He too was uninterested in religious *punya*. The sacredness of the *bhumi* remained entirely political: a gesture of membership in the legitimate community of the land. For both men, and for Golwalkar too, Hindu nationhood denoted the happy coincidence of geography, genealogy, culture, and political purpose, undisturbed by things and people that did not fit in.[157] But on the question of whether Muslims should be counted among such people, there were major differences between Savarkar and Golwalkar on the one hand, and Sarkar on the other. Sarkar's rejection of the importance of an Aryan invasion opened up racial possibilities that neither Savarkar nor Golwalkar was willing to contemplate. Moreover, unlike the two Maharashtrians, Sarkar differentiated between a Hindu state and an Indian state, and Indian statehood—a necessary modern contrivance and a reasoned response to present-day political realities—increasingly mattered to him.

A sharp ambivalence within Sarkar's notion of the historical Hindu Volk shaped his vision of the Indian states that might emerge in the foreseeable future. Like marginal Hindus, Muslims inhabited a racial frontier: with the requisite polemical and organisational work, they could be imagined within the national community, either as an organic part or as a semi-autonomous partner. Savarkar too had allowed for the possibility of Mussalmani Hindus, but from him it was a demand and an implied threat: Muslims must change their ways, and the terms of inclusion would be set by others.[158] It was always exclusion dressed grotesquely as inclusion. Sarkar made few such threats or demands; on the contrary, he tried hard to be accommodating and could be scathingly critical of narratives of the 'alien Muslim'. His organically included Muslim, however, proved a difficult fit, especially as Muslim separatism gathered steam in the 1930s. Under the circumstances,

76 *An Indian Race*

Sarkar retreated from the one-people formula, emphasising a more conservative discourse of 'Hindu–Muslim unity'.[159]

Despite the resemblance to the shallow paeans to Hindu–Muslim fraternity that floated around Bengal in the swadeshi years, that was not an uncomplicated conservatism. It was based on a recognition of the problem of accommodation, i.e., the cultural politics of unity. The rhetoric of 'Hindu–Muslim unity' has today passed almost completely from Indian public discourse, replaced by the concept of 'communal harmony'. The latter suggests a resolved question of communal relations: the Hindus are the majority in the nation-state, Muslims must adapt. The former, however, suggests an open negotiation between semi-autonomous political entities, or two 'communities' that can either unite or face the consequences of disunity. Sarkar wrote from that earlier milieu, grappling with the problem of fusing increasingly slippery and discrete entities into a common Volk—a self-conscious race—through mutually engaged scholarship and equal representation as *Muslims and Hindus*. 'A solid nucleus for Indo-Islamic philology is likely to emerge if an initial investigation be carried on for a period of about five years by three Mussalman and three Hindu scholars under the leadership of a philologist, say, like A. Suhrawardy of Calcutta', he wrote during the Khilafat Movement, urging that Benares Hindu University take the lead in the project.[160] The exhortation that Hindu scholars learn Arabic and Muslim scholars learn Sanskrit was not just a gesture towards an integrated Indian civilisation of the future. It was also a gesture towards the precolonial past, when Hindus did learn Farsi and Muslims like Dara Shikoh studied and patronised 'Hindu' scriptures. It was, as such, a movement towards a new Indian history. Sarkar's cosmopolitanism and his vision of a composite Indian people went hand in hand, precluding his 'Hindu nation' from coming too close to that of Savarkar (who also had a soft corner for Dara Shikoh[161]). The position paralleled his willingness to accept multiple Indian states. Something composite may emerge from joint endeavours, Sarkar hoped, but in the meantime there must be mutual recognition.

A measure of 'Hindu nationalism' is undoubtedly present in Sarkar's ethnographic writing before the Great War. The Muslim conquest of Bengal is seen not so much as a conquest by degenerates or a harbinger of Hindu degeneracy, as enabled by Hindu degeneracy: Muslims become the calamity at the end of a racial-moral sin.[162] Circa 1915, Muslim kingship is still 'the loss of . . . independence' to aliens, persecution of Hindus is the historical norm, the worship of Satya Pir by Hindus is subterfuge, and Sanskrit was the 'lingua franca of educated Indians' before English came along.[163] The ideological debt to Bankim is clear and acknowledged.[164] But even when Muslims are marginal in the India of his imagination, they are not absent: Sarkar observes that a variant of Mangala-Chandi was known as Bibi, and notes that the appellation indicates a married Muslim woman.[165] The 'Bengal frontier' remained available for migrations of rituals, names and identities, and in 1942 he precisely anticipated Richard Eaton's theory of the parallel production of Hindus and Muslims.[166]

Nor were Sarkar's Muslims particularly villainous. He—with Haridas Palit—saw Muslim interventions as a democratising factor that had helped, not disrupted, the development of folk culture in Bengal:

> The Bengali language . . . owes its elevation to a literary status to the Mohammedans. Instances of Bengali translation of Sanskrit and Persian books at the order of Mussalman chiefs are not rare. They served to remove the supercilious spirit in which Bengali was looked upon by the Sanskrit-loving Brahmanas and Hindu Rajas.[167]

Clearly, the Hinduness of 'Bengali culture' was not without internal complications. 'All Bengalis are half-Hindu and half-Muslim', he insisted as late as 1944.[168] Islam and Hinduism were both alien imports in Bengal; aborigines—the truest Bengalis—conquered and modified the new religions even as they became Hindus and Muslims.[169] Once again, the celebration of impurity as anti-colonial racial substance created room for innovation. 'Indian' might be a confused contrivance and 'Hindu' more authentic, but what mattered to Sarkar were the innate cosmopolitanism of the mongrel and political effectiveness in the present time. His use of 'Hindu' was the correction of an Orientalist taxonomical-political error. It was also a deliberate imprecision with ethnic categories to strengthen a polemic.

Over the course of the 1910s, Sarkar rearranged his older outlook, concluding that after an initial externality, Muslims became integral to Hindustan.[170] Simultaneously, he theorised the openness of the Hindu world to Muslims. When Sarkar read the *Sukraniti* for the origins, boundaries and content of the 'Hindu race', he did not read uncritically. The authors of the *Sukraniti*, he observed, equated *yavana*—which in his own time meant Muslims—with non-Vedic, non-Vedic with alien, and alien with extra-national.[171] But historical *yavanas* were separate in faith only, Sarkar insisted, and even their faith differed only in its references and not its structure. *Yavana* beliefs were *recognised* by a larger community of the land, even if they were recognised as autonomous. There is a tension here between autonomy and alienness: what is autonomous may or may not be alien. Sarkar's narrative of *mlechcha* identity has a similar simultaneity of exclusion and inclusion: *mlechcha*s were often soldiers in the service of Hindu kings, and had their uses in the political body.[172] Here again, military service was a forum of inclusion and the state an instrument of binding together those who were ritually disparate, forming a new caste or race of the soldier/citizen. The state stood above the nation but it also produced the nation by managing its component races; in each capacity, it was a secularising mechanism.

That secular imaginary of the Volk was broadly compatible with Sarkar's early sense of insiders and aliens, which was itself closely tied to freedom. He observed approvingly:

> The poets of the Sukra Cycle have displayed a pre-eminently modern conception by thus allowing freedom of religious convictions and practices but compelling obedience to one and the same system of non-religious laws throughout the realm. On the one hand, religious neutrality or toleration which implies a diversity of creeds, and on the other, uniformity or unity in economic, political and other secular interests,—these are the notions ... regarding the Yavanas as well as Mlechchas.[173]

At the level of the state, then, non-unity of the people did not constitute an insuperable problem of citizenship. Sarkar was considerably more liberal than Savarkar here: he made no demands that the citizen identify his *punyabhumi*. He had no difficulty in choosing 'Abdul' and 'Ismail' as the names of hypothetical Indians.[174] His model is actually closer to Jinnah's vision of Pakistan at the moment of independence, or even the Congress's India: religious communities could contingently be conceded to be nations, but the state could accommodate multiple civil codes and nations (provided the right nation was in control), and still retain an expectation—articulated as 'hope' or 'directive principles'—that in time, secular citizens would form fully individualised relationships with the nation-state.[175] Religion and the state function as sites of freedom from each other: in matters of faith a man can do (or at least believe) what he wants, and when he deals with the state he operates on an even plane with the *yavana*/*mlechcha*/Brahmin. It constituted an effective rebuttal of Savarkar. By separating peoplehood and religion, Sarkar suggested that cultural and political fusion could proceed without religious synthesis, bypassing the *punyabhumi* trap.

Thus, by the 1920s, Sarkar's understanding of the boundaries of the 'Hindu nation' was considerably more expansive (though the flexibility of race) and also more limited (by the supremacy of the state) than that of those who derived their nation from Bankim and Tilak. He shared, superficially, the reflexive competitiveness of Harbilas Sarda, who in 1906 had borrowed wholesale the language of European social sciences and European anxieties about modern society, and both men accepted the racist premise that race is the language of civilisation.[176] But he was far more sophisticated than Sarda, less given to cranky theories of Hindu colonisation of Britain and America in the ancient past and juvenile claims of being the 'greatest nation in the world',[177] and more inclined towards liberal understandings of political community as well as the 'felt community' of precolonial Hindustan.[178] He did believe that Hindus had colonised and civilised *some* other people, he was not entirely persuaded by his own rhetoric of inclusion, he could not fully resolve the problem of the contingencies of inclusion, and he became less interested in such resolutions after the partition of India. But until then, he tinkered quite heroically with the most vital problem and greatest failure of Indian nationalism, attempting to find a solution that would be compatible with a state that was purposeful, self-constituting and democratic.

The radical possibilities of Sarkar's Hindu nation are strikingly visible in two narratives from the early 1920s. One is an attempt to count Asians among the 'superior races' of the world, in the course of which Sarkar refers to Aurangzeb, of all people, as 'the great Mughal-Hindu'.[179] (Even in 1942, he was ready to claim Bakhtiyar Khilji as a Bengali.[180]) The other narrative was not directly about India at all, but involved a similar intervention in race and history. In a long essay titled 'Revolutions in China', Sarkar analysed Sun Yat-Sen's revolutionary manifesto of 5 January 1912. While he admired Sun's objectives, he balked at the depiction of Manchus as tyrannical aliens in China. As a Han critique of Manchu rule, Sun's manifesto is immediately suggestive of how Hindu nationalists regarded the end (or prospect) of 'Muslim rule' in India. The complaints about despotism, retarded progress, crimes against civilisation, stifled native industry, and the subjugation of an unaggressive nation were familiar to Sarkar. Sun's narrative of unjust taxes echoed both the Hindu-nationalist understanding of the jiziya and the American rhetoric of taxation-without-representation, indicating how intertwined 'indigenous' and 'foreign' narratives of oppression could shape a cosmopolitan-nationalist political discourse. In this discourse, Manchus—and by extension, Muslims—were alienated from China/India not only because they were barbarians, but also because they were colonisers.[181]

Sarkar disagreed vehemently with Sun's notion of the coloniser-at-home, writing:

> The case made . . . against the Manchus does not exhibit a picture of the atrocities of Spanish rule in the Netherlands and Peru or the horrors of the age-long social and political persecution of Jews in every Christian land. The . . . references to the inequities of the Manchu administration . . . would be equally applicable to the . . . indigenous Chinese dynasties. Besides, which [eighteenth-century] Occidental nation was free from . . . serfdom, intolerance, persecution, oligarchy, arbitrary taxation?
>
> [T]he real foreigners are not the Manchus but these [Western] Powers. The Manchu emperors, as Chinese patriots, did for their fatherland the only duty open to them. They closed the country to Eur-America.[182]

He was explicit about the Indian implications:

> The Mohammedan . . . regime in India is similar to that of the Mongols and Manchus in China, because the first Mohammedans came into India as conquerors. But though they have maintained their religious antithesis practically intact, there has been ultimately a great rapprochement between the Hindus and the Mohammedans in language, music, painting, architecture, folk customs, etiquette, and phases of social life. In political and military affairs the distinction between the original inhabitants of India and the new-comers (and the converts to the new faith) was all but obliterated.
>
> Mohammedan rule in India was in no respects the 'government of one people by another.' It was not an alien rule like that of the Hohenstaufens, and later of the Habsburgs, in Italy, or of the French in Indo-China, or of the Americans in the Philippines. The rule of the Mongols and the Manchus in China was likewise not a foreign rule.[183]

Foreshadowing Bose's emphasis on Hindu–Muslim 'synthesis' in Indian nationhood, this is as sharp a movement away from the identification of Indian Muslims as aliens as it is possible to make.[184] Sarkar demolishes not only the Two-Nation Theory and the two-stage theory of pre-colonial Indian history, but along with these, Orientalist misapplications of race. He was especially critical of Vincent Smith, who he came to see as an imperialist hack: a 'gazette writer' fixated on essential differences and Muslim depredations.[185] Smith's work, for the post-Great-War Sarkar, represented the insidious climax of Max Mueller's construction of an Indian race. Countering it with nothing less than an alternative national history, Sarkar defended Hindus and Muslims, Marathas and Mughals, simultaneously. 'Since the thirteenth century', he insisted in an essay on Saracenic transmissions of 'Hindu' knowledge to Europe, 'India has been as much Mohammedan as Hindu'.[186] Muslims from Iltutmish on were comprehensively claimed for the Indian nation, with the rhetoric of a 'Hindu race' and that of 'India' both facilitating the claim.

The formulation came with its own problems. Sarkar's imaginary of Hindu–Muslim contact in the Sultanate and Mughal periods is heavy on Hindu tutelage of Muslims in virtually every area of life,[187] and the picture of Muslim kings in West Asia happily 'propagating Hindu culture' is fantastic even if one considers the sophistication of Islamicate knowledge.[188] Sarkar was not deploying the word 'Hindu' as a doctrinal identity, but he was nevertheless asserting a civilisational claim that competed with the Islamicate.[189] Moreover, the use of 'Hindu' in the 1920s could never be innocent of the meanings the word had acquired in colonial India. Sarkar's attack on Smith did not deny that there had been a 'fact of conquest' that was 'shameful' for Hindus.[190] He refused to let the fact or the shame define Indian history, and sought to reclaim the Hindu for a new national project, but he would have known that the reclamation would be resisted by contemporary Hindus and Muslims. Must Indian Muslims make themselves comfortable with this encompassing Hindu identity? For Savarkar, that comfort was a key test of Indianness. Sarkar was not so crude, but he could not escape the implications of his inclusiveness. Aurangzeb might have blanched at being called a Hindu, and Buddhists of Sarkar's time may have resented his assertion that Nalanda was a 'Hindu university'.[191] The racially open Hindu nation could be a hair's breadth removed from the swallowing nation, threatening the identities—and inevitably, the rights—of those on the margins.

Yet possible solutions were imbedded within Sarkar's ambivalent vocabulary of an Indian race. He could call Aurangzeb a 'Mughal-Hindu', but elsewhere he refers to 'Moghuls *and* Hindus'.[192] This is partly slippage, but it is also the recognition of the socially and politically contextual nature of identity. In the inter-war period, Sarkar's vision of the racial location of Muslims utilised both the organic and the contextual discourses of Indianness: they supported each other by providing an alternative theory at all times. In some contexts and under the pressure of particular political needs, Muslims could be counted as Hindus, and Hindu could be a synonym for all Indians. But they could also be detached. Crucially, even as Muslims were detached from 'Hindus', they remained within a common 'motherland' and political project identified as 'India' or even 'Greater India', stretching across the Hindu Kush to Balkh and consecrated by the blood of Hindu and Muslim troops in Shah Jahan's expeditionary army.[193] History continued to provide for a common race—complete with mingled blood—even when politics functioned centrifugally.

Sarkar was thus more flexible than Savarkar in his understandings of 'Hindu' and 'Indian'. (Indeed, as Savarkar became less flexible, Sarkar became more so.[194]) Because race could coalesce through common political purpose in spite of different origins and faiths, it could provide a platform for renewed political work in the present time, which amounted to the management and production of race itself. The religious 'antithesis' he had postulated in his rebuke to Sun Yat-Sen gave way to an emphasis on mutual influence, and his childhood in Malda retrospectively became an idyll of intimacy with Muslims.[195] He criticised Rabindranath for literary self-isolation from Muslims (and the poor).[196] In an interview in 1945, Sarkar plainly became irritated at the questioner's surprise at his familiarity with Muslim writers and scholars.[197] Even when he proceeded from a construction of India as a country of discrete Hindus and Muslims, Sarkar pieced together a rhetoric of 'joint' culture and politics ('aspirations'), represented prominently by Urdu, which he called 'the most advanced of all Indian tongues' in scientific as well as literary development.[198] Unlike Sanskrit, Urdu (which, he clarified, was also 'Hindustani', now without the extra 'h') was the appropriate lingua franca of the present time. In this work about work, discrete entities merged to produce something hybrid, and that was both *new* and *Indian*, in overlapping fields of cultural-political activity.[199]

Such unity was not a given but an unending pedagogical task. Sarkar was clearly admiring of the innovative curricular and organisational work being done at a 'Muslim' university like Osmania.[200] Like his proposal for the study of 'Moslem achievements in medieval culture' at Banaras Hindu University, such work extended the scope of National Education and corresponded with Sarkar's indisputably Romantic vision of anti-colonial politics from 1857 to the

Khilafat Movement. 'In this history of torture on the one hand and self-sacrifice on the other', he could say, 'the Mohammedans have come out as brilliantly as the Hindus'.[201] The content of the education did not differ dramatically from any Orientalist/European course of study.[202] What set it apart was the political purpose and identity of the scholars: Muslims and Hindus come together as Indians and then advance into the world, preserving the connection between race-making and justice.

There is, here, an acknowledgement of the productive and organisational power of Jinnah's concept of multiple Indias, which is dismissed only to be recuperated.[203] Sarkar's objection to the Two-Nation Theory stemmed primarily from a liberal refusal to let the individual citizen be subsumed by the religious community and prevented from exercising his will.[204] But he also saw demands for a Muslim state as historically unnatural: a mono-religious state would destroy the pluralism that gave Indian society its creative spark.[205] Moreover, partition would mean a transfer of populations, he wrote in 1942, and that would be inhuman.[206] Sarkar demanded, instead, 'joint Hindu–Muslim nationalities for every inch of the Indian soil', in which Hindus and Muslims would continue to transform each other, as they had done historically: 'The Muslimization of the Hindu as well as the Hinduization of the Muslim are the two solid factual foundations of Indian personality, character, institutions and movements'.[207] Allegiance to the state—or states—would provide social cement. The idea was grounded, as usual, in his vision of the state as an agent of justice. Sarkar acknowledged the disadvantaged condition of Muslims in colonial-Indian society and politics: that they were comparatively poor, and underrepresented in councils and associations. Nationhood could not be blind to these inequalities, and he welcomed political platforms tied to their remedy: the Lucknow Pact of 1916, for instance, and the 1923 entente between the Swaraj Party and Muslim politicians. He demanded that Hindu elites be more generous towards Muslims.[208] He thus acknowledged Muslims as a legitimate political formation with which other Indians could negotiate.

By the 1940s, Sarkar had largely abandoned his enthusiasm for a Hindu race that included Muslims, and adopted a pragmatic rhetoric of Hindus-and-Muslims as separate, interested parties in a common Indian polity. Yet that flexibility—his willingness to reconcile the existence of the Muslim League, the legitimacy of at least a portion of its programme, and the rhetoric of late-Mughal Hindustani politics[209]—left a crack in the modern national Self which could be exploited by Hindutva-enthusiasts and two-nation theorists, and into which Sarkar himself slipped occasionally. In 1944, he called Shyamaprasad Mukherjee the most important Bengali politician after Subhas Bose, although he praised Humayun Kabir in the same breath.[210] In his post-Partition writings, there is a hesitation when it comes to including Muslims in an Asian India. 'On the whole', he now wrote, 'Muslim thought in India has been less Asian and more Islamic or theocratic'.[211] The point should not be over-stressed. Muslims remained within his vision of Asian freedom. Given Ataturk and Sukarno, he could not ignore secular-nationalist and socialist developments in the Muslim world; nor did he want to.[212] But Partition had diminished the need to be ideologically creative about the place of Muslims in India itself. Indian Muslims, in these new circumstances, were recast as a minority: objects rather than agents of work.

When Sarkar looked at Asia in the late 1940s, he saw no stable political-military Muslim community, only individual Muslim states that could be manipulated by foreign powers.[213] He did not interpret this vulnerability as a Hindu-Indian opportunity,[214] but concluded that the Muslim world was now an external entity that India must treat like other external entities, according to principles of *Realpolitik* rather than presumptions of an anti-colonial race. Since Pakistan had become a part of this fractured external entity, Indian Muslims were now the ideologically stranded, rather than displaced, objects of a policy question which Sarkar attempted to answer:

> What about Muslims? The Muslims of Dominion India are Indians. The Muslims of Dominion Pakistan are Pakistanis. And that is the end of the matter. The Muslims of Dominion India will accordingly have to get used to the new category, 'Indians.' They are entirely independent of Pakistanis although they happen to be Muslims. The sooner the Muslims understand this *Realpolitik*, the sooner they will learn to place themselves on secular, territorial, anti-theocratic, anti-medieval and the allied paths to progress.[215]

This is, at one level, an inclusive secular nationalism. It resonates easily with the rhetoric of the less virulent Hindu nationalists, such as Sarkar's old friend and target Lajpat Rai.[216] In 1925, Lajpat had declared that '[t]he correct thing for us to do is to strive for a democratic Raj in which the Hindus, Muslims and the other communities of India may participate as Indians and not as followers of any particular religion'.[217] The rhetoric is an eloquent plea for a liberal state, insisting that it is necessary not only for the well-being of society, but also for the sustenance of the individual as a moral actor. The problem, however, is not only that Lajpat's remarks were embedded in a speech in which he—like Sarkar in 1949—implicitly held Muslims responsible for communalism, but also that he spoke from within the self-identified Hindu nation: he was the president of the Hindu Mahasabha. For both Lajpat and Sarkar in this mode, being Hindu was the default (and reasonable, generous) mode of being Indian: so much so that its communal connotations disappeared and it appeared secular. Savarkar may have had the last laugh. At another level, Sarkar's posture after the Partition eliminates the possibility that Indians and Pakistanis could retain any loyalties across the borders of the nation-state. The Romantic race was over, so to speak, but it was the 'Hindu race' that was over, replaced by a narrowly liberal concept of Indianness.

In spite of his fetishised roots in Bikrampur[218] (near Dhaka), Sarkar expected, first of all, that India and Pakistan would simply drift away in opposite directions, and that the ties of affect and identity developed since the thirteenth century—which he had earlier emphasised—could be delegitimised. He expected, secondly, that the nation-state, rather than other forms of community (like religion), must be the exclusive focal point of identity. Here, he approaches the absurdity of what Amitav Ghosh called the 'shadow lines',[219] and it is an absurdity that has to be enforced, and taught, by the coercive state. We have here a drastic reformulation of the pedagogy of governance. There is little doubt that Sarkar came to see Muslims as a problem of mentality and governmentality in independent India. There is, in his post-1947 writings, no comparable discussion of Hindus as a 'problem'; it was understood that they would be loyal citizens of the new Indian state, and that they would be liberal (or amenable to liberal education). There is no perception, or anticipation, of Hindu bigotry directed at Muslims in independent India, either as an ethical dilemma or as a problem of statecraft. This is a major flaw in Sarkar's secularism, because without acknowledging the problem, he could not direct his activist-pedagogical state to fix it.

In 1949, Sarkar called again for a new historiography of India: the period between the thirteenth and the eighteenth centuries, he declared, should be re-examined and reinterpreted in terms that were less 'rosy'.[220] It is unclear what gave him the idea that the dominant nationalist historiography painted this period in rosy hues, particularly since he himself had, in his earlier call for a new Indian history, depicted it as a time in need of rescue from narratives of Muslim oppression. But after the Partition, Sarkar was engaged in an ideological reorganisation: shrinking back from the heroic Romanticism of his middle years to a narrower vision of the racial Self, with all the bitterness that is involved in such readjustments. He was not as sanguine about 'losing' Pakistan as he made himself out to be.[221] His liberalism remained intact (and indeed, became more pronounced), but he gave up a vital part of the experiment with expansive communities of justice.

Conclusion

The widest circle of Sarkar's racial Self was Pan-Asia.[222] It is not for nothing that the alternate title of *The Futurism of Young Asia* is *The Sociology of Races*. In that work, Sarkar sought, up to a point, to construct an Asian race in a negative sense. Asians were a race because they suffered from a common predicament, which had to do with the European insistence on assigning a 'nature' to them. He did not say that there is no Asian nature, but he insisted that the Western reading of Asian nature was incorrect and self-serving. He remained ambivalent about whether the content of racial nature—expressed as culture—was self-contained or subject to borrowing. On the one hand he insisted that cultural phenomena were mainly autonomous, on the other he emphasised there had been significant exchanges between cultures which indicated not only the agency of Asia, but also the historical mutability of race.[223] In the process, Sarkar established a fluid relationship between Asia (geography) and Asian (race) that had broad relevance for anti-colonial nationhood.[224] Asia was wherever Asians lived, and anybody living in this construction of Asia could be 'Asianised'. There was no insistence on a stable or reliably evident biological identity. The breakdown of racial identity remained a live political impulse in all communities, especially on the fringes. By the same token, the margins of the race became an asset: the zone of novelty, growth, renewal and also justice.

For the most part, the Asian formula was applicable to India. Here too, race functioned as a language of external and internal justice: a way of articulating agendas of resistance and correction, in which the inclusive dynamics were more prominent and imaginative than those of exclusion. Where Gobineau had argued that inclusion (articulated as miscegenation) produced the downfall of the race, Sarkar agreed only to disagree: the intelligent mongrel, he suggested, was the survivor-author of history, thriving on fluidity itself, learning to manage its degeneracy and incorporating new material from within and without. Incorporation could be both organic and negotiated, total and contingent. An Indian race—which might claim justice for itself, but also do justice to its components—was thus both a Romantic 'given' and an ongoing political project involving the identification of tasks and negotiating partners. In the 1930s, this understanding of community came increasingly to hinge on the Hindu-Muslim relationship. When that ended in the Partition, a vital frontier of the Indian race was lost, or rather, disavowed by those inclined to be inclusive. With that disavowal, the project of articulating race as justice lost its teeth. Some vestiges lingered in Nehru's foreign policy,[225] but the failure in the domain of the politics of Indian identity was nothing short of catastrophic.

Notes

1 See Subhas Chandra Bose, *The Indian Struggle, 1920-1934*. London: Wishart Co., 1935, pp. 3-35.
2 Edward Said, *The Question of Palestine*. New York: Vintage, 1992, pp. 3-54; Eric Hobsbawm, *Nations and Nationalism since 1780: Programme, Myth, Reality*. Cambridge: Cambridge University Press, 1992, pp. 101-30.
3 Anthony Smith, *The Ethnic Origins of Nations*. Oxford: Blackwell, 1986, pp. 1-18.
4 Robb (ed.), *The Concept of Race in South Asia*, pp. 35-36.
5 *PBHS-II*, pp. 73-74.
6 Robb (ed.), *The Concept of Race in South Asia*, pp. 32, 304-26.
7 Frantz Fanon, *Black Skin, White Masks*. New York: Grove, 2008, pp. xi-xviii.
8 Hannah Arendt, *The Origins of Totalitarianism*. Orlando: Harcourt, 1976, pp. 274-83.
9 Arthur Comte de Gobineau, *The Inequality of Human Races*. Burlington: Ostara, 2011, pp. 29-31; Robb (ed.), *The Concept of Race in South Asia*, pp. 19-27.
10 *VT*, pp. 255-56.
11 *FYA*, p. 249.
12 Ibid., p. 166.
13 On Bankim and nationalist self-criticism, see Sudipta Kaviraj, *The Unhappy Consciousness: Bankimchandra Chattopadhyay and the Formation of Nationalist Discourse in India*. Delhi: Oxford University Press, 1998, pp. 107-57.
14 Forbes, *Women in Modern India*, pp. 157-88; Antoinette Burton, *Dwelling in the Archive*. Delhi: Oxford University Press, 2003, pp. 65-100.

88 An Indian Race

15 On Gandhi and health, see Joseph Alter, *Gandhi's Body: Sex, Diet and the Politics of Nationalism*. Philadelphia: University of Pennsylvania Press, 2000, pp. 3–27.
16 Gwilym Beckerlegge, *The Ramakrishna Mission: The Making of a Modern Hindu Movement*. Delhi: Oxford University Press, 2000, pp. 79–112.
17 Leonard Gordon, 'Divided Bengal', in Mushirul Hasan (ed.), *India's Partition: Process, Strategy and Mobilization*. Delhi: Oxford University Press, 1993, pp. 274–317; Chatterji, *Bengal Divided*, pp. 18–54.
18 Swami Shraddhanand, *Hindu Sangathan: Saviour of the Dying Race*, n.p., 1924.
19 Christophe Jaffrelot (ed.), *Hindu Nationalism: A Reader*. Princeton: Princeton University Press, 2007, p. 9.
20 Ibid.
21 M.S. Golwalkar, *We or Our Nationhood Defined*. Nagpur: Bharat Prakashan, 1947, pp. 21–52.
22 Sumit Sarkar, *Writing Social History*, p. 363.
23 Menon, 'A Local Cosmopolitanism', p. 133.
24 Henrika Kuklick, *The Savage Within: The Social History of British Anthropology*. Cambridge: Cambridge University Press, 1993, pp. 75–118; Gregory Smithers, *Science, Sexuality and Race in the United States and Australia*. Routledge: New York, 2009, pp. 85–89.
25 Kuklick, *The Savage Within*, pp. 27–74; Satadru Sen, *Savagery and Colonialism in the Indian Ocean: Power, Pleasure and the Andaman Islanders*. London: Routledge, 2010, pp. 20–24; Clare Anderson, *Legible Bodies: Race, Criminality and Colonialism in South Asia*. Oxford: Berg, 2004, pp. 1–14.
26 Kathleen Wilson, *The Island Race: Englishness, Empire and Gender in the Eighteenth Century*. London: Routledge, 2003, pp. 54–91.
27 Smithers, *Science, Sexuality and Race*, pp. 84–89; Sen, *Savagery and Colonialism in the Indian Ocean*, pp. 127–56.
28 Greenfeld, *Nationalism*, pp. 367–70; *FYA*, p. 352.
29 *PPS-1905*, p. 123; *FYA*, pp. 33–34.
30 *FYA*, pp. 193–94.
31 Ibid., p. 98.
32 *VT*, p. 548.
33 On empire and white decline, see also Anne McClintock, *Imperial Leather: Race, Gender and Sexuality in the Colonial Contest*. London: Routledge, 1995, pp. 132, 232.
34 *VT*, pp. 548–52.
35 Fanon, *Black Skin, White Masks*, p. 120; Ashis Nandy, *The Intimate Enemy: Loss and Recovery of Self under Colonialism*. Delhi: Oxford University Press, 1983, pp. 1–63.
36 Eric Foner, *Free Soil, Free Labor, Free Men: The Ideology of the Republican Party before the Civil War*. Oxford: Oxford University Press, 1970, pp. 40–72.
37 *VT*, pp. 552–57.

38 Kenneth Ballhatchet, *Race, Sex and Class under the Raj: Imperial Attitudes and Policies and Their Critics 1793-1905*. London: Weidenfeld & Nicholson, 1980, pp. 123-24; Harald Fischer-Tiné, *Low and Licentious Europeans: Race, Class and 'White Subalternity' in Colonial India*. Hyderabad: Orient BlackSwan, 2009, pp. 1-15; Sen, *Colonial Childhoods*, p. 36; Stoler, *Race and the Education of Desire*, p. 95.
39 *VT*, pp. 552-57.
40 The difference between Arendt and Sarkar on this point is that whereas Arendt argued that the colonies attracted a particular sort of degenerate European, Sarkar saw the colony as the source of degeneration. Arendt, *The Origins of Totalitarianism*, pp. 138-39, 157, 337.
41 *VT*, pp. 552-57.
42 The debates on opium in the League of Nations are an example of this. Sen, *Migrant Races*, pp. 146-49.
43 Hegel, *The Philosophy of History*, p. 93.
44 *FYA*, p. 71.
45 See Sumit Sarkar, 'The City Imagined', in *Writing Social History*, pp. 159-85.
46 Nandy, *The Romance of the State*, pp. 121-33.
47 *PPS-1905*, pp. 5-6; Pitirim Sorokin and Carle Zimmerman, *Principles of Rural-Urban Sociology*. New York: Holt, 1929. Sarkar qualified his receptiveness to Sorokin by observing that Sorokin was naïve about where humanity was headed. *BSB-II*, p. 651.
48 *VT*, pp. 177-78.
49 Hughes, *Consciousness and Society*, pp. 78-82, 249-77.
50 *PPS-1905*, pp. 179-80.
51 *VT*, pp. 177-78.
52 Sen, *Colonial Childhoods*, pp. 128-41; Fischer-Tiné, *Low and Licentious Europeans*, pp. 186-232.
53 See P.K. Wattal (ed.), *Population Problem in India: A Census Study*. Bombay: Bennett Coleman, 1934, p. 139; U.N. Mukherji, *Hindus: A Dying Race*. Calcutta: Bhaskar Mukerjee, 1929.
54 *PPS-1905*, pp. 201-3.
55 Ibid., p. 83.
56 *BSB-II*, pp. 530-34.
57 Sumit Sarkar, *Writing Social History*, pp. 216-81.
58 Shraddhanand, in Jaffrelot (ed.), *Hindu Nationalism*, pp. 79-83.
59 *NBGP*, pp. 155-61. Shraddhanand was willing to let widows remarry only if their marriages had been unconsummated. Jaffrelot (ed.), *Hindu Nationalism*, pp. 79-83.
60 Mukhopadhyay, *Prabandha Samagra*, pp. 12-13, 130-34.
61 Tanika Sarkar, *Hindu Wife, Hindu Nation*, pp. 23-52.
62 V.D. Savarkar, *My Transportation for Life*. Bombay: Veer Savarkar Prakashan, 1984, Appendix; Sen, *Traces of Empire*, p. 79.

90 An Indian Race

63 Oswald Spengler, *The Decline of the West*. New York: A. Knopf, 1928; Hughes, *Consciousness and Society*, pp. 368–78.
64 *VT*, p. 187.
65 *PPS-1905*, pp. 70–72; *BSB-II*, pp. 552–54.
66 *VT*, pp. 255–56.
67 Andre Beteille, *Society and Politics in India*. Delhi: Oxford University, 1990, pp. 19–20.
68 Sarkar enthusiastically speculated that the Mauryan era was 'an epoch of inter-racial marriages' in India. *CRTHE*, p. 93.
69 *VT*, pp. 258–59.
70 Ibid., pp. 268–69.
71 Ibid., p. 257; Zachariah, 'Rethinking (the Absence of) Fascism in India', pp. 194–95.
72 Derek Hoff, *The State and the Stork: The Population Debate and Policy Making in US History*. Chicago: University of Chicago Press, 2012, pp. 44–71; Gay, *The Cultivation of Hatred*, pp. 60–61; *PPS-1905*, pp. 173–203.
73 *BSB-II*, pp. 534–35.
74 On Gandhi, see Sarah Hodges (ed.), *Reproductive Health in India*. Hyderabad: Orient Longman, 2006, p. 235.
75 Dona Schneider and David Lilienfeld (eds), *Public Health: The Development of a Discipline*. New Brunswick: Rutgers University Press, 2008, pp. 579–682.
76 *VT*, pp. 285–86.
77 Ibid., pp. 285–86.
78 Schneider and Lilienfeld (eds), *Public Health*, pp. 579–682.
79 Ibid., p. 484.
80 Michel Foucault, *Discipline and Punish: The Birth of the Prison*. New York: Vintage, 1979, pp. 257–92.
81 Satadru Sen, *Disciplining Punishment: Colonialism and Convict Society in the Andaman Islands*. Delhi: Oxford University Press, 2000, pp. 42–48.
82 *VT*, p. 446.
83 Raj Kapoor made *Awaara* barely a decade after Sarkar wrote *Villages and Towns*.
84 *VT*, p. 451.
85 Daniel Pick, *Faces of Degeneration: A European Disorder 1848-1918*. Cambridge: Cambridge University Press, 1989, pp. 37–74, 222.
86 Flora, 'Benoy Kumar Sarkar', p. 252.
87 Sartori, *Bengal in Global Concept History*, pp. 68–108.
88 Joya Chatterji, *Bengal Divided*, pp. 150–90.
89 *NBGP*, pp. 150–53.
90 Chandi Charan Bandyopadhyay, *Vidyasagara: The Life of Ishwarchandra Vidyasagara*. Calcutta: n.p., 1895, pp. 518–20.
91 On sex and wholeness in contemporary Indian polemics, see Menon, 'A Local Cosmopolitanism', pp. 145, 149.

92 *PBHS-II*, p. 33; *PPS-1905*, p. 234.
93 *BSB-I*, p. 237.
94 Benoy Kumar Sarkar, *Love in Hindu Literature* (henceforth, *LHL*). Tokyo: Maruzen, 1916, p. 52.
95 On restraint and *bhadrata*, see Sen, *Traces of Empire*, pp. 99, 231; also Sudipta Kaviraj, *Trajectories of the Indian State*. Delhi: Permanent Black, 2010, pp. 64–67.
96 *FYA*, p. 312.
97 Benoy Kumar Sarkar, *The Beginning of Hindu Culture as World Power* (henceforth, *BHCWP*). Commercial Press: Shanghai, 1916, p. 13.
98 Sumit Sarkar, *Writing Social History*, p. 184.
99 Satadru Sen, 'A Juvenile Periphery: Geographies of Childhood in Bengali Children's Literature', *Journal of Colonialism and Colonial History*, 5(1), 2004.
100 *BSB-I*, pp. 239–41.
101 Sumit Sarkar, *Beyond Nationalist Frames: Postmodernism, Hindu Fundamentalism, History*. Bloomington: Indiana University Press, 2002, pp. 69–72. On Namasudra activism, see Sumit Sarkar, *Writing Social History*, pp. 377–85.
102 Benoy Kumar Sarkar, *The Folk Element in Hindu Culture: A Contribution to Socio Religious Studies in Hindu Folk Institutions* (henceforth, *FEHC*). London: Longmans, Green and Co., 1917, pp. ix–x.
103 *BSB-I*, p. 240.
104 *FEHC*, pp. ix–x.
105 Ibid.
106 *BSB-I*, pp. 350–54.
107 *FEHC*, p. 7.
108 Ibid., pp. 23–24.
109 *BSB-I*, p. 81; Benoy Kumar Sarkar, *Samaj Bigyan* (henceforth, *SB*). Calcutta: Chuckervertty, Chatterjee & Co., 1940, pp. 486–87.
110 *FEHC*, p. 53.
111 Ibid., pp. 82, 108.
112 On Rivers, see Kuklick, *The Savage Within*, p. 119–74; Marcel Mauss, 'W.H.R. Rivers and the Todas', *Annee Sociologique*, 11, 1906–9, pp. 154–58.
113 See Kuklick, *The Savage Within*, p. 8–17.
114 Sen, *Traces of Empire*, pp. 19–36; Edward Said, *Culture and Imperialism*. New York: Vintage, 1993, pp. 19–30.
115 Benoy Kumar Sarkar, *Naya Banglar Goda Pattan* (henceforth, *NBGP*). Calcutta: Chuckervertty, Chatterjee & Co., 1932, pp. 337–40.
116 Romila Thapar, *The Aryan: Recasting Constructs*. Gurgaon: Three Essays Collective, 2008, pp. 38–43, 65–88; Rosalind O'Hanlon, *Caste Conflict and Ideology*. Cambridge: Cambridge University Press, 1985, pp. 255–302; Gail Omvedt, *Dalit Visions*. Hyderabad: Orient Longman, 2006, pp. 17–24, 34–42.
117 P.T.S. Iyengar, *Life in Ancient India in the Age of Mantras*. Delhi: Asian Educational Services, 1982, pp. 8–15.
118 C.V. Vaidya, *Epic India*. Bombay: S.A. Sagoon, 1907, pp. 280–88.

92 An Indian Race

119 He supported Iyengar's refusal to entertain biological or stable cultural differences between Aryans and Dasyus. Benoy Kumar Sarkar, *The Positive Background of Hindu Sociology (Non-Political)* (henceforth, *PBHS*). Allahabad: Panini Office, 1914, pp. 52–57.
120 *BHCWP*, pp. 9–16.
121 Susan Bayly, 'Caste and Race in Colonial Ethnography', in Peter Robb (ed.), *The Concept of Race in South Asia*. Delhi: Oxford University Press, 1995, pp. 167–68.
122 *PBHS-II*, pp. 89–90.
123 Chowdhuri-Sengupta, 'The Effeminate and the Masculine', pp. 282–303; *PPS-1905*, pp. 53–54.
124 *PBHS*, p. 52.
125 *PBHS-II*, pp. 87–88.
126 *FEHC*, p. 87.
127 Nicholas Dirks, *Castes of Mind: Colonialism and the Making of Modern India*. Princeton: Princeton University Press, 2001, pp. 43–60, 125.
128 *FEHC*, p. 108.
129 Ibid., pp. 114–15.
130 M.K. Gandhi, *An Autobiography*. New York: Beacon, 1957, p. 170.
131 Madan Mohan Malaviya, in Jaffrelot (ed.), *Hindu Nationalism*, p. 68.
132 *FEHC*, p. 169.
133 Ibid., pp. 133–34.
134 Bhattacharya, *The Sentinels of Culture*.
135 *FEHC*, pp. 19–21.
136 Ibid.
137 Ibid., p. 74.
138 Ibid., p. 127.
139 *BSB-II*, p. 495.
140 *PBHS*, p. 53.
141 *FEHC*, p. 16.
142 Ibid., p. 65.
143 Giuseppe Flora, *Benoy Kumar Sarkar and Italy*. New Delhi: Italian Embassy Cultural Centre, 1994, pp. 19–20.
144 Sumit Sarkar, *The Swadeshi Movement*, pp. 1–7, 344–94; Joya Chatterji, *Bengal Divided*, pp. 18–54; Sartori, *Bengal in Global Concept History*, pp. 109–35.
145 Jaffrelot (ed.), *Hindu Nationalism*, pp. 3–25.
146 Sen, *Disciplining Punishment*, pp. 264–72; V.D. Savarkar, *My Transportation for Life*.
147 *FYA*, p. 318.
148 Bakhle, 'Putting Global Intellectual History in Its Place', pp. 233–34.
149 V.D. Savarkar, *Hindutva*. Delhi: Hindi Sahitya Sadan, 2003, p. 85.
150 Ibid., p. 9.
151 Ibid., pp. 102–16.
152 Jaffrelot (ed.), *Hindu Nationalism*, pp. 98.
153 Golwalkar, *We or Our Nationhood Defined*, pp. 21–52.
154 Savarkar, *Hindutva*, pp. 10–12, 42–47.

155 *FEHC*, pp. 215–16.
156 *FYA*, p. 121.
157 Golwalkar, *We or Our Nationhood Defined*, pp. 21–52.
158 Savarkar, *Hindutva*, pp. 113–15, 139.
159 *BSB-II*, pp. 546–47, 770–77.
160 *FYA*, pp. 331–32.
161 Savarkar, *Hindutva*, p. 44.
162 *FEHC*, p. 212.
163 Ibid., pp. 24–25, 213.
164 Ibid., pp. 261–62.
165 Ibid., p. 100.
166 Richard Eaton, *The Rise of Islam and the Bengal Frontier*. Berkeley: University of California Press, 1993, pp. xxii–xxiv; *PPS-1905*, pp. 57–62; *BSB-I*, pp. 354–56.
167 *FEHC*, p. 217.
168 *BSB-II*, p. 772.
169 *BSB-I*, pp. 354–57.
170 *BHCWP*, pp. 18–19.
171 *PBHS-I*, pp. 53–54.
172 Ibid., p. 50.
173 Ibid., p. 51.
174 *BSB-I*, pp. 232, 235.
175 Jinnah in Pakistan Constituent Assembly, 11 August 1947, in Stephen Hay (ed.), *Sources of Indian Tradition*, vol 2. New York: Columbia University Press, 1988, pp. 385–87; Austin, *The Indian Constitution*, pp. 75–78.
176 Harbilas Sarda, *Hindu Superiority: An Attempt to Determine the Position of the Hindu Race in the Scale of Nations*. Ajmer: Rajputana Printing Works, 1906, pp. 27–31.
177 Ibid., pp. xxiv, 135–200.
178 Rajat Kanta Ray, *The Felt Community: Commonality and Mentality before the Emergence of Indian Nationalism*. Delhi: Oxford University Press, 2003, pp. 67–74.
179 *FYA*, p. 171.
180 *PPS-1905*, p. 56.
181 *FYA*, pp. 177–79.
182 Ibid., pp. 183–84.
183 Ibid., pp. 196–97.
184 Bose, *The Indian Struggle*, p. 5.
185 *FYA*, pp. 285–95. Five years previously, he had utilised Smith's work and called him 'one of the greatest figures in Indology'. *CRTHE*, p. xvi.
186 Ibid., p. 261.
187 *FYA*, p. 260.
188 Ernst, 'Admiring the Works of the Ancients', pp. 98–120.
189 David Gilmartin and Bruce Lawrence (eds), *Beyond Turk and Hindu: Rethinking Religious Identities in Islamicate South Asia*. Delhi: India Research Press, 2002, p. 2.

94 An Indian Race

190 *FYA*, pp. 285–95.
191 Ibid., p. 171.
192 Ibid., p. 197.
193 On the Mughal expedition to Balkh, see John Richards, *The Mughal Empire*, Cambridge: Cambridge University Press, 1993, pp. 132–33.
194 Bakhle, 'Putting Global Intellectual History in Its Place', pp. 233–34.
195 *BSB-I*, pp. 279–80; *BSB-II*, pp. 771–77.
196 *BSB-I*, p. 72.
197 *BSB-II*, pp. 771–74.
198 *FYA*, pp. 323–24.
199 *BSB-II*, p. 777.
200 *FYA*, p. 325.
201 Ibid., p. 350.
202 Ibid., pp. 331–32.
203 Ayesha Jalal, *The Sole Spokesman: Jinnah, The Muslim League and the Demand for Pakistan*. Cambridge: Cambridge University Press, 1985, pp. 126–73.
204 *NBGP*, vol. 2, p. 113.
205 *PPS-1905*, pp. 329–44.
206 Ibid., pp. 335–36.
207 Ibid., pp. 329–44; *BSB-II*, p. 772.
208 *NBGP*, pp. 275–82.
209 Ray, *The Felt Community*, pp. 360–95.
210 *BSB-II*, p. 635.
211 *DIWP*, pp. 123–24.
212 Ibid., pp. 134–35; *PB*, pp. 25, 97–98; *PPS-1905*, pp. 44–46.
213 *DIWP*, pp. 134–37.
214 Bandyopadhyay, *Vidyasagara*, p. 114.
215 *DIWP*, pp. 159–60.
216 By 1922, Sarkar had decided that Lajpat Rai was insufficiently militant, and wrote a scathing review of Rai's book on Indian anti-colonialism. *FYA*, pp. 342–43.
217 Lala Rajpat Rai, Presidential Address to the Hindu Mahasabha, excerpted in Jaffrelot (ed.), *Hindu Nationalism*, pp. 69–70.
218 *BSB-II*, pp. 755, 844–48.
219 Amitav Ghosh, *The Shadow Lines*. New York: Viking, 1989.
220 *DIWP*, p. 160.
221 Ibid., pp. 157–58.
222 Duara, 'The Discourse of Civilization and Pan-Asianism'.
223 *FYA*, pp. 105–8.
224 Ibid., pp. 2–9.
225 B.R. Nanda, *Indian Foreign Policy: The Nehru Years*. Honolulu: University of Hawaii Press, 1976, pp. 1–23.

2
Wars of the Emasculated

Historically speaking, nations are born in wars. Nationality is in essence a militaristic concept. If there is any spirituality associated with nationalism it is the spirituality of war or the categorical imperative of Kshatriyaism.
— Benoy Kumar Sarkar, 1925–26[1]

With few exceptions, male Indian nationalists from the 1890s on defined their predicament in terms of two intertwined shortcomings: the lack of manhood and the lack of a state. The more cosmopolitan among them read the problem as part of a wider Asian predicament: the condition of the 'little man' cowed down by the hulking physicality of the imperial West. The powerlessness of their nation in the world was, after all, an extension of their own powerlessness in the streets and beds of colonial India. They and those with whom they identified were forever at risk of being assaulted or brushed aside by soldiers, sailors, policemen and railway guards, not to mention civilians wearing the most basic badge of the racist state: white skin.[2] Moreover, powerlessness in the world naturalised their humiliation in their own country, because as the sovereign state became the necessary fulfilment of nationhood, it became self-evident that only those endowed with agency abroad truly deserved the dignity of manhood at home.

Already in the 1890s, Indian men looked to Japan for compensation. Bhudeb Mukhopadhyay lauded Japan (and China, inaugurating a Sinophile strand within Indian nationalism that survived into the 1950s) for having demonstrated that European individualism and science—the keys to resisting Europe—could be imported discerningly and filtered through indigenous institutions, preserving both dignity and national essence.[3] It was after the Japanese naval victories over Russia, however, that manhood-in-the-world came dramatically to the rescue of the castrated-at-home. Calcutta University's Eden Hindu Hostel, Sarkar wrote, became a window through which Japanese artillery was audible.[4] The equation of 'Asian' with 'weak' and 'effeminate' was undermined, because not only had an Asian race prevailed over Europeans, it had done so in the form of a state, equipped with all the paraphernalia of modern statehood: steel ships, admirals, the rhetoric of strategy and national interest. Miraculously, this development had coincided with the radicalisation, intensification and popularisation of Indian anti-colonial agitation, especially in Bengal. For Bengalis armed with pens, newspapers and unreliable bombs, 1905 was at least retrospectively the Year of the Asian Man. Lending substance to Pareto, Gini and Spengler, new and relatively history-less people like the Japanese—and Bengalis—could now be shown to be the virile conquerors and successors of a senile, decadent albinocracy.[5] As H. Stuart Hughes has noted, Europe had its own 'generation of 1905': reactionary intellectuals who read Nietzsche, felt stifled by history, and looked ahead to war as a form of release and rebirth.[6] They (Spengler in particular) too became a part of the prism through which Sarkar saw his Asian predicament.[7] The gaze was returned; a German critic of *The Futurism of Young Asia* remarked that Sarkar 'reminds us in many ways of our Oswald Spengler'.[8]

Much of Sarkar's writing on Asia and internationalism emerged in a period bracketed on one side by the Great War and his stay in Japan and China in 1915-16, and on the other by the Japanese invasions of China. When he began, Japan was already a colonial power, and its disregard for Chinese sovereignty as egregious as that of the Western powers. Such 'equality' sat uneasily with Sarkar's admitted Sinophilia:[9] no reconciliation could be credible here. Rather than attempt to reconcile Japanese aggressiveness with Chinese passivity, Sarkar generally made a temporal separation: the Chinese predicament represented the humiliating Asian present, while Japan was a model of the future. There was, however, considerable ambivalence. While Japan appeared as the Asian champion, the methods of its power and the politics of its self-identification—particularly its tendency to affiliate itself diplomatically with the Western powers—also raised the spectre of deracination. Sarkar had few lasting illusions about Japanese imperialism: 'there can be no enthusiasm in Asia for this kind of liberation', he mused in 1942 after the fall of Singapore and Burma.[10] China was a more pliable extension of the Self: it could be either India's Asian fellow-victim, or a vision of greatness that, while imperial, was neither distant from Asia nor tainted by a recognisable colonialism. Relying largely on comparative mythology, Sarkar argued in 1916 that China and India were essentially similar, for reasons that 'must be explained by other circumstances than facts of history': even before the advent of Buddhism, there existed 'a common psychological basis endowing the two races with a common outlook on the universe'.[11] But unlike the two poles of Japan and India, China was an unanswered question: 'The world is waiting to see if the modernizing of China is to be effected along Indian lines, i.e., through slavery to alien domination or along the Western and Japanese lines of unhampered and independent development', he wrote a decade later.[12]

Sarkar's interest lay in appropriating Asia for his vision of a manly, or 'energistic', Indian nation.[13] This could be done in two ways. One was to participate vicariously in Japanese imperialism. The other was to extend, as far as possible, a historical Indian claim upon Japan, not to mention China. Radhakumud Mookerji and Phanindranath Bose had already shown their eagerness to make such claims upon Southeast Asia.[14] Consequently, the India that Sarkar envisioned became hard to separate from the rhetoric of conquest. It cannot be brushed away as metaphorical; for Koreans and the Chinese, 'conquest' was already real. Even as a metaphor, Sarkar's 'conquest' was ideologically loaded: not only was it tied to domination, it was deployed as a natural and implicitly biological aspect of being a man, akin to sex.[15] His fondness for biological analogies for political behaviour lent itself easily to reactionary statecraft and fantasies.[16] The German political scientist Karl Haushofer—retired general, former advisor to Japan, teacher and friend of Rudolf Hess, director of the Duetsche Akademie, and finally a victim of the Nazi regime[17]—described geopolitics as a choice between 'stimulating penetration' and 'exploratory rape'.[18] Haushofer and Sarkar were mutual admirers;[19] both wanted German support for Asian decolonisation, and saw close links between Asian freedom and the freedom of subjugated/cramped nationalities within Europe.[20]

Haushofer was not a 'Nazi strategist' as Manu Goswami has somewhat carelessly asserted,[21] but he justified Japanese expansionism in terms of *Lebensraum* and Social-Darwinist predicaments.[22] Mass emigration and settler-colonialism were linked strategies of national-economic growth.[23] As Woodruff Smith notes in his study of German imperialism, *Lebensraum* ideology originated in *liberal* anxieties about emigration, depopulation, deracination and weakness.[24] Nevertheless, the utilisation of Japan to construct a state based on militarism and imperial fantasy, a manhood based on violence, and a race based on conquest indicates, firstly, the limits imposed by *ressentiment* on liberalism. In Europe and in Germany in particular, such limits constituted an interwar outlook: that of a humiliated nation longing for blood, fire and 'wholeness' even as it experimented with liberal democracy.[25] Similar but not identical considerations saturate Sarkar's Romantic yearning for a state of war. Second, it reflects the fascination that Japan—the first modern Asian state, the perpetrator of terrible atrocities, and the victim of unspeakable horror—has held for Indian onlookers in the twentieth century, right up to the more or less simultaneous moments when Japan lay devastated and India emerged from colonial rule. From Rabindranath Tagore to Radhabinod Pal, Japan was an object of desire and alarm: a sign of what was missing from the colonised nation, a theatre of revenge, and simultaneously, a representation of the cannibalistic nature of the world in which they moved. They spoke from Indian realities; the Japan they imagined was never very far away. Not surprisingly, the desire to walk in Japanese shoes (with Hindustani hearts) proved unsustainable for nearly all of them.

The State of War

In the early 1920s, Sarkar reviewed several new books on Indian politics. These included Verney Lovett's *A History of the Indian Nationalist Movement*.[26] Lovett was an Indian Civil Service (ICS) man with unambiguous political sympathies. He had co-authored the Rowlatt Bill and prepared the official history of Indian sedition for the colonial government in 1918.[27] He dismissed out of hand the idea of dominion status for India, calling its British advocates naive. India, he explained, could not be kept in the empire without direct British rule, because even Moderate nationalists were closet Extremists.[28] Sarkar began his review by noting that Lovett was a straightforward imperialist. He then agreed with Lovett's assessment that there was no real difference between Moderate and Extremist in Indian politics: you were either a 'patriot' or a 'traitor'. He continued:

> From a reading of the book one rises with the conviction that a state of war exists in India between the people who are its natural leaders, and the foreigners who have managed to get possession of the country. This belligerency . . . is not recognized as such in international law, because the rebels have not yet been able to smuggle, purchase or steal enough arms and ammunition for one or two dramatic military demonstrations. But India's efforts to attain political emancipation in the teeth of the formidable opposition of the enemy are patent to all who study warfare and the 'halfway houses' to war. The . . . book is a record of this struggle, especially of the crisis that is coming to a head, from the other side of the shield.[29]

Sarkar thus read Lovett's book with satisfaction: there was a convergence between what the imperialist saw and what the nationalist wanted to see. From his position within a regime looking to justify its repression, Lovett described the nationalist challenge as a radical, unified and effective threat, and implied that it was nothing short of a war against the empire. Sarkar was happy to agree, because the rhetoric of national war strengthened his position that India was not only an extant nation, but nearly an extant state. A prerogative and sign of statehood, war set political violence and the community that practised it above the illegitimacy and insignificance of mere terrorism. The lack of wider recognition for this state of war was, therefore, irritating to both Lovett and Sarkar, and the latter needed something substantial and undeniable to reify his people.

But where might the 'disarmed' find their militarism, by which Sarkar meant the ability, the will and an undeniable eagerness to make war? Where was the spectacle, without which the rhetoric of war fell flat? In London in 1914, Sarkar supposedly presented the young revolutionary Kedarnath Chatterjee with a pistol and ammunition,[30] but for middle-class nationalists, the best armoury and theatre was usually the past. Anticipating Romila Thapar, Sarkar denied that Ashoka's Mauryan state had been pacifist, or that 'the citizens of India' at the time had been bound by Buddhism: *dhamma* was not Buddhism.[31] In his extensive writings on early Indian religion, he downplayed whatever was mystical and 'quietist', highlighting the rational, worldly, activist, organisationally inclined elements, from humanitarian intervention to the killing of tyrants.[32] These became signs of civilisational virility, and virility a mode of gendered citizenship. In ancient Indian political thought, he insisted in 1921, *paurusa* (manliness) trumped *daiva* (fate): the former reflected 'intelligence and might', and the latter impotence.[33] The Gupta era was 'an epoch of all-round success in arms and arts', and that, for Sarkar, made it 'the period to conjure with even in the twentieth century'.[34] 'Arms and arts' constituted the heart of a successful national culture, and '[Kalidasa] was as great a nationalist or patriot or jingo as was the Roman [Virgil]'.[35]

The direct model was Europe and America between Napoleon and the Great War, where virility compensated for bourgeois anxieties about melancholy, pessimism, decadence and degeneracy.[36] Sarkar welcomed Hemchandra Banerji's odd but enthusiastic poem about America, in which the poet wrote: 'Her *hu-humkar* yells cause the earth to quake / Disembowel she would the globe, as it were / and reshape it fresh at her own sweet will'.[37] *Hu-humkars* (war-cries associated with Indian epic literature) and world-disembowellings (the assertive American foreign policy since the war with Spain)[38] did not alarm Sarkar in the least; they were the stuff of creative disorder. The moribund Indian Ocean must be dredged into an invigorating new Atlantic, he insisted.[39] The 'jingo' state, with its immediate association with the overwrought machismo of Theodore Roosevelt and Kipling, could become the old India, if not the new one. The *Arthashastra* provided a handy link:

> The compiler was Kautilya, a Bismarck or Richelieu of India. The militarism of the Hindus would be evident to every reader of this book. Women with prepared food and beverage were advised to stand behind the fighting lines and utter encouraging words to the men at the front. This is out-Spartaing Sparta. There is here indicated a real 'universal' conscription like the one ... witnessed during the recent World-War.[40]

Packaging Sparta, Richelieu and the Great War in the same paragraph was not so much carelessness with European history as a carefully formulated counter-history of India:

> It is alleged that the Hindus have ever been defective in organizing ability and the capacity for administering public bodies. Epoch by epoch, however, India has given birth to as many heroes, both men and women, in public service, international commerce, military tactics, and government, as has any race in the Occidental world. Warfare was never monopolized by the so-called Khatriya or warrior caste in India, but as in Europe, gave scope to every class or grade of men to display their ability.[41]

Sarkar's dismissal of the idea that war was a Kshatriya preserve is more than a critique of Orientalist scholarship.[42] Like the pre-Great-War German interest in a new officer corps that extended beyond the Junker aristocracy,[43] and (more complicatedly) Bhudeb's regret that 'self-defeating' Hindus had left war to only one segment of society,[44] it also indicates a view of war as the definitive national activity, that allows the nation to discover and become itself. The idea of a warrior-caste is rejected precisely because it goes against modern notions of horizontal citizenship and popular sovereignty. War becomes a basic democratic phenomenon—an experience of citizenship in which all can participate—but democracy is not entirely voluntary: '[T]here was nothing against the Bramana [sic] class *as such* being drafted for the regiments', Sarkar wrote about the Mauryan state. 'The whole nation could be drilled at need'.[45] The discipline of the drill and the draft, as much as the wildness of the *hu-humkar*, revealed energism, which was a valuable cultural development in its own right and an essential ingredient of modern statehood.

What was energism? Sarkar equated it with 'shakti-yoga' and the motivating force in world-history, epitomised by Vivekananda.[46] Elsewhere, seeking to escape Marxist materialism, he described energism as an alternative materiality: a quality 'of the organic body, nature of flesh and blood, health-basis of struggles'.[47] It was a physiologically rooted willingness to act in the world, unrestrained by paralysing scruples about truth and falsity.[48] Amal Mukhopadhyay has fairly described Sarkar as a theorist of man's struggle to control his animal aggressiveness.[49] More than control was at stake, however. To drop out of the 'world' and be relegated to the 'private' sphere of the home and the shrine was also to be stripped of manhood. Sarkar was no crude woman-hater: he strove to temper the notorious misogyny of Manu into a palatable Victorian patriarchy, depicting the Manusmriti as 'gallant' and 'reverent' to women even as it provided a Dionysian alternative to the suffocating femininity of Christianity.[50] More important than Manu was what Nietzsche made of Manu. Sarkar quoted Nietzsche from *The Antichrist*: 'All those things which Christianity smothers with its bottomless vulgarity, procreation, woman, marriage, are [in Manu] treated with earnestness, with reverence, with love and confidence'.[51] Energism was the gendered citizenship of the rebel against the Christian West.

Like other Romantic nationalists, Sarkar was highly inconsistent in his relationship with Nietzsche. He conceded that colonised Indians were 'emasculated and demoralised', and India 'an asylum of incapables, a land of vegetating animalcules, or of mere stocks and stones'.[52] Salvation through energism was possible, but it was intertwined with the rediscovery of the state, particularly since 'Nietzsche finds greater truth in the mercilessly correct view of inter-statal relations given by the Hindus than in the hypocritical statements of Occidental statesmen whose actions belie their words'. Indeed, 'Old India has contributed its hoary Manu as the master-builder in order to boss the super-men who are to architecture the Occident of the twentieth century'.[53] The master-builder, however, bossed from a deep well of humiliation. The energism and militarism that Sarkar theorised rested on the *ressentiment* that informed his vision of a world of race and power: in a tactical misunderstanding, what Nietzsche abhorred became, for Sarkar, something to cultivate.[54]

That deviation from Nietzsche was rooted in Sarkar's conviction that the disease could generate the cure. Empire was demoralising but *productive* of rebellion: 'Such spheres are necessarily the eternal storm-centers of the world'.[55] Moreover, he suggested (citing a cluster of resolutions passed by the American Friends of Freedom for India in 1920), particular colonial institutions—such as the stationing of an 'unnatural' body of troops (men without wives) in India—had generated visible forms of gendered demoralisation: a plague of venereal disease, homosexuality, and a prostitution in which Indian women were set apart for the use of white men.[56] The idea that military prostitution threatened the masculinity of native men has not received much attention in the scholarship on the Contagious Diseases and Cantonments Acts.[57] Sarkar's writing indicates that it was a humiliation that closely fit the connections between nationalism, patriarchy and sex in a racial hierarchy.[58]

Combating this degradation required a compensating spirit, which Sarkar identified as resentment itself. Hate took on inherently positive connotations corresponding to health and wholeness. The 'alleged mentality' of being anti-war was a thing of the past, he observed enthusiastically in 1926, adding that '[a] fresh and young war-spirit is abroad in every nation'.[59] And when the Blitzkrieg raged, Sarkar wrote:

> A healthy mind reacts not only love-wards but also hatred-wards. War ... is not a disease. It is as normal as peace.[60]

The previous world war had transformed the resentment of the emasculated into something potent, he perceived, not least because it had opened up new arenas of manhood. This was not limited to Asia. In Germany, Peter Fritzsche has observed, the Great War produced (at least initially) an outpouring of pleasurable, purposeful identity which could be recalled for the purposes of National Socialism.[61] '[T]he war', Sarkar wrote, 'has given Asia the one thing she needed— a complete change in the diplomatic grouping of powers and in the values obtaining in the political psychology of all nations'.[62] The reference to political 'psychology' is worth noting. It is, on the one hand, a fashionable deployment of psycho-science. On the other, it refers to operationalised ideology in imperial relations: the racism of imperial powers, and the inclination of the colonised to resist the assumptions of automatic privilege or deference they had been taught. The need for revenge, in that useful twist on Nietzsche, becomes the stuff of vigour: to be prized, not avoided, in the colonies. In the modern world, *ressentiment* is the only alternative to slavery and hegemony.

That, of course, is a Fanonian formulation of the purifying and constructive power of violence, which presumes that violence does not so much derive from an extant position of strength, as generate strength.[63] Sarkar's effort to systematise the idea is visible in his use of the word 'vindictiveness'. Railing against Orientalist characterisations of the Chinese as docile, he wrote:

> If the Chinese have not been an aggressive people, one would have to define afresh as to what aggressiveness means. The people and the rulers of China have exhibited warlike and vindictive habits in every generation. The martial characteristics of [the] Chinese have really been as conspicuous as those of the proverbial fighting races of India.[64]

Sarkar's vocabulary is not a casual imprecision with language; nor should it be taken as quaint jargon with no meaning beyond the text. The insistence on a violent Orient is an attempt to restore Asia to world-history by restoring history—imagined as masculine aggression—to what Sarkar revealingly called the 'Concert of Asia'.[65] The moral inversion, however, is not fully credible even to its own articulator. A note of hysteria creeps into Sarkar's praise of 'vindictive' China, and into his declaration that ancient Indian *rishi*s were expert at 'burning, killing and fighting'. (His embarrassed biographer Haridas Mukherjee explained that such language should not be taken literally, but merely as a sign of Sarkar's 'human manner'.[66]) Also, the counter-discourse that Sarkar puts forward never cuts the tie with Orientalism: he falls back above on the Martial Races theory,[67] and his major work on China—which he begins by rejecting essential differences between East and West—is subtitled 'A Study in the Tendencies of Asiatic Mentality'.[68] Consequently, Sarkar puts himself in a position where he must both deny and affirm the Yellow Peril: Asians are aggressive and manly, but also the hapless victims of white-racist imperialism.[69]

Cracks then begin to appear in the rhetoric of vindictiveness and in the culture of the state of war, with Sarkar revealing the ambivalence of his desire:

> Reprisals and retaliations are undoubtedly justifiable weapons in literary as in material warfare. It is out of vindictiveness that people resort

to them. And surely Asia today is pervaded by the spirit of revenge; for the mal-treatment that she has received at Eur-America's hands is profound and extensive, really 'too deep for tears.' But no system of values can look for permanence on a war-basis. War is a force in social economy only because it raises issues and clarifies the surcharged atmosphere. Life's dynamics however must proceed to erect new structures on the new foundations created by the change in status quo.[70]

Elsewhere, he suggests that vindictiveness is a form of impotence, speaking in the same breath of the onset of militarism in the colonised world, the decline of 'vindictive' nationalism, and a new 'uplift' to a 'spiritual plane'.[71] Militarism in this counter-formulation is the *opposite* of vindictiveness.

The tension was extended through two simultaneous narratives of war. In one, Sarkar made vengeful threats. In the other, he wrote of conquests that were not so much vengeful as natural. 'Real life consists of the urge to capture the present and the future world', he wrote in 1926. 'And, by venturing to conquer the world, one can bring such a life to its fulfillment'.[72] Naturally, therefore, white racism would force Asians to strike back.[73] Asians would refuse to die like savages, and the West would have to come to terms with their natural determination to survive, which was inseparable from action and expansion.[74] There was no simple causal link between Asian tenacity and Western racism. Rather, the two were pieces of the larger problem of race/empire, which would generate a backlash in the form of economic boycotts and race-war. Sarkar cited Ludwig Gumplowicz's theory of *Rassenkampf*, or 'race struggle', both as a critique of Western racism and as a defence of the Asian urge to conquer,[75] and in the middle of a call for 'cosmopolitanism', declared: 'Young Asia wants Eur-America to remember the historical fact that the duration and extent of oriental aggressions into Europe have been greater than those of [the] European into Asia'.[76] It would be difficult to find a better example of the contorted nature of the cosmopolitanism of *ressentiment*. Having articulated a reasonably consistent position of justice premised on equality, Sarkar slips into a self-defeating rhetoric of threats, taunts and muscular nationalism: 'remember, we humiliated you more than you humiliated us'.

The equality (if not surplus) of historical humiliation was necessary, because a large part of Sarkar's polemic is a plea for Orientals to be recognised as humans and kinfolk of Europeans. If there is something pathetic about this, it is a colonial predicament: a residue of the mendicancy that Sarkar decried in Moderate politicians, which could not be disguised by the ink expended on 'conquest'. With military conquests unavailable or restricted to Japanese adventures, Sarkar had to get by on metaphors. Writing of the science of Young India, he insisted that 'Jagadish Chunder Bose's comprehensive analysis of [biological] "responses" . . . is but the theoretic correlate of the modern Indian *sadhana* for conquest and expansion'.[77] Europe was already India's *sadhana* in the colonial era: it certainly was Sarkar's. But that *sadhana*—perilously close to mimicry—could be imbued with dignity only if it was recast in terms of *digvijaya*, i.e., injected with militarism, vindictiveness and 'spirit', which meant the spirit of the nation-state and not some metaphysical irrelevancy.

Asian conquests could thus be differentiated from European conquests, but only tenuously. Both were natural, except that one was also legitimised and energised by justice. Since nationhood in this perspective meant 'conquer or be conquered', there was, potentially, the Japanese option: joining the colonisers in their project of racist imperialism. After the creation of the League of Nations, Ramsay MacDonald (whose sympathy for Indian aspirations Sarkar appreciated)[78] had proposed that some European colonies in Africa be made over to India under the League's provision for 'mandates'. MacDonald wrote that either the plan would fail and be reversed with no harm done, or it would 'stamp India with a dignity which would command for it a position of unquestioned equality amongst the federated nations of the Empire'.[79] Sarkar scoffed at the idea, not out of solidarity with Africans, but because he believed that Indians had already done their bit for British imperial ventures.[80]

For a man who wanted India to be counted as an actor in the world, MacDonald's proposal could not have been without appeal. Sarkar himself had insisted that international relations were normatively, not pathologically, a matter of *matsyanyaya*: the 'law of the fish' (i.e., the axiom that big fish eat little fish).[81] There can be no doubt about what side of the fish-law he wanted to be on. But he recoiled from the condescension implicit in MacDonald's proposal, and from the language of the 'experiment', which cast the colony in the role of a specimen even as it gave it the trappings of power and prestige. Moreover, the plan involved the League of Nations, for which Sarkar had contempt: he increasingly saw it as a European-imperialist front and an infringement of the principle of sovereignty.[82] (The UN would be only somewhat less disappointing.)[83] His rhetoric of Asian decolonisation was, after all, premised on an unequivocal declaration that '[t]he expulsion of the West from the East is the sole preliminary to a discussion of fundamental peace terms'.[84] The League had no place within this militancy. Conquest and expansion were worthwhile only if initiated by Asians themselves, in their own interests.

Sarkar's anti-imperialism was thus complicated, if not compromised, by his militarism. His vision of continuous revolution and productive conflict was interwoven with fantasies of conquest; self-making through engagement across borders incubated the desire for domination. While he refused to assign any spiritual content to the Indian nation, war became a spiritual experience (not yet experienced), producing freedom (that remained elusive). His 'theory' of *vishwashakti* must be seen in this context: the worldly man was a historically savvy nationalist who could manage *vishvashakti* in accordance with *Rassenkampf* and *matsyanyaya*.[85] 'The eternal problem of today is, as our *Mahabharata* has taught for all ages, to study the science and art of Macht, i.e., shakti or power', Sarkar wrote.[86] It is not that he was unaware of a moral problem in identifying with aggressors over victims, but the colonised man's need for power outweighed or inverted moral considerations. Internationalism became inseparable from coercive acquisition: praising Ashoka as an internationalist, Sarkar explained that he meant 'nationalist, i.e., an imperialist'.[87]

The Japanese Conundrum

For an ideologue who saw 1905 as the turning point in the history of the modern world, wanted to believe Spengler's theory of the decline of the West, but would not concede that civilisation was doomed,[88] Japan was irresistible in more ways than one. Its naval victories over Russia were literally spectacular: people looked on, especially in the colonies. They made connections between their own struggles and the battles of Port Arthur and the Tsushima Straits, between their own racial-political predicament and that of the Japanese.[89] This resurgent Asian Self could be owned by the emasculated at the level of the body: the Japanese diet was relatable to what Indians ate, Sarkar noted happily.[90] It was not, however, an easy claim to sustain. The Japanese themselves appeared ambivalent towards their admirers, and the admirers were fickle.

For Sarkar, the Japanese were admirable not only because they had defeated Europeans in war, but also because they had shown themselves to be masters of their own cultural fate, having bypassed crucial philological roadblocks on the way to modernity. 'Japan did not wait for the revolution of scientific terms in the Japanese language before she proceeded to assimilate the standard European and American works on medicine, engineering, and metallurgy', he observed.[91] Having sought precisely this type of development in National Education, Sarkar reiterated the relevance of the manoeuvre to Indian modernisers and institution-builders: '[N]o philologist has yet ventured to assert the capabilities of the Japanese language as an instrument of modern expression are richer than those of any of the Dravidian or the Aryan languages of India'.[92] As in linguistics, so in science and technology: since the Meiji restoration, Japan had not waited for a colonial spoon-feeding. Such bypassing was not merely academic. It was the opposite of feminine passivity: it required improvising continuously in one's own national interest. When European knowledge was acquired by Asians through self-motivated tactics, it ceased to be European. The state of war was thus already, definitively, free.

Whether that freedom belonged to Japan alone, or to other colonised people as well, remained unclear. Taraknath Das, Sarkar's fellow-Japanophile, enthusiast of Greater India and master of *vishwashakti*,[93] asked himself whether Japan was 'a menace to Asia', and responded with an unconvincing '[i]t is our belief that she has no [hegemonistic] ambition'.[94] Sarkar was even more evasive and sought to dismiss the question: asking whether Japan was a friend or foe of Asia was like asking whether England and Germany were friends or foes of Europe, he remarked in 1932.[95] This was disingenuous; Japan's role in Asia had no European counterparts. Sarkar glumly noted that resurgent Japan had become Britain's junior ally in Asia and agreed 'to help England put down revolutions among the Hindus and Moslems of the British Empire'.[96] For those seeking Asian decolonisation, the Japanese were evidently not a reliable asset. But because they mattered as a strategic calculation to Europeans and Americans, they also mattered to the political position that Sarkar was assembling, which had to do with restoring a broken model of the world at least as much as it had to do with justice.

The establishment of links between Asian and European affairs was a vital part of Sarkar's project of returning a margin to its rightful place in world-history. Haushofer, building upon the British geographer Halford Mackinder's paranoia about an alliance between the 'Land People' of Eurasia and the 'Sea People' of the Pacific, had already cast Japan as a key ally in European competitions.[97] Even when it was less than impressive, therefore, a militarised Japan ensured that Asia was not relegated to passivity in its own history. The Japanese may act against the interests of their fellow-Asians, but they *acted,* and on the world stage. That was ideologically valuable. Moreover, in spite what Tokyo had promised its British ally, the hope remained that Japan would function at least occasionally as a voice for racial justice in the world, as it had done at the Paris peace talks after the Great War.[98] Japanese diplomats had, of course, spoken in their own national interests. Nevertheless, the rhetoric was of racial equality, and Sarkar extended it into a larger context of Asian subjugation:

> The only protests can come from Japan in regard to Eastern Asia . . . But they are bound to be too feeble. Little Nippon is dazed by the extraordinary changes that have taken place. Even her own independence may be in danger. She cannot any longer look for self-defence in the mutual competition among the Great Powers . . . The complete annihilation of German influence in the Pacific and the Far East is certainly not an unmixed blessing to the Japanese people or to the Asians as a whole.[99]

Japan thus remained the Great Coloured Hope, and the very tenuousness of that hope—Japan's 'dazed' condition—provided a point of identification for other Asians struggling to come to terms with modernisation and weakness. Sarkar continued, for instance, to seek a balance between his empathy for China, the Asian victim that was potentially a great power, and his admiration for Japan, the Asian victimiser that was already a major power but otherwise a victim, bullied by the West since Perry's arrival in Tokyo Bay in 1853. 'Altogether . . . Japan has been "more sinned against than sinning" in her Chinese policy', he observed, 'but of course, so far as the infringement of China's sovereignty and territorial rights . . . is concerned, it is useless to weigh the powers in the balance and find which is the greater sinner'.[100] On the eve of its invasions of China in 1933 and 1936, Japan was both a winner and a loser in the world. Not all independent powers were equally powerful, Sarkar warned Young India; the Asian emperor was not securely dressed.[101] Even in the spring of 1942, with Japan apparently irresistible in battle, Sarkar predicted that the white powers—including Germany and Russia—would eventually combine to reverse the gains.[102]

Sarkar's ambivalence about just what (and who) modern Japan represented gives away his uneasy conscience over what it meant to be a winner in the world. Rabindranath's critique of Japanese imperialism—that it had reproduced the worst Western pathologies—would have been comprehensible to him, although he would have rejected it.[103] Welcoming the expansion of suffrage in Japan in 1925 as a victory over a feudalism that Indians could recognise (he referred to the older Japanese elite as 'Zamindars and Nawabs'),[104] Sarkar voiced the hope that democratic rights would bring a greater consciousness of responsibility, and that Japan would become *less* aggressive on the world stage. He added: '[D]emocracy and government by public discussion, criticism and party-spirit, temporarily and superficially a source of weakness although it is, furnishes in the long run the surest foundations of a people's well-ordered and richly diversified energism'.[105] Sarkar's narrative of Japanese 'energism', however, was more internally conflicted than Rabindranath's, because he accepted the imperatives of competing races and nation-states. The Yellow Peril became the 'white peril' in Sarkar's disturbed rhetoric, explaining and partially excusing Japanese behaviour:

> The elementary need of self-preservation thus happens to induce Japan to resist by all means any further advance of Eur-America penetration in the Orient. The nightmare of this 'white peril' is the fundamental fact of Japanese politics, internal as well as international. Japan can hardly be blamed for trying to snatch a few pieces of the Far Eastern loot for an Asian people.[106]

Sarkar implied that for Koreans and the Chinese, loss of sovereignty to other Asians was less damaging—and less historically meaningful—than the aggression of Europeans. But Japanese policy remained a form of looting, and he acknowledged that while some in Japan had called him 'Indian brother', he had also heard much anti-Indian abuse.[107] Sarkar could not bring himself to embrace Japan. 'No individual or people that holds slaves abroad can be a genuine democrat or exponent of freedom at home', he would write later.[108]

Even Sarkar's interpretation of the Russo-Japanese War betrayed his ambivalence. He knew that in the realm of statecraft, racial purpose and solidarity remained elusive: 'The problem of each Asian people will . . . have to be fought out separately against its own official enemies'.[109] Thus, whereas the ideological and polemical significance of the rise of Japan was great, the political significance was doubtful. Spengler might be wrong; Sarkar was unconvinced that the West was weakening.[110] In a similar vein, the Japanese victory was both miraculous and mundane, and Sarkar was uncertain which was more desirable. The victory was politically miraculous. It was at the level of the miracle that Japan's emergence as a modern Asian nation and a world power was fragile, unreliable, suffused by pessimism. But as a sociological and racial phenomenon, it was mundane, because the mundane was the level at which the mumbo-jumbo of racial difference fell apart and produced a reliable basis for dignity:

> [T]he Asian civilization with which Japan started on the race about 1870 was not essentially distinct from the Eur-American, but . . . it was slightly poorer and 'inferior' . . . because it had not independently produced the steam engine. Thus, scientifically speaking, there is nothing miraculous in the phenomenal developments of new Japan.[111]

That split between the miraculous and the mundane informed Sarkar's attitude towards Japan as a racial entity that was Asian but not necessarily *of* or *with* Asia. It generated a sharp resentment towards the perceived Japanese tendency to leave Asia behind for the company of Europe. A miraculous Japan was an attractive image for colonised Asians because it carried the possibility of transcending the handicaps of race, but it also allowed Japanese elites to assume that they had already transcended race and taken on a different destiny. The Japanese in Calcutta behaved like whites, Sarkar noted bitterly.[112] The more powerful and 'miraculous' Japan became, therefore, the harder it became for the colonised to identify with it. Even Japanese militarism had suffered from 'imperialist psychology' and physical degeneracy: '[When] the rank and file of the imperial people gets used to ease-loving habits [of being served by colonial subjects] . . . bushido morality, military ethics, or the knighthood pattern ceases to function'.[113] Moreover:

> Since 1905 Japan herself has indeed been anxious to proclaim to the world that she is different from, and superior to, the rest of Asia in her ideals, institutions, and methods. But this notion is confined within the circle of a few diplomats, professors who virtually hold diplomatic posts, and such journalists as have touch with prominent members of Parliament. It is . . . preached in foreign languages . . . by those intellectuals who . . . write for Eur-American statesmen, scholars, and tourists. The masses of the Japanese, and these diplomats themselves at home are always conscious of the real truth.[114]

The real truth—the racial-political predicament—was thus both strength and weakness, with the latter predominating. The ambiguity reminded an Indian nationalist of a familiar weakness:

> [Japan] must varnish her yellow self white in order that she may be granted the dignity of a ruling race. The Japanese bankers and officials, captains and policemen are therefore compelled to have the Eur-American paraphernalia of public life. This is abhorred by most of them in their heart of hearts.[115]

Intriguingly, the complexity of fitting Japan into his map of resurgent Asia compelled Sarkar to reverse his general tendency to distinguish between the inert masses and the dynamic vanguard, and fall back upon a more conventional concept of national authenticity: the masses were wise, the elites foolish or hypocritical. In an instability within Sarkar's narrative of modern, manly 'Young Asia', the Japanese masses became the repository of a racial knowledge the elite had forfeited. There were then two kinds of deracination: a bad/weak one which was politically aligned with colonialism, and a better one which was nationalist-cosmopolitan but also flawed, in the sense that it lapsed easily into the former category. The former was associated with power and insider-status, but the latter—while marginalised by the existing racial order—was tainted and embarrassed by the nakedness of its desires. Modern Japan was necessarily a fantasy of the militant Indian nationalist, but not necessarily a flattering one.

Sarkar's critique of his Japanese counterparts quickly became a critique of mimicry, sycophancy and self-hate that Bankim would have appreciated.[116] It came with the old nationalist dilemma of how to be similar while also being dissimilar: Asians must have states, states must have railroads and battleships, but precisely for those reasons, perhaps their citizens should wear dhotis. 'Japan has learnt by bitter experience that the white nations would not admit her into their caste of first class powers if she were to appear to them in "native" *kimono* and *geta*', Sarkar remarked.[117] He was not especially interested in what the Japanese wore, of course. Clothes stood for political affiliation, and deracination was mainly a matter of disloyalty.[118] Clothes, like the 'Asiatic mentality', stood also for an awareness of colonial power relations, i.e., for the consciousness of humiliation.

What Sarkar was implying, like Bankim and (differently) his own contemporary, the satirist Sukumar Ray, is that national consciousness in a colonial world is false unless it comes accompanied by a paradoxical sense of shame, and by the desire to assert a contrarian pride and to take the side of other humiliated people.[119] The perception that the Japanese had turned their backs on the humiliation of colonised Asians is also why Sarkar identified more strongly with China than he did with Japan. China remained a civilisation even when it was politically 'fallen', but Japan never escaped the suspicion that it was a well-armed barbarian on the fringe of Asia. Sarkar read the condition of modern Japan—not accepted by the West, and self-distanced from Asia—as an insularity, which, for him, was a particularly unfortunate predicament for a nation. To be insular was the condition of the savage, the backward and the literally unworldly: the opposite of his cosmopolitan-nationalist-masculine vision of civilisation.[120] It was, in fact, a double isolation, because the Japanese state was apparently cut off not only from the world but also from its own society, which remained Asian. These layered isolations constituted a sickness, which could be described in the language of modern medicine:

> [Young Asia] ... does not condemn Japan, but rather pities her isolated condition. The establishment of another Japan on continental Asia is the only possible therapeutic for the current international pathology. And to this the political doctors of Young Asia are addressing themselves.[121]

The call for 'another Japan on continental Asia' may appear similar to the rhetoric of Japanese imperialism,[122] but it is the opposite: Sarkar wanted a 'Japan' that was self-identified with the aspirations of the Asian mainland. He elaborated:

> Every inch of Asian soil has to be placed under a sovereign state of the Asian race, no matter whether sovietic-communal, republican, monarchical, democratic or autocratic. For the present there is the urgent call for at least another Japan of fifty, sixty, or seventy million people on continental Asia, able to work its own mines, finance its own administration, and man its own polytechnic colleges.[123]

The desire for another Japan' gives away Sarkar's inability to come to terms with Japan as it existed. As an icon of modern Asian statehood, Japan was too valuable to eschew from the fantasy of freedom, and he wanted more. But by declaring that he wanted a *continental* Japan, he implied that he wanted a Japan that was integral—politically, geographically and culturally—to Asia. The specifications of this imaginary country return us to Sarkar's 'militarism': he had calculated what numbers and institutions are required for victory. Such planning was a common form of fantasy for middle-class Indian youth in this period, when the state was in the hands of other men. A young Nirad Chaudhuri, planning a free Indian military down to the calibre of the guns but straying down to the river to admire British warships, is another example of this armchair citizenship of the colonised male.[124] Sarkar and Nirad both admired Curzon as a model statesman-scholar-writer.[125] The bête noir of Young Bengal was the 'avatar of the power of youth', Sarkar enthused. Imagining virility had to be a matter of precision and articulate pleasure: a literary war-game.[126]

Indian Men and Japanese Ships

Indian aspirations remained at the heart of the game: Japan and China mattered to Sarkar because *he* could 'go there' in the past as well as in the present. He made frequent equations between Bushido[127] and 'Kshatriya culture' (which he also identified as 'Prussianism' and the 'spirit of Sparta'), pointing to the Mauryan military as evidence.[128] He was engaged in rejecting the sealed boundaries of race and culture, so that what was evidently Japanese or Indian could be appropriated or exported convincingly, and Kshatriyas and Mauryan charioteers could sail on Japanese battleships. Far from diluting Indian nationhood, Sarkar's insistence on similarity produced openings through which the nation could enter the world. The manoeuvre was not limited to guns: he corresponded with Irawati Karve about higher education for women, sending her material about Japanese institutional models and taking pride in her work in Pune.[129] Education, for the acolyte of Satish Mukherjee, was another form of war.

It should be remembered that Sarkar's internationalism was explicitly a type of nationalism. The *vishwashakti* of the twentieth century remained not just resistance to the albinocracy,[130] but a gendered vision of agency, exploration and appropriation. 'It should', he wrote, 'be . . . our life's creed boldly to venture out into the world, discover which of the inventions, experiments, ideals, politics and laws of different nations are . . . worth having, and introduce them to the Indian world through the Indian intermediaries'.[131] Foreigners had called him the 'Indian Columbus', Sarkar declared after returning to India in 1925. (He also admitted that they had jokingly called him 'Hindu Culture Sarkar' and 'Young Asia Sarkar'.[132] Columbus remained vulnerable to the laughter of natives.) He told the Bangiya

Sahitya Parishad in 1927 that when Europeans and Americans had asked him why he travelled, he had replied that it was to fight, arm-wrestle and test his strength.[133] Only then had they accepted him in their midst. Haraprasad Shastri, president of the Parishad, greeted him as a *digvijayee* who had brought home the wealth of the world.[134] 'The utilization of *vishwa-shakti* in the interest of one's own self-assertion and progress is to remain the principal urge for each and every state, region, race, group of party throughout the world in the choice of its allies and enemies', Sarkar wrote at the moment of Indian independence. 'This is the *Realpolitik* of Dominion India's orientations to Asian politics'.[135]

Sarkar's Bushido–Kshatriya equations were not primarily a theory of Asian essence. They underlay his narrative of 'Greater India', incorporating Asia. Sarkar began citing Radhakumud Mookerji before the Great War,[136] and it was in an essay titled 'Greater India' that he insisted, 'Hindu thought is even now governing the Bushido morality of the Japanese soldiers'.[137] Not even China was safe:

> The Kushans were Scythians or Tartars of Central Asia naturalized on Indian soil. Through them the northern frontiers of India were extended almost as far as Siberia. Along with this territorial expansion, Hindu missionizing activity was greatly enlarged owing to direct political sovereignty or spheres of influence. It was through this 'Greater India' on the land side that China . . . came within the sphere of influence of Hindu culture.[138]

After Pearl Harbor, Sarkar remained aware that Radhakamal Mookerji, like Haushofer, had described Japanese expansionism in terms of an 'Asian Lebensraum'.[139] He was himself expansive, telling an interviewer in 1943 about the importance of nurturing Greater India in Asia and Africa.[140] Sometimes the anti-colonial man checked himself: in 1916 he tempered his vision of past conquests by suggesting a benign 'Indian missionizing in foreign countries'.[141] In 1949, when the fantasies of *digvijaya* had dimmed, Sarkar clarified: 'Indian Asianism is . . . but a new phase of India's expansion in interhuman contacts and nothing more'.[142] But *Realpolitik* remained the explicit organising principle of contact. Greater India reflected an irresistible desire to be in and of the world, and it was not premised on reciprocity (let alone altruism). It appealed to Sarkar not only because it took Indians out into the world under their own agency, reversed the racist politics of 'Asian exclusion', and supported his vision of a healthy (expanding) population, but also because it brought home to India what was most competitive in 'Asian culture', feeding his determination to (re)claim the world as India's oyster.

Greater India did not preclude acts of academic generosity: greatness could be shared. China could be endowed with an empire, 'Greater China', which included Tibet, Sikkim, Burma and Vietnam, in a way that would have horrified Burmese or Vietnamese nationalists of Sarkar's time. (Quite a few places were made over promiscuously to both China and India.)[143] That an Indian nationalist would concede so much to China indicates the temporal and historical distance from independence: Indian foreign-policy considerations were remote enough from Sarkar's thinking in the 1910s and 1920s that he *could* be magnanimous towards China, which already had a sovereign existence, although India was (he insisted) more institutionally developed.[144] Mainly, however, it suggests a fondness for grand narratives of civilisation and 'influence' that steamroller the littler narratives of resistance and peoplehood. Little narratives had no use when they could not be incorporated into big countries. What mattered was that Chinese 'imperialism' in the past, like Japan's in the present, was a pre-packaged state, a culture and a militarism that enabled specific and overarching affiliations simultaneously.

For a colonised elite that had already made a virtue out of the need to learn from the world, an important principle of pedagogical power was at stake in these formulations of the past. In a time when Indian (and Chinese) students, intellectuals and revolutionaries travelled to Japan to *learn*, and Japanese intellectuals like Okakura came to India to *teach*, Sarkar reversed the direction of tutelage by imagining a past in which Japan and China were the pupils and India the teacher.[145] Chinese 'vindictiveness' in the past and Japanese militarism in the present could be made to stand on Indian foundations. *Matsyanyaya*, Sarkar remarked in an essay on China, is a 'Hindu political philosophy'. Asian militarism was an Indian invention, he insisted, although he came to *matsyanyaya* more directly through Darwin, Spencer and Ernst Haeckl than through Kautilya.[146] To be fair to Sarkar, it should be noted that he was writing before the Japanese military acquired its particular notoriety: Manchuria, Nanjing, Bataan and Manila had not yet been established in the discourse of race and atrocity.[147] He was groping for a form of cultural contact that was not closed to the two-way traffic of knowledge. But in its language, this contact slipped into the terrain of 'hegemony' and 'colonies', racism crept into the assumptions of unequal borrowing, mimicry and inauthenticity, and it did not shy away from coercion. The colonial model of 'international' contact retained a fierce hold on a man in Sarkar's historical position:

> Hindu activity in China was promoted by sea also through Indian navigators, colonizers, and merchant marine. This maritime enterprise gave to India the cultural hegemony ultimately over Burma, Java, Siam, Annam, and Japan.[148]

The references to maritime activity are not throwaway lines in the work of a scholar excited by the Russo-Japanese War. As an Indian nationalist, Sarkar would have been conscious of the importance of sea power in the history of the British Empire. He, like Radhakumud, would have 'felt' the lack of a navy as a major aspect of the nation's weakness, and regarded navies of the past—Chola 'armadas', Maratha 'admirals'—as evidence of historical dignity.[149] Warships of the past and present represented movement itself: the ability to leave a landlocked inferiority and travel, armed and erect, across a blue liquid curvature that had been colonised by white men as much as any land. This too was a transgression of empire, which was predicated on unequal movement. Only some races could travel at will: then as now, all passports were not equal, permission to enter was not granted on an equal-opportunity basis, and Sarkar himself had once been trapped in India by a denied passport.[150] The heroic broke out. Wanderlust was in Vivekananda's blood, Sarkar insisted: 'he was a world-tourist'.[151] He admired Bose, in part, because Bose got around: he left the home/prison of colonial Calcutta, trekked to Europe, caught a submarine to Southeast Asia, and then a rode a bomber into the blackness beyond Formosa. The salience of the travelling native in Pan-Asianist imaginaries has been noted by Dilip Menon and Javed Majeed;[152] mobility was almost inherently an act of war. The Chinese were admirable because they were not a 'stay-at-home, and war-dreading people', Sarkar wrote, and ancient Indian greatness was marked by 'constant coming and going' between Pataliputra and the wider world.[153]

Sarkar did a great deal of travelling himself, but such exceptional and vulnerable mobility only reinforces the awareness of inequality, produces a sense of statelessness and generates an insatiable appetite for more movement. Vivekananda is a case in point, as Sarkar himself noted,[154] but the observation can be made for other colonial elites who went, or wanted to go, abroad. When Rabindranath flew to Iran and Iraq in 1932, he was highly conscious of the connection between his borrowed KLM wings, the masculine vigour of the Dutch pilots, his own status as a brown man and a colonial subject, and his kinship with the victims of British aircraft then engaged in bombing the region.[155] Only some races have warships of their own. In his admiring interest in the Japanese naval build-up of the 1920s,[156] and even his remarks on the rise of America, Sarkar made the connection between the modern technology of mobile warfare, racial self-assertion, and only secondarily, justice. White Americans would not meet the fate of the Aztecs and Incas because they were 'militarized and navalized to the nth term', he remarked.[157] He understood that the power of modern weaponry was the power to articulate race itself, but refused to disavow the privilege. His remarks on America retained a suggestion that Native Americans did not count because they had not turned the embryo of race into a *political position* of race, backed up with ships. They were landlocked, self-isolated from the world, and therefore naturally fated to die. Thus, although Sarkar was concerned with justice, the concern was limited by his investment in modern civilisation. Only the modern/civilised of the world were fully deserving of justice; only those who could think in terms of world war were fully deserving of 'world peace'. For others, calculations applied that were not far removed from Gobineau and Darwin.

Beyond Hiroshima

In 1946, Michio Takeyama, a Japanese veteran of the war that had just ended, wrote a novella titled *Harp of Burma*. Ostensibly written for teenagers, *Harp of Burma* was entirely more 'serious' under the surface, rooted in the experience of traumatised veterans and a devastated society in ways that go far beyond the fellowship and sanitised violence of most war stories for adolescents.[158] John Dower has noted that Takeyama's novella is an early sign of the Japanese attempt to come to terms with defeat and occupation.[159] It is also an attempt to come to terms with the state of war itself: a tentative questioning of the model of modernity and citizenship that Japan had embraced since the later nineteenth century, which Sarkar embraced also, although not without qualms.

Harp of Burma follows a unit of Japanese soldiers in Burma when the tide of the war had already turned against Japan. The Japanese in Burma were then caught up in a calamity. Overextended, supply lines cut, air power exhausted, pushed into an unwise new invasion (of India), and with Japan itself besieged, they were reduced to a starving, sick army retreating before the British-Indian drive towards Malaya.[160] They were very far from the Tsushima Sea of Sarkar's imagination. Takeyama does not dwell on their misery: he gives us, for the most part, a story of homesick but cheerful soldiers that could easily have been published before the war. There are no references to the intense resentment of officers and hatred of the army that we find in post-war Japanese veteran's literature like Hiroshi Noma's novel *Zone of Emptiness*,[161] and there is no brutal occupation; the Burmese themselves are absent from much of the story.

Two thirds of the way into the book, however, there is shift. One Japanese unit, having surrendered to British troops who treat them humanely, decides to encourage another unit to surrender rather than fight another futile and bloody battle. They dispatch a corporal named Mizushima to talk to their fellow-Japanese. Mizushima fails to return from his mission, and his old comrades, interned in a Prisoner of War (POW) camp, are unsure whether he is dead or alive. Then an unrecognisable Buddhist monk appears near the camp fence, and although he will not speak to them, he sends them a letter. This letter—Mizushima's letter, detailing what had happened to him—forms the final one-third of the novella.

It is, as Mizushima's old comrades declare, an astonishing letter, not only because of the fate that Takeyama imagined for his emissary, but because of its ideological significance for the Japanese model of Asian resurgence. Mizushima had reached the other Japanese unit, but the soldiers had called him a coward and traitor and thrown him out of the cave they insisted on defending to the death. Failing to head off the battle and wounded in the shelling, he wanders through the jungle and is rescued by head-hunting cannibals, who nurse him back to health but, naturally, want to eat him when he is better. Through a combination of luck and diplomacy, he manages to avert this fate, only to have the cannibal chief insist that he marry his daughter. This danger too is averted (the chief withdraws the offer when he learns that Mizushima has never taken a human head), and Mizushima is allowed to leave.[162] The soldier falls in with Burmese monks, witnesses Burmese funeral rituals, immerses himself in the beauty of the land and the culture, and stumbles across fields strewn with the Japanese dead, who he tries in vain to bury. There are too many, he concludes in despair. He spies on a British military hospital and mortuary, then enters a Buddhist monastery; he enters also a statue of the Buddha through a hidden entrance in the Buddha's foot. He finds himself transformed: he realises he has become Burmese and is no longer pretending in order to hide out among them. He resumes his abandoned task of cremating and burying the bodies of dead soldiers, absorbing their desolation into himself. 'I shall not return to Japan', he writes in his letter.[163]

Mizushima's letter is a dense text, in part, because it overlaps existing narratives of empire. The story of being captured by cannibals who might either eat you or marry you is, for instance, not simply comedy, but a recognisable trope that we find from John Smith in the New World to Dudhnath Tewari in the Andaman Islands: a narrative of the fear, attraction and nervous amusement produced by the prospect of falling out of civilisation and being swallowed by the jungle beyond the colony.[164] Such narratives also convey, as Obeyesekere and Said have suggested, the European subject's secret desire for apotheosis, and the construction of the tropics as a world where ordinary whites suddenly became gods or supermen.[165] There were coloured versions of these fantasies—the Indian middle class of Sarkar's era had its own, typically formatted as children's literature[166]—and Japanese modernity and imperialism had generated a particularly vivid one. The opening of the Japanese soldier's eyes to the beauty of the occupied country parallels John Flory's love of Burma; Takeyama, like Orwell, was suggesting that disillusionment with empire—and falling out of the community of colonisers—opens new windows of love, aesthetics and identity.[167]

It is an important text also because Takeyama suggests the possibility—and necessity—of transformation, not just of the citizen-soldier but of the nation-state itself. Like an Orientalist Buddha, Mizushima says:

> Our country has waged a war, lost it, and is now suffering. That is because we were greedy, because we had only a superficial idea of civilization. Of course we cannot be as languid as the people of this country, and dream our lives away as they often do. But can we not remain energetic and yet be less avaricious? Is that not essential—for the Japanese and for all humanity?[168]

Takeyama understands that the chances of rebuilding the nation-state along those lines—'energetic and yet [not] avaricious'—are slim. It remains uncertain whether the 'traitor' who refuses to return to his homeland, refers to himself as a Burmese monk, but continues to use the pronoun 'we' to refer to the Japanese, is or is not a deserter. The soldier who has been systematically torn down by the experience of misery, death and redemption must live outside the nation-state, burying the victims of the nation in an endless task that is both a penance and a healing of the world: a different medicine from what Sarkar had prescribed for Japan.

Takeyama was not alone in thinking along these lines in post-war Japan. Whereas he drew his inspiration from Buddhism, the philosopher Hajime Tanabe looked westwards, towards Christianity in general and Kierkegaard in particular. Unlike Takeyama, Tanabe was well-known in the world of letters: he had lectured extensively in Europe, especially Germany. He and Sarkar had, in fact, been in Germany at the same time: the early years of Weimar, with its characteristic swirl of republican politics, labour radicalism, angry veterans and anti-democratic *ressentiment*.[169] Tanabe had been a member of Heidegger's circle of colleagues, and he (along with other faculty at Kyoto University) was subsequently accused of having entertained fascist sympathies. But it was during the war that he developed his philosophy of metanoesis or *zange*, which emphasised the total self-abnegation of the individual. Tanabe wrote:

> *Zange* is . . . a balm for the pain of repentance. Through *zange* we regard ourselves as truly not deserving to be, and therefore enter fully into a state of despair leading to self-surrender. After the submissive acknowledgment and frank confession of our valuelessness and meaninglessness, of our rebelliousness in asserting ourselves despite our valuelessness, we rediscover our being. In this way, our being undergoes at once both negation and affirmation through absolute transformation.[170]

James Heisig has argued that those who accused Tanabe of facilitating Japanese militarism by devaluing the individual missed the point of *zange*, which is rooted in Tanabe's broader concept of the 'logic of species'. A large part of the logic of species is a theory of the relationship between the individual, society and the world, and the implications of this relationship for freedom and responsibility. The individual, for Tanabe (as for Sarkar), did not spring unmediated from the world in the form of a world-citizen or cosmopolitan. The community—usually articulated as the nation/state—remained a necessary medium. This dynamic might be read as an endorsement of the reality of the nation and its prioritisation over the individual. Tanabe, however, emphasised two positions that deflate that interpretation. One is that the community is not closed or insulated: it exists to facilitate contact with the world and interpenetration with other communities. The other is that the individual must be free both *from* the contingencies imposed by the community, and *for* the contingencies of community.[171] Moral responsibility thus devolved clearly to the level of the individual actor. The logic of species is thus a very different conception of nationhood and citizenship from the logic of the fish, with its 'natural'—and hence amoral—flows of power.

For Tanabe at the end of the war, *zange* was a process of introspection and repentance: a necessary death that would produce rebirth and regeneration in the form of love, and as Heisig noted, the possibility of a radically reoriented world-history 'aimed at world peace'.[172] The self-obliteration of the individual—the Mizushima phenomenon—would not recuperate or reinforce the community; it would initiate its reformulation and repositioning in the world. Such prescriptions were not altogether ignored in post-war Japan, just as the concerns of 'rubble literature' were not insignificant forces in post-war Germany.[173] As Dower has noted, however, introspection and repentance were generally marginal responses to the catastrophe of the vindictive community: 'we were deceived by our leaders' was the more pervasive response in Japan (as in Germany). The very structures of state, community and national culture that had earlier been mobilised for war were remobilised for the post-war state.[174]

For Indian nationalists, the Japanese experience at the end of the Second World War continued to be a spectacle. Although less exciting than what they had imagined in 1905, it again provided opportunities for contemplating the Asian state of war as a political and moral entity. There was little rubble in India, but Japanese rubble, like Japanese warships, could be utilised to modulate the distances between East and West, Self and Other, the citizen and the state, the nation and the world. For some, the model of insurgent Indian nationhood that fell into place after what Sarkar called 'the event of 1905' was destabilised suddenly by the events of 1945. It is useful, at this point, to remember Justice Radhabinod Pal at the Tokyo War Crimes trials. Pal was the sole Indian on the tribunal; he was also the only judge to find all the defendants 'not guilty'. He soon became a hero for the Japanese right-wing, although the left too has staked its claim.[175] Pal's famous (or infamous) dissenting judgment was based on two main planks: he argued that the criteria for guilt were established *ex post facto* (he objected especially to the punishment by death of individuals who had not been proved to have committed specific criminal acts), and he pointed out that the victorious allies had turned a blind eye to their own atrocities.[176] Ashis Nandy has made the intriguing suggestion that Pal was motivated more by his understanding of 'Hindu law' than by his knowledge of international law.[177] Pal was, in fact, not only a highly accomplished jurist, but also an amateur historian of ancient India.[178]

That brings us back to Sarkar, who shared Pal's scholarly interest in ancient Indian cultural codes. They were similar men in many ways: of the same age, with similar backgrounds and professional trajectories in the interwar colonial state, erudite, worldly, reformist, anti-communist, impatient with tradition, and for that reason, also obsessed with seeking out reassuring continuities between the ancient and the modern. Like Sarkar in Europe and America, Pal in Tokyo was something of a fraud, representing a nation-state that did not quite exist. Pal's intervention at the International Tribunal was, very likely, supported by a political sympathy for Japan that Sarkar would have understood instinctively. But if we look closely at Pal's remarks in Tokyo, we find that he wrote: 'The name of Justice should not be allowed to be invoked only for the prolongation of the pursuit of vindictive retaliation'.[179] As an indictment of Western bona fides, this is familiar; as an ideology of international justice, it is not.

In his study of Pal in Tokyo, Nandy has emphasised that the Indian judge was *not* excusing the crimes of the Japanese leadership, and suggested that his position reflected his 'Hindu' conviction that 'responsibility, even when individual, could, paradoxically, be fully individual only when seen as collective and, in fact, global'.[180] On the one hand, only individual perpetrators could be punished, and acts committed on the battlefield could not be contextualised (and thus either excused or magnified by, say, pointing to a greater good or evil). On the other hand, Japan's crimes did not belong to the Japanese alone, but to the modern world. Even after making allowances for Nandy's tendency to essentialise Indianness, it is fair to say that in 1945, those Indians who were most inclined to empathise with Japan were backing away simultaneously from 'vindictiveness' as a political faith, and from the imperatives of a national masculinity invested in a state bound only by *matsyanyaya*.

For Sarkar, the Second World War left a mark of dubious depth. He remained an apologist for Japan, which, he continued to argue, had been India's ally during the war and a strategic asset for both Bose and Gandhi.[181] But he was clear-eyed about Japan's imperialist goals, and conscious of the price paid by Indians in the Bengal famine.[182] In spite of a social-scientific fascination with disaster, Sarkar was shocked into certain revisions of his view of modernity and the nation-state:

'World-War II which compelled the hyper-civilized peoples to march back to the caves in which the paleolithic races had flourished furnishes us with an occasion for re-examining the foundations of [the] traditional view of science and philosophy regarding the illiterate', he wrote shortly before his death.[183] In a related vein, he revised his faith in 'charismatic' individuals who might seize the *vishwashakti* of their time,[184] and consequently, his vanguardist vision of Young India. The expertise of the intellectual and administrative elites of the world had proved to be terribly narrow, he observed. As an active force in society and politics, this gendered expertise—now seen as a pathological 'hypercivilisation'—could not be equated with 'human values' and 'culture', or prioritised over the values and knowledge of illiterate peasants and labourers of dubious gender.[185]

Sarkar made his remarks as the Constituent Assembly of India was nearing the completion of its task. At that critical moment in the history of modern India, he urged Nehru, Ambedkar and their colleagues to follow through on their radical inclinations:

> It is impossible to assert that the peasant as a class in his moral obligations and sense of duty towards [society] is on a lower plane than members of the so-called educated class. The rights of the illiterate ought to constitute in social psychology the foundation of a new democracy. A universal suffrage independent of all considerations as to school-going, ability to read and write or other tests should be the very first postulate of social economics. It is orientations like these that democracy needs today if it is to function as a living faith.[186]

This is a different idealist from the exponent of a 'virile' education who, after the Great War, described elite militarism as the engine of democracy and the proving ground of citizenship, and who, as late as 1941, had written that 'world-peace can only be the greatest calamity for mankind', akin to slavery.[187] He had not disavowed the masculine state; he prescribed a foreign policy for India that Kissinger would have admired.[188] But the romance had gone out of the state of war.

Conclusion

It is useful to remind ourselves how remote an observer like Sarkar was from the concerns that animated Tanabe and Takeyama, and also how relevant they were to him. A reader of Sarkar or Nirad Chaudhuri (or Bankim for that matter) might immediately notice a paradox: the war-obsessed nationalist represented a nation with no experience of war.[189] That lack of war functioned as an innocence or naiveté, but it would be foolish to resort to the cliché that those who have experienced war become anti-war. More relevant is that for Sarkar and other Indian nationalists, the lack of an easily identifiable history of war was precisely that: a historical lack that corresponded with a problem of freedom. Freedom became inextricable from the cultivation of conflict,[190] both intra-national/intra-state and international/interstate.

Theirs was thus a specific reaction. Sarkar's equation of peace with slavery reflected not only his location in a colonised country without a recent war, but also his Hobbesian view of politics, in which peace merely signified the aftermath of the last defeat. This outlook was only partially affiliated with Völkisch thought, pre-Great-War Romanticism, and the Japanese cult of race-spirit-state-military unity. In Europe, that attitude could survive and even flourish as an interwar mentality, but the turning-away had already commenced: as Paul Fussel noted, it was difficult, in 1918, to mutter *Dulce et decorum est pro patria mori* ('It is sweet and honorable to die for one's country') without a wince of irony.[191] Even ostensibly 'pro-war' literature, like Ernst Jünger's *Storm of Steel*, could be shot through with doubt: the nationalist war-veteran comes very close to rebelling against the nation-state, saying, 'The state, which relieves us of our responsibility, cannot take away our remorse; and we must exercise it'.[192] In India, however, irony derived not from masculine excess, but, as the body of satirical writing indicates, from the colonial curse of effeminacy.[193] A large part of Indian nationalism remains, in spite of Sarkar's moment of hesitation in 1949, essentially a permanent pre-war attitude: that of a nation waiting for its war. It is hardly a coincidence that Savarkar, who read the Gita as a history that might teach the nation the transformative value(s) of war, insisted on calling the 1857 revolt the 'First War of Independence'.[194] With such an unconvincing 'first war', another was badly needed, and the cosmopolitans among the nationalists felt the need most acutely.

It can be said—following Appiah—that cosmopolitanism necessarily begins with a primary commitment to one's own community.[195] But the gregariousness that Appiah saw in his Ghanaian-nationalist family is not the major mode of cosmopolitanism for middle-class natives contemplating their place in the world when manhood is at stake. What made emasculation such an effective curse is that colonialism in India had generated the desire for organised violence but not the opportunities, even in the age of revolutionary terrorism. A few revolvers and bombs only affirmed the condition of impotence, and the third century BCE was not an adequate compensation. Solace had to be found in the contemporary world of battleships and howitzers, even if these were in the hands of those whose political 'colour' was unstable and disappointing.

Notes

1 *PB*, p. 16.
2 Elizabeth Kolsky, *Colonial Justice in British India: White Violence and the Rule of Law*. Cambridge: Cambridge University Press, 2010, pp. 69–107; Jordana Bailkin, 'The Boot and the Spleen: When Was Murder Possible in British India?' *Comparative Studies in History and Society*, 48(2), 2006, pp. 462–93.
3 Mukhopadhyay, *Samajik Prabandha*, pp. 35–36, 105–6, 122.
4 *NBGP*, p. 214.
5 *PPS-1905*, pp. 1–3, 33–39, 112, 320.
6 Hughes, *Consciousness and Society*, pp. 337–78.
7 *BSB-I*, pp. 446–48.
8 Ibid., p. 17.
9 'China and Japan are a great weakness of my life', he wrote. Benoy Kumar Sarkar, 'China, Japan and Young India', *Atmashakti*, 24(2), 1927.
10 *PPS-1905*, p. 125.
11 *CRTHE*, p. 5.
12 *PB*, p. 194.
13 *DIWP*, pp. 121–34.
14 Mookerji, *History of Indian Shipping*, pp. 99–129.
15 *VT*, pp. 80–81.
16 *PBHS-II*, pp. 35–39.
17 Haushofer's wife was a 'half-Jew', and his son Albrecht—who worked as a diplomatic advisor to the government—thus a *Mischling*. Although the family was long protected by Hess, Albrecht was implicated in the Stauffenberg plot to kill Hitler and executed. Harassed by the occupation regime after the war, Haushofer and his wife committed suicide in 1946. On Sarkar and Haushofer, see *VT*, p. 130.
18 Karl Haushofer, *Geopolitics of the Pacific Ocean: Studies on the Relationship between Geography and History*. Lewiston: Edwin Mellen, 2002, p. 219.
19 *BSB-I*, pp. 17–18.
20 There were differences: Sarkar also tied Asian decolonisation to the liberation of Europeans under German domination. *PPS-1905*, pp. 283–84. But Haushofer ensured that the Deutsche Akademie remained sympathetic to Indian nationalists in spite of Hitler's indifference and hostility, and may have channelled Sarkar's geopolitical thinking to Subhas Bose in 1934.

It was to meet him that Sarkar went to Munich in 1931. Taraknath Das, whose career as a travelling revolutionary paralleled Sarkar's in many ways, seems to have introduced them. Taraknath Das, *Foreign Policy in the Far East*. New York: Longmans, Green and Co., 1936, pp. 43-72. Also see Flora, 'Benoy Kumar Sarkar', pp. 96-104, 355.

21 Goswami, 'Imaginary Futures and Colonial Internationalisms', p. 1485.
22 Haushofer, *Geopolitics of the Pacific Ocean*, pp. vii, xi, 207.
23 Hobsbawm, *The Age of Empire*, p. 36.
24 Woodruff Smith, *The Ideological Origins of Nazi Imperialism*. Oxford: Oxford University Press, 1986, pp. 21-24.
25 Gay, *Weimar Culture*, pp. 1-22, 70-101.
26 Verney Lovett, *A History of the Indian Nationalist Movement*. New York: Frederick Stokes Company, 1920.
27 On the Rowlatt Act, see Minault, *The Khilafat Movement*, pp. 66-67.
28 FYA, p. 334.
29 Ibid., pp. 335-36.
30 Mukherjee, *Benoy Kumar Sarkar*, pp. 70-75.
31 FYA, pp. 274-75; CRTHE, pp. 88-91.
32 FYA, pp. 101-3; CRTHE, pp. 85-87.
33 PBHS-II, pp. 31-32.
34 FYA, pp. 104-5.
35 Ibid.
36 Gay, *The Cultivation of Hatred*, pp. 96-98.
37 FYA, pp. 311-12.
38 Walter LaFeber, *The American Age: United States Foreign Policy at Home and Abroad since 1750*. New York: Norton, 1989, pp. 181-217.
39 NBGP, p. 220.
40 FYA, pp. 7-8.
41 Ibid., p. 251.
42 Dirks, *Castes of Mind*, pp. 3-18.
43 Hobsbawm, *The Age of Empire*, p. 319.
44 Bhudeb Mukhopadhyay, *Samajik Prabandha*, pp. 28-33.
45 FYA, p. 273.
46 PB, p. 15; PPS-1905, pp. 215-19.
47 NBGP, pp. 352-53.
48 BSB-II, p. 510.
49 Amal Kumar Mukhopadhyay (ed.), *The Bengali Intellectual Tradition*. Calcutta: K.P. Bagchi, 1979, p. 228. 'Man has everywhere and always been fundamentally a beast', Sarkar mused. CRTHE, p. xiii.
50 FYA, pp. 150-51.
51 Ibid., p. 151.
52 Ibid., p. 166.
53 Ibid., p. 150.

54 Friedrich Nietzsche, *The Philosophy of Nietzsche*. New York: Modern Library, 1927, p. 617.
55 *FYA*, p. 246.
56 Ibid., pp. 70–72.
57 Philippa Levine, 'Re-reading the 1890s: Venereal Disease as Constitutional Crisis in Britain and British India', *Journal of Asian Studies*, 55(3), 1996, pp. 585–612; Ashwini Tambe, *Codes of Misconduct: Regulating Prostitution in Late Colonial Bombay*. Minneapolis: University of Minnesota Press, 2009, pp. 26–51; Ballhatchet, *Race, Sex and Class under the Raj*, pp. 96–122.
58 Beteille, *Society and Politics in India*, pp. 15–36.
59 *PB*, p. 277.
60 *VT*, pp. 510–11.
61 Peter Fritzsche, *Germans into Nazis*. Cambridge: Harvard University Press, 1998, pp. 6–7.
62 *FYA*, p. 23.
63 Frantz Fanon, *The Wretched of the Earth*. New York: Grove, 2004, pp. 1–51.
64 *FYA*, pp. 184–85.
65 *CRTHE*, p. 236.
66 Mukherjee, *Benoy Kumar Sarkar*, p. 49.
67 Heather Streets, *Martial Races: The Military, Race and Masculinity in British Imperial Culture 1857-1914*. Manchester: Manchester University Press, 2004, pp. 1–17.
68 *CRTHE*, p. xi.
69 *FYA*, p. 65.
70 Ibid., p. 107.
71 Ibid., p. 31.
72 *NBGP-I*, p. 182; *GYI*, pp. 119–20.
73 *FYA*, p. 66.
74 de Gobineau, *The Inequality of the Human Races*, pp. 1–35.
75 *FYA*, p. 193.
76 *FYA*, p. 174; *CRTHE*, pp. 233–36.
77 *FYA*, p. 82.
78 *BSB-I*, p. 386.
79 Ramsay MacDonald, *The Government of India*. London: Swarthmore Press, 1919, pp. 213–20.
80 *FYA*, p. 339.
81 Ibid., pp. 285–86.
82 *VT*, pp. 557–58; *PB*, pp. 212–24.
83 *DIWP*, pp. 146–51.
84 *FYA*, p. 25.
85 Bandyopadhyay, *Vidyasagara*, p. 36.
86 Benoy Kumar Sarkar, *The Sociology of Population* (henceforth, *SP*). Calcutta: N.M. Ray Chowdhury & Co., 1936, p. 13.

128 Wars of the Emasculated

87 CRTHE, pp. 88, 93–94.
88 PPS-1905, pp. 281–83; BSB-I, pp. 446–48; Spengler, The Decline of the West, pp. 3–40.
89 Nirad Chaudhuri, The Autobiography of an Unknown Indian. New York: The New York Review of Books (NYRB), 1951, p. 320.
90 PPS-1905, p. 141.
91 FYA, p. 81.
92 Ibid.
93 BSB-II, pp. 769–70, 792–95.
94 Taraknath Das, Is Japan a Menace to Asia? Shanghai: Taraknath Das, 1917, p. 56.
95 NBGP, pp. 306–7.
96 FYA, p. 26.
97 Haushofer, Geopolitics of the Pacific Ocean, p. vi.
98 Margaret MacMillan, Paris 1919. New York: Random House, 2003, p. 306.
99 FYA, p. 29.
100 Ibid., p. 234.
101 NBGP, pp. 308–12, 324–28.
102 PPS-1905, pp. 124, 285.
103 See Rabindranath Tagore, The Spirit of Japan. Tokyo: Indo-Japanese Association, 1916; Mishra, From the Ruins of Empire, pp. 233–37; Goswami, Producing India, pp. 254–55.
104 PB, p. 312.
105 Ibid., p. 322.
106 FYA, p. 21.
107 NBGP, pp. 319, 329.
108 VT, p. 546.
109 FYA, pp. 17–18.
110 NBGP, pp. 5–10.
111 FYA, pp. 18–19.
112 BSB-II, p. 717.
113 VT, pp. 550–54.
114 FYA, p. 19.
115 Ibid.
116 Kaviraj, The Unhappy Consciousness, pp. 27–71.
117 FYA, pp. 19–20.
118 Sen, Colonial Childhoods, pp. 187–210; on clothes and colonial culture, see Bernard Cohn, Colonialism and Its Forms of Knowledge: The British in India. Delhi: Oxford University Press, 1997, p. 106.
119 Sen, Traces of Empire, p. 37.
120 Sen, Savagery and Colonialism in the Indian Ocean, pp. 1–24.
121 FYA, p. 20.
122 John Dower, War Without Mercy: Race and Power in the Pacific War. New York: Pantheon, 1986, pp. 203–33, 262–90; John Dower, Ways of Forgetting, Ways of Remembering. New York: The New Press, 2012, pp. 65–104.

123 *FYA*, p. 25.
124 Chaudhuri, *The Autobiography of an Unknown Indian*, pp. 303-4.
125 *NBGP*, pp. 390-94.
126 The pleasure is palpable in Sarkar's discussion of military strategy in the Pacific and Indian Oceans. *PB*, pp. 290-98.
127 Dower, *War Without Mercy*, p. 157; Carol Gluck, *Japan's Modern Myths: Ideology in the Late Meiji Period*. Princeton: Princeton University Press, 1985, pp. 259-60.
128 *FYA*, pp. 279-80; *CRTHE*, pp. 85-87.
129 *NBGP*, p. 438.
130 *PPS-1905*, p. 285.
131 *GYI*, p. 8.
132 *BSB-I*, pp. 216-17.
133 *NBGP*, pp. 395, 427-28.
134 Ibid., Appendix II, pp. 449-50.
135 *DIWP*, p. 137.
136 *PBHS*, p. 202.
137 *FYA*, p. 250.
138 Ibid., p. 257.
139 *PPS-1905*, p. 198.
140 *BSB-I*, p. 411.
141 *CRTHE*, pp. 255-56.
142 *DIWP*, pp. 137, 139-41.
143 *FYA*, pp. 232, 257.
144 *NBGP*, p. 330.
145 *FYA*, pp. 10, 19.
146 *FYA*, p. 193; Gay, *The Cultivation of Hatred*, pp. 38-53.
147 Dower, *War Without Mercy*, pp. 43-45.
148 *FYA*, p. 257.
149 Mookerji, *History of Indian Shipping*, pp. 116-82; *CRTHE*, p. 241.
150 Home Department, J.P. Blair to Secretary, Government of India, 27 April 1929, Letter no. 128PSD.
151 *PPS-1905*, p. 213.
152 Dilip Menon, A Local Cosmopolitanism', p. 136; Javed Majeed, *Autobiography, Travel and Postnational Identity: Gandhi, Nehru and Iqbal*. Houndmills: Palgrave, 2007, pp. 10-50.
153 *FYA*, pp. 184-85; *CRTHE*, pp. 95-96, 236-37.
154 *DIWP*, p. 124.
155 Rabindranath Tagore, *Journey to Persia and Iraq*. Calcutta: Viswabharati, 1932, pp. 23-25.
156 *PB*, p. 294.
157 *FYA*, p. 54.
158 Michio Takeyama, *Harp of Burma*. Rutland: Tuttle, 1966.
159 John Dower, *Embracing Defeat: Japan in the Wake of World War II*. New York: Norton, 1999, pp. 502-3.

160 Gordon, *Brothers Against the Raj*, pp. 513–14, 534–37.
161 Hiroshi Noma, *Zone of Emptiness*. Cleveland: World Publishing Co., 1956.
162 Takeyama, *Harp of Burma*, pp. 89–113.
163 Ibid., p. 95.
164 Sen, *Savagery and Colonialism in the Indian Ocean*, pp. 159–70.
165 Gananath Obeyesekere, *The Apotheosis of Captain Cook*. Princeton: Princeton University Press, 1992, pp. 8–22; Said, *Culture and Imperialism*, pp. 19–30.
166 Satadru Sen, 'A Juvenile Periphery'.
167 George Orwell, *Burmese Days*. Orlando: Harcourt Brace Jovanovich (HBJ), 1962.
168 Takeyama, *Harp of Burma*, pp. 129–30.
169 Gay, *Weimar Culture*, pp. 1–22.
170 Hajime Tanabe, *Philosophy as Metanoetics*. Berkeley: University of California Press, 1990, pp. 2–5.
171 James Heisig, 'Foreword', in Hajime Tanabe (ed.), *Philosophy as Metanoetics*. Berkeley: University of California Press, 1990, p. xvii.
172 Ibid., p. xiv.
173 Maja Zehfuss, *Wounds of Memory: The Politics of War in Germany*. Cambridge: Cambridge University Press, 2007, pp. 1–31, 176–78; Sen, *Traces of Empire*, p. 119.
174 Dower, *Ways of Forgetting, Ways of Remembering*, pp. 246–55.
175 Ashis Nandy, 'The Other Within: The Strange Case of Radhabinod Pal's Judgment on Culpability', *New Literary History*, 23(1), 1992, pp. 45–67.
176 Dower, *Embracing Defeat*, pp. 469–74.
177 Nandy, 'The Other Within'.
178 Radhabinod Pal, *The History of the Law of Primogeniture with Special Reference to India, Ancient and Modern*. Calcutta: Oriental Press, 1923.
179 Radhabinod Pal, *Crimes in International Relations*. Calcutta, 1955, pp. 193–94.
180 Nandy, 'The Other Within'.
181 *DIWP*, pp. 101–3.
182 *BSB-II*, pp. 510–13, 684–89, 717.
183 *DIWP*, p. 166.
184 *SHHM*, p. 74.
185 *DIWP*, pp. 166–68.
186 Ibid.
187 *VT*, pp. 513–14.
188 *DIWP*, pp. 137–44.
189 See Chaudhuri, *The Autobiography of an Unknown Indian*, pp. 318–28; Sen, *Traces of Empire*, p. 84.
190 Benoy Kumar Sarkar, 'Demo-Despotocracy and Freedom', *Calcutta Review*, January 1939, p. 110.
191 Paul Fussel, *The Great War and Modern Memory*. Oxford: Oxford University Press, 1975, pp. 3–35.

192 Ernst Jünger, *Storm of Steel*. New York: Penguin, 2004, p. 241.
193 Sen, *Traces of Empire*, pp. 37–57.
194 Vinayak Chaturvedi, 'Rethinking Knowledge With Action: V.D. Savarkar, the Bhagavad Gita, and Histories of Warfare', *Modern Intellectual History*, 7(2), 2010, pp. 417–35.
195 Appiah, *Cosmopolitanism*, pp. xvi–xviii.

3

A Romance of the State

The sociologist, as a student of interhuman relations or social mobility is convinced that in health matters compulsion—no matter at what stage—is an absolute necessity.[1]

— Benoy Kumar Sarkar, 1941

Freedom as Therapy

Benoy Kumar Sarkar was not a Nazi, in spite of his willingness (in 1934) to praise Hitler as a great 'teacher', and (in 1939) to call Germany 'a state *of* the people and *by* the people'.[2] He was not a fascist either. But colonial intelligence described him as a propagandist for fascism,[3] and the insinuation has adhered to him even in the writings of his admirers. 'Was B.K. Sarkar a fascist?' wondered Flora, suggesting that Sarkar's Italian enthusiasms reflected the frustration of an intelligentsia that had failed to gain traction over peasants, and the desperation of a visionary of 'development' confronted with insurmountable problems in the mobilisation of capital.[4] During Sarkar's stay in Italy in 1929–31, he became enamoured of the Mussolini regime.[5] He befriended Croce, Gini and other right-leaning intellectuals, admired fascist youth organisations, and got drawn into a scheme—backed by Gini and Mussolini's brother—for an 'Italo-Indian Institute' that would be a front for Rome in India.[6] Yet Croce had already lost his own enthusiasm for fascism,[7] and the planned institute was aborted because Mussolini's government found Sarkar untrustworthy.[8] The skepticism was not baseless. 'The world has come to realize that there is a limit to dictatorship and absolutism', Sarkar had written in 1925 when the Italian opposition forced Mussolini to make political concessions.[9] 'Fascism as a moral force has to justify its existence among the people', he had added, repelled by the murder of the socialist Giacomo Matteotti the previous year.[10] He had raised a sardonic eyebrow at the rhetorical excesses of Hitler and Ludendorff during their trial for conspiracy in 1923.[11] If anything, he was a critic of fascism, albeit a mild one. Nevertheless, when a chapter must be prefaced with the observation that the subject was not a Nazi, it indicates a problem that cannot be dismissed as merely a desire for economic growth or trains that run on time. The problem involves the imaginary of individuality, freedom and statehood in the final decades of colonial India, when the nationalist vanguard sought to combine transformation, citizenship and democracy in a single institutional framework.

Sarkar made no attempt to define freedom. The historical diversity and contextuality of freedom made such attempts futile, he wrote more than once.[12] But in the period between the Great War and Indian independence, when Sarkar imagined free India, he was clear about its constitutional shape: he wanted an inclusive, liberal, democratic state, in which the individual citizen would have all the rights associated with the Enlightenment. The Enlightenment and its institutions were a universal resource, and universal access to that resource was central to his politics of anti-colonial redress. Sarkar's vision of liberal statehood, however, is so fraught with tension that it barely holds together. He desired the individual more as an agent of 'creative disequilibrium' than as a repository of rights or an entity in need of protection. To reconcile the universalism of his racial posture with the observable 'facts' of Indian backwardness, Sarkar relied on a 'lag', i.e., the different locations of nations on a common timeline of progress and liberty.[13] The role he envisioned for the state, particularly in 'latecomer' nations like India, had to do with such lags: while they lasted, the vanguardist state would compensate for the backwardness of society, even if it had to put the individual in a re-education camp or a hospital.[14]

It is not that this is an unreasonable or 'flawed' vision of freedom. It requires no radical departure from Mill, who himself made an explicit connection between backwardness and coercion: 'The early difficulties in the way of spontaneous progress are so great . . . that a ruler full of the spirit of improvement is warranted in the use of any expedients'.[15] It is that Sarkar posits notions of identity, citizenship and governance in which there is a normative confusion between the state, the nation and the community, and the individual can never be certain where he is located. Where Mill imagined a discrete regime that dragged a laggard population into progress, Sarkar's state weaved in and out of its identification with the people: it was both 'of' the people and actively engaged in producing the people. The latter dynamic worked on two levels. As Bernard Yack has suggested, the discourse of popular sovereignty produced the people not only as a political community occupying the space of the state, but also as a supra-political nation that might override or reconstitute the political domain of citizens.[16] Sarkar's democracy was thus also normatively authoritarian and potentially fascist. He was—and we are—left with a dilemma within a postcolonial nationhood that is ultimately a project of liberation: the individual is both essential to freedom and a problem of freedom.

The problem is constituted by interlocking but not fully reconcilable formulations connected to the urbanisation unfolding around Sarkar. Like Durkheim, the Czech sociologist-statesman Tomas Masaryk and to some extent the anthropologist Robert Redfield (who saw the 'Folk' and the 'Urban' as discrete poles, with the individual occupying the latter), Sarkar regarded industrial urbanity as the text of a potentially fatal misalignment between the individual and society.[17] Unlike them, he welcomed the crisis: his needs were imbedded in a sharper sense of lack. Since that lack might be summarised as modernity itself, it is not surprising that Sarkar anticipated some, but not all, major aspects of the thinking of Talcott Parsons and other modernisation theorists: he was uninterested in voluntarism as an alternative to state action, but very interested in the production of individuality as an asset to the state. Fittingly, his thoughts on the relationship between the state and the individual are most fully articulated in the relentlessly comparative, statistically underpinned *Villages and Towns as Social Patterns*, published in 1941. In 1939, he had called for the 'emancipation' of provincial Bengal from the political, economic and cultural domination of Calcutta and its established elites.[18] The resemblance to fascist anti-urbanism is misleading: 'ruralism' was 'a thing of the past', Sarkar had insisted more than a decade earlier.[19] Unlike Radhakamal Mookerji, Sarkar did not see the village as a viable site of national development.[20] The village was a ghetto in the world: unless one could get away, there could be neither modernity nor freedom. In his later work, the urban emphasis had been honed rather than jettisoned: the modernising village would follow the lead of the industrial city.[21] There was, moreover, a consistent rejection of the 'village Indias' associated with Rabindranath, Gandhi and nineteenth-century Orientalism. 'The peasants and artisans of villages do not happen to possess a charmingly romantic soul', Sarkar observed, adding (in a rebuke to Spengler) that peasants were not ahistorical, and that the city was the 'origin and ever-flowing source of the blood' that 'makes the peasant, his farm and his village'.[22]

Sarkar's colonial metropolis was the site not only of state-driven changes in the caste hierarchy, but of rapid changes in class status brought about by capitalism. He refused to condemn such transformations, but his unease with nouveaux riches and parvenu elites is palpable:

> As long as money rules, everybody in each income-group tries by hook or by crook to elevate his or her position to the next higher rung. [T]his evolution of classes has been featured with the evolution ... of diverse forms of evil. Family *mores* are profoundly affected by the craze for class uplift. Bits of the human psyche can be opened up through many vanities.[23]

Contemptible bourgeois mobility was connected directly to the plutocracy of electoral politics, and indirectly to corruptions and criminalities. The city was not just an artifice to be contrasted with the natural village: it had a nature of its own, which was both liberating and threatening, and which corresponded with the psychological nature of humanity. It was up to the vanguard to study and manage this nature, through the enumerative modalities of scholarship and governance.[24]

What should be the objective of management? In the modern city, Sarkar suggested, capitalism and industrialisation produced individuality—which he equated with humanity itself—willy-nilly. The twofold problem was that this individuality/humanity was either not recognised as legitimate by the existing elites (and thus wasted), or genuinely deviant (and thus counterproductive). The task before the vanguardist state involved a double pedagogy: educating the poor to a proper individuality, while educating the elite to be politically and socially inclusive, i.e., to recognise the working-class capacity for citizenship. Following Spengler's lead, Sarkar described the city as a dynamic force that 'municipalises' its individual residents until they would rather die of starvation than live in villages.[25] Since such morbidity is undesirable, the vanguard must manage transformation in ways that produce freedom and well-being, not delinquency and degeneration.

The city thus became a metaphor of the modern nation. After the Great War, municipal administrations were the most 'independent' level of government in colonial India, substantially under the control of Indian politicians.[26] Under the circumstances, what Sarkar called 'municipal democracy' (with its characteristic combination of popular pressure from below, bureaucracy from above, and plutocracy throughout) was not limited to C.R. Das's Calcutta, but constituted a larger model of governance that had to be rationalised, not destroyed, by a new elite not invested in the plutocracy.[27] Serving Vivekananda's vision of *daridra-narayan* or the common man as God, the municipality itself became godlike in its benign omnipresence as it went about ensuring the quality of milk and regulating the use of toxic chemicals.[28] Also, reimagining the Indian city as an engine of improvement allowed Sarkar to dismiss the racist discourse that might be described as Kipling's 'cities of dreadful night', or the 'drain inspections' of Katherine Mayo. Sarkar did not deny that Calcutta and Bombay had dirty drains. Dirt had its ideological uses. Whereas Mark Harrison has suggested that Indian politicians obstructed colonial initiatives in urban sanitation after the Montagu-Chelmsford reforms,[29] Sarkar pointed out that British-Indian expenditure on public health was pitiful compared to what the German state spent.[30] The implication was that Indians—scientists-as-administrators, individuals conscious of their historical role in the world—could manage their dirt (and dirty) better than the British could. Moreover, Sarkar was able to argue that the problems of the colonial city—filth, disease, crime, neuroses, disrupted families, street children—had nothing to do with racial difference, climate or geography. They had been ubiquitous in the West also, and only recently reduced by interventionist governments.[31] The pathologies and cures were both embedded in a common modernity, in Bombay as in Berlin. That commonality was a way out of the ghetto.

The megacities of the modern world, Sarkar observed, were essentially similar: they produced individuals (creative or delinquent) on the one hand, and municipal democracy on the other. India was no exception, and he embraced that universality as freedom itself. The individual subject was a necessity of freedom-in-society, being a self-conscious actor in the world. Sarkar's fascination with hereditary and environmental influences on human behaviour fell far short of a crude determinism: 'Until morbidity, physical or mental, can be demonstrated by unquestionable tests the individual is responsible for his choice of . . . saintly or . . . scoundrel-like behavior', he wrote about urban criminality.[32] Also, the relatively unindividuated subjecthood centred on the patriarchal family that Dipesh Chakrabarty has theorised for Indian nationalism was for Sarkar a reactionary and retrograde weakness.[33] The family and similar 'traditional' formations were not legitimate constraints upon individuality, but challenges to overcome.

The freedom of the individual was thus a confrontational dynamic basic to national progress and racial equality. Moreover, crime and revolution were located in the same processes of individualisation, which was inherently rebellious in a colony where criminals were 'tribes', rebels were 'hordes', and society a lump of 'communities'.[34]

Yet not only was the individual at the helm of the state a potential tyrant, the population constantly challenged the nation either with its useless non-individuality or with a lethargic, selfish or disruptive subjectivity. The state could be engineered to contain these possibilities, but not without considerable powers of coercion. When India became independent, Sarkar grumbled:

> The greatest drive in our character is . . . to be found in the chase, maddening as it is, for personal glorification, power, position and purse. A new therapeutic has to be devised.[35]

There are compelling overlaps between Sarkar's ideas about 'therapy' and the coercion that scholars of colonial medicine have highlighted in relations between patient-natives and the doctor-state.[36] Sarkar slipped frequently into a quasi-colonial identification with oppressors and oppression itself.[37] Italy and Germany had embarked upon ambitious projects of 'internal colonization', he noted approvingly in 1936, adding that India would need to follow suit.[38] Sarkar was referring to state-directed economic mobilisation: specifically, the fairly benign *Bonifica* scheme for reclamation of 'useless' or 'unhealthy' land, which he observed in Italy in 1929.[39] There was, however, considerable ideological overflow. The rhetoric of internal colonisation was a long-standing feature of German imperialism, and the line between empty and populated Lebensraum was fuzzy.[40] In 1949, Sarkar endorsed the reclamation of the Andaman Islands as a 'prospective colony for Indians'.[41] The unhappy implications for the indigenous population—excluded from Indianness and individuality—need not be recapitulated here.[42] Such unhappiness was irrelevant to Sarkar. The world was witnessing a *digvijaya* (triumph) of democracy, he wrote in 1940–41. Whoever won the world war, the world would be more democratic.[43]

It is in that context that we might examine Sarkar's fondness for Germany, which went further than the conventional inclination of nationalists in the colonised world to be well disposed towards enemies of the coloniser. It was not absolute; Germany was a part of the albinocracy.[44] Nevertheless, it bordered on delusion: after 1945, Sarkar declared that the diffusion of captured German soldiers, scientists and military technology around the world amounted to a triumphant 'German invasion in men, ideas and inventions'.[45] He bitterly accused Gandhi, Nehru, the Congress, and the Indian foreign-policy establishment of being pro-Soviet and biased against Germany, Japan and Italy.[46] *Ressentiment* gave Sarkar an immediate ideological affinity with German Romanticism.[47] It gave him, for instance, a similarly convoluted outlook on Nietzsche: what was the place of the 'free' individual in the Volk and the state, if none could be dispensed with? The boundaries of the state became the limits of individuality. We find Sarkar concluding, ultimately, that the individual needed the state to make him an individual, and a reinvented community to sustain him in his individuality. For all his antipathy towards constructions of India as a 'spiritual' culture, Sarkar could not give up the Geist: the state itself became the guarantor of the 'national spirit' of the citizen.

To understand the ramifications of that imaginary, it is useful to look at Detlev Peukert's analysis of the relationship between the state and society in Nazi Germany. Peukert suggested that by aggressively invading those areas of society that had hitherto been 'private', the German state inadvertently brought about a retrenchment of the private sphere. Individual dissent and freedom were secreted but also contained within this remapped privacy. Simultaneously, by blurring the lines between the public and the private, the regime opened up the state to semi-autonomous agents, compromising its own coherence and control.[48] In India, the problems were not identical: here, bourgeois privacy was itself underdeveloped. To produce the individual citizen, the state would have to create as well as violate the private world, while remaining vigilant against 'traditional' formations hostile to private and public alike. This is consistent with Sarkar's conception of 'Young India'. The 'old' masses, by definition, had to be awakened to individuality and modernity by the 'young' vanguard for the liberal nation to come to fruition. What is startling, however, is the suggestion that the vanguard itself needed the state to contain it: to prevent it from dissipating into the world of movement, to guard it against the treasonous aspect of cosmopolitanism, and to prevent it from becoming another unidentifiable mass. Needless to say, these considerations have serious implications for masses that show a reluctance to 'awaken', and for elites that reveal their inclination to dissipate.

Sarkar's state is thus an instrument of containment, packed with disciplining institutions as well as 'spirit'. It need not be Nazi Germany or a crude fantasy of homogeneity. But the scholarship on fascism, totalitarianism and state coercion that has followed in the wake of the Third Reich—the work of Hannah Arendt, Giorgio Agamben, Peukert, Robert Gellately, and others—is nevertheless valuable in examining Sarkar's thinking, not least because independent India has generally privileged the state and the community over the individual in its structure of rights, laws and government. With its roots in *ressentiment* and its desire for the signs of the coloniser's power (especially the state), anti-colonial nationalism tends to create the individual as well as the mob, potentially consigning the former either to the violence of the mob, or to the lawlessness of the state of exception.

The Nature of Indian Individuals

In April 1936, in Rangoon to address the Convention of Religions (organised to mark the centenary of Ramakrishna's birth), Sarkar outlined his vision of the role of the individual in history:

> Man as an individual or in groups has had but one function, and that is to transform the gifts of the world into which he is born, namely, Nature and society, into the instruments of human and social welfare. It is not Nature, region or geography that in the last analysis determines man's destiny. It is the human will, man's energy, that re-creates the topography and natural forces, humanizes the earth and spiritualizes the geography. Then, again, it is not the group, the clan, the nation or the society that ultimately forces the individual to submit to the social *milieu*, the group *mores*, the tradition, and the status quo. It is rather the individual personality that compels the *mores* to change and the *milieu* to break, that subverts *status quo* and reforms tradition.[49]

This is easily recognised as another articulation of *vishwashakti*, in which talented individuals emerge to refashion their historical moment.[50] Sarkar was positing individuality as an unruly asset of liberalism: it was necessary for freedom, threatened by the other paraphernalia of freedom (such as the community and the state), and it was, in some circumstances, itself a threat to freedom: an element in need of restraint.

The simultaneity of the desire and the fear surfaces very strongly in Sarkar's view of women and sex in modern India. Sanjam Ahluwalia has argued that middle-class Indian men who interested themselves in sexuality and birth control in the early twentieth century were generally hostile to female agency, and sought primarily to subordinate women's bodies to elitist constructions of 'national interest'.[51] Sarkar, however, remained unapologetically liberal on the 'women's question':[52] dismissive of differences between European and Indian womanhood,[53] and broadly supportive of equality for women in the family, education and the professions. Even in 1907, when swadeshi opinion had become ambivalent towards *srti-swadhinata* ('women's liberation'),[54] he used the National Schools of Malda to promote the inclusion of women in political agitation—a fact duly noted by colonial intelligence.[55] Over time, sexual freedom became central to this vision of equality. Describing the community-enforced celibacy of Hindu widows as a 'sterilisation' that was both unjust and unwise, Sarkar demanded (in the language of racial hygiene and public health) that Indian women become, and be accepted as, autonomous agents of sexual choice, divorce and remarriage.[56] In all these areas, Indian social and governmental institutions needed reform, he held, without caveats about national freedom having to come first. The pursuit of reform was itself independence; ensuring that women were equal and free was 'individualisation'.[57] Sarkar's long-standing advocacy of romantic-sexual love was another facet of this desire for autonomous individuals who were whole—and free— women and men.[58] Such women already existed in the cities; society had to facilitate their proliferation and accommodate their presence.

At the same time, 'free' women unnerved Sarkar. He described their emergence not only as individualisation, but also, taking his cue from Ferdinand Tönnies, as 'masculinisation'.[59] The radical concept of sterilisation-by-family was turned on its head and reconciled with an increasingly masculine universal norm of labour.[60] Feminism was *both* 'nothing but the participation by women in all the so-called male activities', and a 'pathology', Sarkar suggested: a neurosis intimately connected with juvenile delinquency, criminality and venereal disease, which had to be 'sociologically appraised as the cost of civilization or price of progress'.[61] The new individualised/masculinised women, he wrote, were 'society women', not 'community women'.[62] Quite apart from Sarkar's association (again derived from Tönnies) of 'society' with the city and 'community' with the village,[63] an additional meaning was imbedded in the word 'society' when used in this context: it designated not only the public sphere of national life, but also the realm of elite arrogance, frivolousness and selfishness.[64] Moreover, the society woman was 'artificial', Sarkar wrote, as opposed to the 'natural' woman of the old-fashioned type: 'Under the regime of masculinization the ...

woman natural is replaced by or transformed into the . . . woman of artificial will and impulses, the woman of conventions, contracts and business intercourse'.[65] Within and without the family, such women brought conflict and chaos, upending older relationships, hierarchies and roles. As usual, Sarkar refused to condemn conflict and chaos: these were the engines of freedom, and artifice was the stuff of statecraft and the will to innovate. He showed little interest in the psychiatrist Paul Möbius' desire to preserve 'natural' women as the counterparts of 'cultured' men, or in Indian critiques of the 'artifice' of modern European civilisation that an earlier generation of social theorists—like Bhudeb Mukhopadhdyay—had articulated.[66] But it was clear to him that family and 'community' were no longer adequate as structures within which conflict and chaos might be contained and utilised. They were, indeed, counterproductive: '[T]he greatest breeding centres of criminals are, first, the family, and secondly, the street-corner or the neighborhood'.[67]

New structures of family life were needed that could break up the older communities and also manage the free individual. The structures could be literal. Indian homes were undifferentiated jumbles of living spaces, Sarkar complained, producing architecturally abetted immoralities:

> In Calcutta neighbours can very often shake hands with one another through the windows. [T]here can hardly be any privacy in many housing conditions. The sex-triangle can be easily fostered by the family, joint and large as it is, comprising often, in addition to the husband, wife and children, the families of married sons, as well as the near or distant relatives from both sides. Interhuman relations of this and allied types can hardly lead to sanity in morals, manners and sentiments. If many of the behaviors or reactions are not technically declared as crimes it is simply because everybody interested in the phenomena is careful enough to avoid contacts with the police and the court of law. This situation describes the folkways not only of the working classes . . . but of highly placed officials, publicists, intellectuals and other *bhadralok* groups.[68]

Sarkar's ideal of domestic architecture was clearly European-bourgeois, with its particular segregations and its normative expectations of privacy and, paradoxically, surveillance. Significantly, he was not arguing that the modern city had destabilised a better 'native' model of domesticity, but that it had highlighted a problem of 'housing-morality' among Indians of *all* classes. This led him to call for a particular kind of state, which might make good an ideological shortcoming in the people: 'Other circumstances remaining the same, a more energetically patriotic state or an administration with a consciously goalful plan of action could show much higher results [in] housing reform, etc. than the present regime'. He added that the status quo 'requires to be combated by every student of sociations and progress'.[69] The rhetoric of 'students' is worth noting: the same state (and statesman) that teaches also studies. The individual subject had to be objectified immediately.

Even more than women, youth represented an individuality that excited and alarmed Sarkar. He wrote with great social-scientific exactitude about the nature of youth: in particular, the interconnected social, political, psychological and biological characteristics of different age groups. Only those between the ages of 16 and 30 were capable of change, he wrote; only they could be 'creators of the as-if', i.e., imagine transformation.[70] *Villages and Towns* is dedicated to 'Youth, the remaker of the world and the embodiment of creative disequilibrium'. Sarkar's enthusiasm was aligned with a powerful strand of youth-worship within Indian nationalism.[71] It was, however, also affiliated with dispersed and often contradictory developments, such as the construction of juvenile delinquency as an individualised defect,[72] and post-Boer-War European youth movements (from the Boy Scouts to the Hitler Youth) driven by fear of racial deterioration in the city.[73] Peukert has pointed out that a basic function of these youth movements was to normalise war.[74] Closer to home, it reflected the discourse of 'seditious' teenagers caught up in anti-colonial militancy, and the social-scientific and clinical discourses of adolescence and child-psychology which self-consciously modern Indians had embraced as part of the intellectual and legislative contests of dyarchy.[75] Sarkar himself expressed his support for laws like the Bombay Shops and Establishments Act, which sought to limit child labour and provide poor urban children with 'opportunities for leisure and recreation'.[76] To acknowledge the dynamic individuality of youth—patriots as well as degenerates—was to show yourself as a dynamic individual, if not young.

But dynamic youth bent on transformation alarmed their older compatriots, in India as in Europe. The politician and journalist Panchcowri Banerji complained in 1916:

> Thanks to Surendra Nath Banarji and his crew, [patriotism] has ruined many a student. [E]very big agitation requires young men. [I]t is the boys

who possess any real capacity for work. No wonder, therefore, that they should now suffer from slightly swelled heads. [This] is the main cause of all the anarchism, assassinations and arrests of the present day.[77]

While the colonial police obviously concurred,[78] so did the wider discourse of modern youth. The European youth movements were mechanisms for the socialisation of the disorderly and the déclassé, and it is hardly a coincidence that they dressed their members in uniforms.[79] Post-war German memorialising literature suggests that fascist youth culture in the 1930s was highly uneven: full of bullies and conformists, but also full of the indifferent, the fickle and the outright resistant.[80] Containment was clearly necessary, and since youthful individuality was inherently 'wild', it was a need that would never exhaust itself. Sarkar's interest in scientifically conceived, carefully regulated pedagogical structures should be seen in this light.[81] This pedagogy was not a strait-jacket for youth. The colonial school, from Aligarh and the Chief's Colleges to the Ramakrishna Mission, National Education and Santiniketan, also created the individual, by making a scientific intervention in heredity and the environment, and *liberating* youth from the retarding constraints of family and 'community'.[82] Modernised, disciplined and disciplining education sought to manage the young individual in the process of ushering him into the state, pursuing that magic combination of privacy and openness.

Vishwashakti is, after all, a theory of managed individuality as much as it is a theory of freedom. It is in the nature of the individual to struggle against society, Sarkar suggested; this struggle generates not only freedom but society itself, in the form of culture and the state. He wove the notion into a conception of human nature: 'The . . . instincts, ambitions, urges or drives lead to four different spheres of creation. These spheres . . . constitute culture in the most generic sense. The state, law, politics, society and allied forms and relations of human life are derived from the urges [of conquest]'.[83] Even when groups—such as nations or classes—appeared to be the agents of struggle/conquest, they could be treated analytically and governmentally as individuals, subject to the laws of human nature.[84] Only those who exhibited this nature were true political subjects, fit for freedom. Fitness itself took on two overlapping meanings: to be individual by nature was a sign of imminent (or potential) statehood and sovereignty, but it was also to be already free. Indians had forfeited individuality and freedom simultaneously: one could afford to ignore the desires and priorities of the individual when one had no political responsibilities, but it was unnatural and contemptible.

Sarkar's fondness for Nietzsche can also be understood in the context of this project of re-naturing Indians. Re-naturing was nothing but a rediscovery of the Self, he suggested when he cited Nietzsche's preference for Manu over the 'slave religion' of Christianity.[85] By 1941, Manu had been rejected as a destroyer of women's individuality: a healthy Indian society, Sarkar now wrote, 'can come into its own only when the marriage laws of Manu . . . have been practically annihilated root and branch, i.e., when the Indian males have become more humane, normal and reasonable'.[86] Nietzsche, however, was not jettisoned, being central to the articulation of individuality and freedom in the tropics.[87] Nietzschean affectations and distortions allowed the white man to set himself apart from the natives, to experience himself as being 'beyond society', and enabled near-mythical episodes of apotheosis.[88] By appropriating Nietzsche for India, Sarkar indicated his awareness of a model of modern personhood that was essential to *both* racialised and cosmopolitan individuality: to the sovereignty of the national man engaged in *Realpolitik* and the worship of the powerful nation-state, as well as to the transcendence of the nation. Simultaneously, approval of Nietzsche's contempt for Christianity not only undermined a pillar of empire, it indicated Sarkar's refusal to be identified with the slaves in the world. This remained a fundamental limit of his radicalism.

Consequently, Sarkar's individual was an unreliable democrat. His insistence that the French Revolution—which he saw as more Romantic than rational—was irrelevant without Napoleon indicates a conviction that the charismatic and even oppressive leader could (or must) be rehabilitated within the revolutionary state.[89] Revolutionary nationhood and the national citizen were poised on the edge of an inviting authoritarian chasm. We have here a glimpse of Bose, who Sarkar regarded as the true radical of his historical moment.[90] Sarkar was not, however, advocating despotism. The individual could not be allowed to swagger in splendid isolation; he—and she—had to be harnessed *for* the community and *to* the state. Indian models were available. Sarkar wrote about Bhartrihari: 'His "whole duty of man" was oriented not only to the sensuous elements in life but also to the moral or social obligations'.[91] When the search for individuality in ancient India confronted Sarkar with a literature that often lacks identifiable authors, he turned the difficulty into an advantage: it is not that individuals were absent, but that they were adept at working together within

A Romance of the State   145

councils and committees.[92] It was a rejection of another Orientalist construction: a 'bad' individuality that prevents the development of civic responsibility, and hence citizenship and politics, in the Orient. In the process, Sarkar reclaimed the possibility of history and nationhood, expressed as usual in metaphors of war with a Teutonic twist:

> Verily, life is a grand war in Indian estimation. And yet this conception of the 'Armageddon' of life is not a Hindu patent. 'The Siegfrieds of the *Nibelungenlied* e.g., of Hebbel's plays and Wagner's operas, are [similar] in their obstinately aggressive individuality.[93]

Without such individuality, Sarkar clarified, there could be no energism. Producing individuals therefore had to be a basic objective of the modern state, which—in America, France, Germany, the USSR but not India—had already embraced the imperative of mass education. Education would effect a qualitative change in revolutions and republics, taking them beyond particularistic grievances and into the universal realm of racial equality and national sovereignty, i.e., true liberalism. He wrote:

> Since 1870 education has become universal all through the civilized world except only in dependencies, protectorates, and the spheres of influence. As a result of this . . . [people] will act more as the 'moral agents' of Immanuel Kant and not as the mere creatures of environments and historic circumstances. The will is becoming more and more self-legislative and free. The idea of *swaraj* as sovereignty and democracy will grow into a commonplace phenomenon in the normal psychology of individuals.[94]

A relationship of escalation was thus established between revolution, education and democracy: revolution may have to precede mass education in India and China as it had in France and Russia, but mass education accelerates and intensifies revolution by imbedding it in a democratic individual self-consciousness. The ubiquitous references to 'psychology' in Sarkar's narrative of politics and history are not a coincidence. They reflect his debt to Pareto[95] and to a newly prestigious discipline, but more than that, they reflect his conviction that freedom was a *mentality* of the fully formed individual. (Ancient India was a land of psychologists, he insisted.)[96] Freedom from colonialism took on a layered meaning: it was freedom from a particular situation of political oppression, but it was also the liberation of the individual *into* a permanent revolutionary mentality, and the liberation of the nation from a passive relationship with history into new, self-directed possibilities. The latter is essentially the phenomenon of freedom-at-midnight. Liberation from history and reconnection to world-history turn out to be the same thing.

Recuperating the individual was a particularly pressing problem in India because here the colonial regime had abandoned the individualising function of the state. The more impressive Indian accomplishments in physics and chemistry in the twentieth century, Sarkar observed, had come when individual Indians had struggled heroically against their institutional milieux, or sought out contacts in countries other than Britain.[97] Science and the scientist in modern India were inherently individualistic and revolutionary. Here, we find again the convergence of a critique of the colonial state, a desire for cosmopolitanism, 'pluralism', and national rejuvenation. We find also an acknowledgement of the connection between individuality and progress: it is individual 'manipulation' of the community or institution that drives progress. Sarkar called it 'political engineering': an unsentimental deployment of the will.[98]

That formulation complicates Sarkar's ideal national community, because it must constantly evaluate whether the manipulative individual is helpful or disruptive, and whether the 'world-conquering' freedom of the individual threatens freedom in society. But there is a clear expectation that liberal nationalism will contain Romantic excesses:

> It may be considered to be a fit theme for self-congratulation that Young India's mentality is not prepared to submit to the Periclean or Napoleonic dictatorship of its own 'enlightened despots,'—howsoever great and good the results already attained by it or howsoever *necessary* it may have turned out to be for historical and environmental reasons.[99]

It will also contain excessive self-interest, such as the 'mania for money-making' and the desire to take credit for research and innovation.[100] Patriotism, not greed, could be the basis of individual pursuits that produce wealth and power. Yet containment is never complete. Sarkar's vision of reform as war, the naked desire for the instruments of reform/war, and conviction that the individual is the most basic such instrument recuperate the powerful individual who has merged not just with the nation but also with the state. The state is the producer, the culmination, the showcase and the container of the free individual; not much remains of the latter when he cannot be shown to be serving the nation-state. The liberal state shelters, and shelters in, the shadow of the dictator, and because it does not disavow democracy, it is inevitably itself the dictator.

The Sheltering Cage: 'Demo-Despotocracy' and India

'The state has grown into the greatest dynamo of material well-being', Sarkar wrote in 1925, but that remark does not do justice to his expectations.[101] Statehood was, in some contexts, more important than nationhood: harder, more tangible, undeniable once extant. The lack of a state indicated not only weakness in the world, but also the inability to close the historical lag evidenced by weakness. In the contemporary Indian context, however, the state—as an idea and an institution—was very unevenly developed. Apart from Sarkar, its only major polemicist was Gandhi, and he was for the most part an ideologue of the anti-state.[102] One can, of course, find a theory of the state in Bankim's reworking of Krishna (1886), or even earlier in Michael Madhusudan Dutta's *Meghnadvadh Kavya* (1861).[103] Sarkar wistfully read Bankim's Krishna as a '*Duce* or . . . *Führer*',[104] but the dictatorship of Krishna and Ravan, like that of Gandhi's Ram, could only be oblique and metaphorical, of doubtful relevance in the world of policy.

In the decades preceding 1945, however, Indians acquired extensive experience of statecraft as a set of practices. Since the Minto-Morley reforms, if not earlier, nationalist politicians and political parties had been oriented towards controlling the organs of the state. We see this in the Lucknow Pact of 1916,[105] it becomes inescapable in the dyarchy councils, the post-war urban administrations, the history of the Swaraj Party, and the ministries after the 1937 elections.[106] During the Second World War, we have the additional instance of Bose's government-in-exile in Southeast Asia. (Unlike many governments-in-exile, Bose—who cut his teeth in Calcutta's 'municipal democracy'—ran a real administration, with taxes, conscription, punishments, and a population of increasingly unhappy 'overseas Indians'.)[107] In all these situations, there was an intertwining of authoritarianism and autonomy. In part, this had to do with the location within the colonial state (or the Japanese Co-Prosperity Sphere): freedom from colonial diktat coexisted with awareness of the limits of that freedom. In part, however, it reflected the perception that even limited freedom was dependent upon authoritarianism for its sustenance and expansion. The experience of independence could not be separated from authoritarian statecraft.

Sarkar's polemic reflected that context even as he strained against its limits. He believed that the insurgent Indian state should be free not only in the sense of being its own agent in the world, but also in conforming to established models of liberal democracy. He had no interest in governance that was narrowly ethnic in its identification, and he clearly favoured a secular state with readily apparent boundaries between private identities and public concerns.[108] The state need not be the focal point of the life of the individual, Sarkar had suggested early in his career: there was more to life.[109] The emphasis on the state as the preeminent institution of human existence increased sharply after the Great War, influenced by the radical reorganisation of Europe in that period. The rhetoric of 'pluralism' continued to function as an ideological hedge, however, keeping Sarkar from getting drawn fully into political fundamentalisms. He welcomed Kemal Pasha's revolution in Turkey, seeing it as 'a significant landmark in the life of the oppressed nationalities' and a successful defiance of Europe, but grimaced at Ataturk's intolerance of parliamentary opposition.[110] 'Kemal Pasha has been behaving like Mussolini', he remarked unhappily in 1926.[111] Pluralism remained the modern citizen's way of negotiating with the state:

> Pluralism rests fundamentally on the idea that the 'real' is hardly ever general, universal or absolute but essentially individual, personal and relative. The very fact that the life of an individual or a group can be regulated by many other than the standardized norm or conventional mores to which tradition is used, challenges the despotism or infallibility of any recognized system of moral, social or political absolutism.[112]

Yet within this avowal of the liberating and liberal state, we find much ambivalence, which became sharper in the late 1920s. The more infatuated Sarkar became with the hard state, the more ambiguous he became about the implications for the individual. When he wrote of the restriction of individual freedom by the state, as in the Soviet Union, he almost never got into issues of legitimacy.[113] Even the colonial state, which Sarkar explicitly equated with terrorism, was never categorised as illegitimate.[114] More relevant than legitimacy was necessity. It is unclear whether this was an endorsement or the recognition of a reality; there is no meaningful distinction. 'The rajya is a *necessary* institution' (emphasis original), he drew from the *Sukraniti*.[115] It is always the state that 'needs', effectively needing itself. Coercive governance is 'a moral necessity ... in all war-conditions', Sarkar insisted, and given his investment in a permanent state of struggle/conquest, the need never fades away.[116] 'Special circumstances' become the norm. We have in this vision of the needy state the kernel of Agamben's state of exception.[117] It also foreshadows Gellately's description of Nazi Germany as a 'prerogative state', or a state based on extraordinary but permanent prerogatives that flow from an absolute national interest—a need— that crowds out liberal considerations.[118]

Those considerations retained their foothold. In 1903, while still a teenager, he became a member of the Dawn Society, the group that incubated National Education, Greater India and mistrification.[119] Composed of nationalist students (Radhakumud Mookerji was a particularly active member), the Society epitomised the tension between democracy and pedagogical visions of governance. Its goal was to 'discover' and train citizens (a basic need of the unrealised state), but not all citizens were equal in their rights, since not all students are equally capable. Yet the Dawn Society, with its overtly parliamentary rules and procedures, was thoroughly liberal. Also, because the mature Sarkar came to admire Pareto more than any other contemporary thinker, it is easy to peg him as anti-democratic. But whereas Pareto was a Machiavellian obsessed with power and contemptuous of democracy, he was also a liberal, and his support for Italian fascism was less than wholehearted.[120] When Sarkar wrote about Italy in the mid-1920s, he portrayed Mussolini as a genius (who had lost his nerve lately) but fascism as a betrayal of Mazzini's 'message of social justice and personal freedom', adding: 'Mazziniano embodies today all the forces that are arrayed against fascism—socialistic, democratic, republican'.[121] The orderliness of Milan was the order of the prison-house, and Mussolini's attempts to muzzle the press reminded Sarkar of the British Raj.[122]

Italy fascinated Sarkar precisely because it resembled colonial India: it too had a deficit—a need—of modernity. In *The Politics of Boundaries*, he elaborated on this point:

> Indian patriots have much to learn by observing the steps which Italy has been taking to educate out of a medievally minded, feudalistic and agrarian people the type of a modernized industrial culture-state such as Western Europe, America and Germany have been able to develop. Italy's experiments in nation-making, economic development and modernism represent ... the cultural bridges over which semi-primitive, semi-developed peoples will have to pass.[123]

Sarkar falls back here upon the rhetoric of colonialism to describe the Indian condition, qualifying it only with a 'semi' or two, but he understood that the Italian solution to backwardness was itself 'colonial' in its reliance on the undemocratic.[124] The means mattered to him, because the ends could not be divorced from considerations of freedom. Democracy and freedom were both connected and separate for an interwar intellectual and anti-colonial nationalist like Sarkar. In his earlier ruminations on Indian political thought, he highlighted the allowances for popular consent, legitimate resistance and the overthrow of despots.[125] The pre-Mauryan republics were 'valuable assets' even when they were 'a nuisance, obstructing the achievement of an all-Indian nationalism'.[126] Nothing was more valuable than freedom, he reiterated on the eve of the Second World War.[127] As the remarks on Mazzini indicate, fascism became particularly problematic when it conflicted with democratic traditions that were themselves intertwined with nationalism. Stalinism was even more problematic: 'Tremendous doses of *a-satya, a-shiva and a-sundara* are associated with . . . the Soviet regime', he wrote under the heading 'The Annihilation of Freedom' when Germany and the USSR went to war.[128]

Like Croce, whose belated turn as a democrat came with an aristocratic reluctance to embrace the label, Sarkar felt compelled to weigh the pros and cons of the democratic tsunami he believed was sweeping the world in the interwar years.[129] Can you handle industrial democracy, in which workers will confront owners on equal terms, he teasingly asked his readers in 1932.[130] On the one hand, he saw in the democratic state an enhanced capacity for the general well-being of society, and understood that democracy had incubated the authority of two generations of social scientists.[131] On the other, he saw a heightened potential for mediocrity, uniformity, tyranny, and the 'excessive demand for well-being'.[132] Tocqueville's reservations about democracy were reasonable, he observed, adding: 'Democracy represents by all means a progress upon the stage of non-democracy, but is inevitably a condition of certain evils not known or apparent in that stage'.[133] Even as he encouraged the Constituent Assembly to establish a republic based on universal suffrage, he remained sceptical about bourgeois democracy:

> Bribery, sex-exploitation, extension of patronage to the unfit and other undesirables, promotions based on backbiting and secret informations, distribution of orders for goods among relatives and party-members,—these

are some of the normal features of municipalized urbanism. The milieu is vitiated from top to bottom by deliberate injustice and palpable inequality.[134]

Sarkar thus remained slightly 'above' democracy, and it did not matter very much whether the model was Soviet or bourgeois. What mattered were the needs that democracy served. This explains Sarkar's apparently naïve comments about a *digvijaya* of democracy at the very moment when totalitarian regimes had demonstrated what they were capable of. Since democracy was not inherently good or synonymous with freedom, Sarkar could speak of unsavoury regimes as being 'democratic'. The *digvijaya* was actually of a particular kind of state: what Sarkar, in 1939, called 'demo-despotocracy', or the modern regime in which democracy and despotism had fused.[135]

Demo-despotocracy is not merely a clumsy neologism. It indicates a particular, normative, relationship between the state and the individual.[136] Sarkar derived the idea in part from William Hocking, who argued that the coercive state was a necessity of both reason and collective will: 'as we demand reason, we must employ force'.[137] Unsurprisingly, Sarkar's critique of democracy veers repeatedly into the discourse of the clinic.[138] Democracy generates individuality in the form of the expert-administrator, located within modern bureaucracies, who investigates and compels:

> What is needed in India is more officials . . . per 1000 inhabitants. A very large number of these officials must be technical experts, i.e., men and women trained in medicine, hygiene, farming, veterinary science, nursing, midwifery, pedagogics, vocational guidance, and such other items.[139]

Simultaneously, it generates individuality-in-sickness and problems of governmentality, which the clinical state must confront and solve.[140] The process is related to a notion of passive consent that amounts to a tautology of democracy: if there is a state, there must be popular consent, and implicitly, individual consent. 'An undemocratic state is as great a contradiction in terms as an undespotic state', Sarkar wrote in 1939, meaning that the absence of active resistance was tantamount to consent.[141] A basic aspect of his 'pluralism' is that power is diffused in the people and a plurality of institutions. Thus, even in authoritarian regimes, power is democratic in its nature and distribution, and fascism and colonialism can be described as triumphs of democracy. British India was a demo-despotocracy, Sarkar argued, not because of dyarchy or the Government of India Act of 1935, but because the ruled had given their passive consent:

> The transfer of power [to the East India Company] was an act of free choice on the part of the Indian peoples or princes. The people, the folk, the *demos* did not revolt against the transfer.[142]

The idea that Indians had passively consented to a 'transfer of power' is a bizarre reading of the history of colonisation. The notion of passive consent, however, made it possible for Sarkar not only to accept the authoritarian state as democratic and legitimate, but also to be blind to signs of resistance, and indeed, to see small acts of resistance as illegitimate or insignificant.

Sarkar's idea of demo-despotocracy is thus both perceptive and naïve. It is perceptive because it acknowledges the coercive fabric of modernity. Sarkar understood that modern states are controlled by bureaucratic, economic and 'knowledge' elites, and that when the individual citizen is 'necessarily' coerced, the source of the coercion is not quite external: '[I]n the dictatorships of today the people is not something antithetical to the ruler, the authority, but a part and parcel of a synthetic organization which combines the two in one solid structure'.[143] He was writing at a time when the FDR administration in America had already raised the spectre of bureaucratic-political overreach within liberal democracy.[144] But it is naïve because he misunderstood the relationship between the totalitarian state and the people. Noting that modern despots like Hitler and Stalin acknowledged popular sovereignty like any democrat, he concluded that 'the despots are incessantly being kept alive to the interests of the masses and dominated by their demands at every step'.[145] By presuming a relationship of identity and even equality between the state and the governed, he missed the element of terror in totalitarian governance. He remained unwilling to recognise totalitarianism as something different from garden-variety authoritarianism, not to mention the New Deal.

Moreover, Sarkar's effectively reactionary vision of class and justice—the fact that he was 'for' the working class but 'against' an overturning of the relations of production—ensured that he saw the managerial state as a social necessity.[146] The different classes, with their different needs, would continue to exist in his free society, and while a 'friendly alliance' between the classes was desirable, the potential for class conflict would remain. That conflict could be managed by the state, which would 'take all social classes along with it in its march towards progress'.[147] The state and citizenship (a super-need) would be the glue holding the classes together. This led Sarkar close to fascism. About Mussolini's Italy, he wrote in 1932:

> [A]nti-socialists from Bismarck to Mussolini . . . have only rejected the vices of socialism and absorbed its virtues. While the vice consists in class antagonism virtue consists in increase in the freedom of the people, better employment facilities etc.[148]

Whose freedom did Sarkar have in mind? The answer can only be the individual who has already accepted the contingencies of docile citizenship.

The prioritisation of docility in the thinking of an intellectual committed to productive conflict and *matsyanyaya* is both jarring and understandable. The state resolves the contradictions: it behaves according to the principles of *matsyanyaya* beyond its borders, but eradicates (or rather, manages) fish-rule within its territory. In the process, it becomes the biggest fish of all. Bholanath Bandyopadhyay has remarked that for Sarkar, the state was only a means to an end that can be described as freedom.[149] Bandyopadhyay is, I think, wrong in this assessment. Freedom, for Sarkar, came to be inseparable from an accommodation reached with the state, i.e., identification with the state to the extent that being swallowed by the 'fish' changed nothing. The state produced the individual, nationhood and freedom, but in the process, it produced itself and its needs. It was thus an end in itself: troubling but necessary.

Only an Indian state would enable the individual Indian to emerge fully. It should come as no surprise that Sarkar's vision of that state is explicitly pedagogical: 'Statesmen should . . . recognize that the very institution of the republic is itself a powerful educative agency, and that actual participation in the work of government is an integral schooling for democracy'.[150] Here, Sarkar is obviously aligned with a broad principle of republican governmentality, as well as a colonial-nationalist governmentality in which the vanguard (contingently 'the people') perceives that it has jumped the gun by embracing a political form with which the masses (potentially 'the people') have not identified themselves. In those circumstances, democracy itself becomes a disciplining agency. That function structures Sarkar's view not only of the Indian future but also of the past. It shapes, for instance, his praise of Shivaji, who he cast not as an anti-Muslim icon but as a sign of the individual's will-to-statehood, 'political engineering', and democracy in the service of the Indian nation: a mobiliser of 'low-class' Marathas.[151] Democracy, like individuality, *must* serve the nation; it is useless if it does not.[152]

By the 1920s, when Sarkar wrote about Shivaji, the democratic nation-state he imagined for India was resolutely 'pluralistic'. He articulated his 'world-conquering' nationhood in multiple Indian languages, including Urdu.[153] Nevertheless, pluralism had to be managed and promoted by the state or quasi-state institutions: to be *ordered*, not dispersed, along federal lines.[154] That discrepancy reflects an uncertainty within Sarkar's vision of a free Indian state: for all the declarations that unity is unimportant, there is a persistent fear of fragmentation, and a corresponding obsession with control. Sarkar's appreciation of linguistic-literary 'academies' in India, and his desire for a 'National Culture Department,' reflect his desire for the bureaucratic organisation of culture, bringing to India a feature of the European nation-state. He could praise Bankim's 'love of individuality' and call for the organised management of culture in the same breath: if he saw a conflict, it was either to be accepted wryly as the price of freedom, or more enthusiastically as 'creative disequilibrium'.[155] Bankim became Nietzsche, Krishna became Zarathustra (and alternately, August Comte), and Zarathustra/Comte became a New Deal bureaucrat in Sarkar's imagination of the highly developed state of *ressentiment*, compensating for and helping—not overtly restraining—the underdeveloped citizen.[156]

Germans and Others

Sarkar admired Germany, in part, because he believed that Bismarck's anti-revolutionary calculations had nevertheless ensured a measure of dignity for all: the old, the sick, workers, children, and even the dead.[157] Through interventionist schemes of education/mistrification and social welfare, the German state had produced civilisation in its fullest sense. Moreover, Sarkar's reputation and self-perception as a 'world scholar' matured during his long stints in Germany in the 1920s and early 1930s, when Berlin was a vital node in a network of Indian 'internationalists'.[158] It is not surprising that Sarkar would be fascinated by the evolution of the German state between the world wars. In the long clash between the communists and the right in the Reichstag, he reserved greater disdain for the former, seeing them as a Soviet fifth column.[159] He also absorbed the German resentment of the Treaty of Versailles. '[M]illions of Germans have been given away in subjection to neighbours on all sides', he observed in 1926, establishing a political bond between Germany and India.[160] (A personal factor is embedded here: Sarkar's wife Ida was a Bavarian-Austrian from South Tyrol, a German-speaking region 'given away' to Italy. She perceived her situation as a kind of statelessness, and Sarkar's sympathy belied his conviction that ethnicity must adapt to borders.)[161] He remained a cautious observer, noting that the 'German atmosphere today is fearfully nationalistic'.[162] But in his Indian eyes, Germany became a colonised country. 'The treatment of the Saar is an object lesson in colonialism', he wrote, and 1918 was a 'catastrophe . . . which has kept [the] German mentality in chains'. Nevertheless, the 'German mind seems to be united in the decision that submission is no longer to play any part in Germany's relations with the nations that have overpowered her in arms'.[163] He described anti-occupation sentiment in the Ruhr in the familiar language of *satyagraha* and *hartal*s.

Despite the apparent spinelessness of the Wirth administration in Weimar (which had brought on 'the nadir of national depression'),[164] Germany still mattered to Indian nationalists. In Bengal specifically, Sartori has suggested, 'Germany' was a long-standing trope of cultural classicism, philosophical idealism and technological modernity, resonant with the emerging national Self.[165] A common enmity with Britain meant taking pleasure in German wars.[166] It was not a universal response; it did not compare in fervour or significance with the pro-Japanese sentiment in Bengal after 1905. Precisely when Sarkar wrote his early paeans to Germany, Sukumar Ray lampooned German militarism as well as its Indian echo in a poem about a belligerent Bengali everyman: *Saat German, Jagai eka / Tobuo Jagai larey*[167] ('Seven Germans versus Jagai alone / But Jagai fights on'). For Sarkar, however, belligerence was no laughing matter: it was a necessary element of citizenship and the state of war. Moreover, he had made an intellectual investment in German history, knowledge and the language itself.[168] Germany came to represent for him an alternative whiteness not so much to be followed blindly as to be recognised as a modern relative: a city cousin.

Sarkar saw no sharp disruption between the Weimar Republic and the Third Reich: a perspective that is apparently grotesque but not without substance. It is somewhat aligned with the thinking of Gellately, who has pointed out continuities in the policing apparatus across the temporal boundary of 1933: early Nazi round-ups of communists were based on police lists prepared in the Weimar period.[169] Also like Gellately, Sarkar highlighted the continuation of democratic politics and plebiscites, suggesting that the Nazi regime and the German population engaged in an intimate dance in which public opinion was assiduously courted by the leadership.[170] Unlike Gellately, however, Sarkar refused to see the Nazi state as something other than 'normal', or to question the nature of that normalcy. In 1936, when the Nürnberg laws had already been deployed, he continued to regard Germany as proof that late-comers to modernity and power could 'catch up with the go-aheads'.[171] In 1935, 1936 and again in 1938, he described the Nazi Winter Relief programme as a model of progressive state action on the one hand and social service on the other,[172] missing—or rather, ignoring—not only the compulsion that went into such programmes, but the wider context of intimidation and force in which they were embedded.[173]

The refusal to react sharply to the Nazis was a common Indian non-response, having to do with distance, proximity in time and more pressing calamities close to home. Gandhi's remark that the Jews should have committed mass suicide is perhaps the best-known example of this failure, Faisal Devji's intervention notwithstanding.[174] (Nehru, pointedly shopping at Jewish-owned stores, was an exception.) In general, Indians who took an anti-Nazi stance did so because of communist or pro-Soviet affiliations, and not because of a particular revulsion towards the Reich.[175] For Sarkar, however, ignorance and indifference were not the major factors. Modern Germany represented for him, first and foremost, a Romantic annex of the liberal and materialist models of community. As such, it had room for the Titanic individuality of his world-makers. Second, situated as he was in the Weimar Republic, Sarkar saw a society convulsed in struggles to determine the relationship between the classes; between the home and the world; and between the people, the state and the charismatic leader. Alert to the unloved nature of the Weimar regime and the isolation of its cultural elite, he saw a process in which threats to democracy were intertwined with populism and 'creative disequilibrium'.[176] Consequently, he remained relatively well-disposed towards the Third Reich, perceiving it not only as an understandable reaction to the excesses of Versailles, but also as the emergence of a new form of democracy. Finally, Sarkar—with his insistent sense of history—linked the German turmoil of the interwar years to a deeper past that was not too deep, going back only to the Napoleonic wars. Even when Germany invaded the Soviet Union, it remained an exciting model of a relatively young, self-regenerating, 'world-conquering' race.[177]

What was happening in Germany was, Sarkar believed, the climax of a statecraft in which the state had become fully race-conscious. This race-consciousness was not so much a matter of discrimination as of 'scientific' governance: maintaining control over conflict, regulating the processes of assimilation, and all the while pursuing the best interests of the political community of the people. As Sarkar became increasingly interested in the science of population, he embraced the biological aspects of the pursuit: medical models of nationhood, degeneracy, purification, hygiene, healthy and sick organisms, parasites in the body politic, blood and cells.[178] The malaise of the Indian political condition became evident in the Indian body, which slouched, yawned, fidgeted, and sniffed its ear-wax when it should be erect and still like Europeans.[179] Biopower and its rhetoric were productive necessities: they produced a people, a public and a body-language of citizenship and power. Hygiene, thus, was 'an important item in the pedagogics of the great powers'.[180] Nazi Germany became a shining example of progress-through-public-health: a polity realising itself through 'that revolutionary zeal, that faith that can move mountains'.[181] The limits of the polity were located in individual citizens and non-citizens who were either normal or deviant.[182] Exclusion and objectification of the individual thus became a basic, natural, but also progressive/scientific, function of the nation-state.

In Germany, Sarkar wrote admiringly as the Nazi programmes of sterilisation and murder of 'defective individuals' neared their completion,[183] the state had become alert to 'the need of preventing hereditarily diseased progeny as an item in human welfare', and 'criminality is being correlated with biological degeneracy in a definite measure'.[184] He grasped the coercive aspect of eugenics and state medicine, but accepted it, divorcing population-making from racism and attaching it to the reasonable needs of the state. He had followed American eugenics—programmes for the sterilisation of 'degenerates', criminals, the 'feeble-minded', and racial and sexual 'deviants'—with approval.[185] 'In every human society the demands of eugenistic prophylaxis are as indispensable as those of individual prophylaxis against contagious diseases', he declared.[186] Because eugenics and social hygiene were supposedly preventive rather than reactive, he saw them as better—not just more effective, but also more progressive—than conventional rituals of medicine and law. 'The problems of progress . . . are directly and indirectly associated with eugenic topics', he noted.[187]

It would be unfair to ignore that Sarkar's enthusiasm for 'the Hitler state' became tempered over the 1930s, or to say that he approved of the murder of Gypsies and Jews.[188] He observed that Jews were unrepresentative of European civilisation, akin to Untouchables, but warned Indian travellers not to absorb European anti-Semitism.[189] In Calcutta during the war, he and his wife gathered a circle of German Jews around themselves; 'we don't recognize caste', he remarked.[190] He believed that the Nazis had 'flagrantly misused' the anthropology of Aryan identity in their persecution of European Jews,[191] and observed: 'It is questionable if the latest variety of race-prejudice embodied in the anti-Jewish legislation of the Nazi regime is capable of [preventing sex between Aryans and Jews]'.[192] That, however, was the extent of his critique of Nazi policy. He accepted its implications at two levels. At one, Sarkar sought a clear-eyed reconciliation between what he saw and what he wanted. The world was increasingly democratic, democracy was not synonymous with justice, and the democratic state would produce its victims. Unlike Gandhi, he offered no alternatives, except the vague hope that in India the inclusion of the proletariat in parliamentary democracy would produce a less destructive state.

At another level, the powerful interventionist state was the necessary price of freedom in a world of *matsyanyaya*, especially for Germany and India, which, unlike the United States (US) and Britain, had recent histories of ignominy and no oceans to protect them. (This is a corollary of the Haushofer—Mackinder theory of a conflict between 'land people' and 'sea people'.[193]) The German state was also glamorous, much like Japan not in spite of the havoc it had wreaked, but because of the havoc it could wreak. Havoc, as Leni Riefenstahl and Goebbels both understood, was inseparable from the aesthetics of order. In this vision of a national-security state looking inwards as well as outwards, communities and individuals that held themselves aloof were nuisances at best, or at worst, foreign bodies in an insistently biological model of the nation/state. That model was not a new consideration in Indian nationalist thought. Bhudeb had rejected it in 1892, calling it beguiling but superficial.[194] Sarkar, a secular man, was more receptive. He adopted it from F.W. Coker, and as usual, found a niche for it in the *Sukraniti*. The dissectible animal-state was too attractively modern to forego.[195] What for Bhudeb was a foreclosure of moral agency was for Sarkar an invitation to clinical intervention. But the model complicated his insistence that the state is a voluntary and artificial association in which minorities are normatively protected by the contract itself.[196]

Sarkar had no illusions about German racism, and he was conscious of the colonial presumptions of German policy towards the non-European world.[197] He cannot have been ignorant of the near-extermination of the Herero.[198] Nevertheless, in the aftermath of Versailles, he not only saw Germany as not-Britain and anti-Britain, he slipped into equating the condition of not having colonies with being not colonialist and even anti-colonialist. The enthusiasm was partly pragmatic. *The Futurism of Young Asia* was written with European readers in mind, and the promotion of a common political mission for Germans and Indians was among other things a work of propaganda: an attempt to turn Germany from one political-historical side to the other. Sarkar attempted to seduce his readers with benefits: there was money for Germany in Indian freedom, a grander historical role and new avenues of competition. The generous sprinkling of German phrases, references to German history and literature, and invocations of familiar aspirations ('a place in the sun') served the same function.

Sarkar's engagement with Germany was not driven entirely by strategy and bio-politics. It had also to do with his refusal to relinquish a nationhood of 'spirit': he sought, after all, not just to produce Indian states, but to awaken an eternal but dormant nation through the agency of the state. In that sense, Sarkar's worldview, like that of Nehru and to some extent Rabindranath,[199] was both prosaic and Romantic: 'If [we examine] the beginnings of Romanticism in Europe we need only understand that Romanticism has been a native Asian commodity as well', he wrote.[200] Sarkar's enthusiasm for Romantic art and literature in India reflected his conviction that history alone was not sufficient 'proof' of nationhood.[201] Romance was essential; the vanguard must breathe life into the bones of history. Romantic culture was a particularly valuable form of propaganda, because when effective it became realised as the fabric of nationhood. To paraphrase Anderson, the imagined community is not an unreal community.[202]

What Germany had demonstrated in the years between 1870 and 1918 is that while the Romantic produces nationhood, the imperatives of nationhood generate realism in culture, which further 'realises' the Romantic nation. Ostensibly realist literature could serve Romantic purposes, Sarkar wrote about his contemporary Bengali writers, placing them alongside their German forbears:

> All these writers embody in a subtle manner the discontent which prevails among the intelligentsia with the existing state of things. Each one is looking forward to the new social order, a new art-philosophy, a new *Weltanschauung*. The poets are . . . dealing not so much with the Romantic past as with the living present. One noticeable trait of the current poetry is the importance given to the different cities and villages, landscapes and historic sites as themes for imaginative portraiture.[203]

In India, as in Germany, realism in descriptions and depictions of landscape literally formed a national terrain, which was simultaneously populated by national bodies.[204] About Dwijendralal Roy's nationalist anthem *Dhane dhanye pushpe bhara* (1905), Sarkar enthused in 1922: 'A chauvinism such as this is as elemental as human blood'.[205] Bringing Bankim into the picture, Sarkar added:

> The romantic handling of the past with a leavening of nationalism, love of individuality, and the sturdy spirit of freedom which characterize the robber-stories of Goethe and Schiller and the romances of Scott has certainly been a common feature of India's modern fiction, saturated with idealism as it is. In this sense *Vande Mataram* is the message not only of [*Anandamath*] but virtually of every literary work, novel or drama, conceived in the background of mediaeval history.[206]

Sarkar was not always kind to Bankim, who he considered too burdened by history to be a prophet of freedom, and eventually accused of propagating pseudo-scientific nonsense about geography and race.[207] But in Sarkar's analysis of *Anandamath*, colonial India is a 'Rousseauesque state of nature'.[208] That jab at the British allowed him to posit a similarity between the forest-and-bandit Romanticism of German nationalist mythology, and the historical wilderness of India, which generated its own bandits. Bandits were simultaneously primitive and desirable; they were undoubtedly individuals, but they had to be brought into a docile relationship with the state, without eradicating either their romance or their existence in the real world of politics and statecraft. Here Sarkar referenced the work of the Gujarati writer G.M. Tripathi, who had taken it upon himself to update Puranic literature: '[W]e are presented with a realistic picture of men and manners such as the eighteen *Puranas* . . . have perpetuated for us'. Sarkar's praise indicates his investment in a Romanticism that recovered the Indian past in a form that is actually more prosaic than poetic, stripped of flying chariots but not of the fantasy of nationhood, and thus usable as history.

The best art, Sarkar was convinced, also taught a form of citizenship that was much needed in India. About R.G. Gadkari's anti-alcohol melodrama *Ekach Pyala*, he approvingly commented: 'This drama is a study in the drink-evil and domestic misery,—and can always be used in the propaganda for prohibitionism'.[209] Unlike Gandhi, who also sought to banish the 'drink-evil', Sarkar imagined a politics of moral instruction that also expanded the domain of the state. He was not hostile to 'art for art's sake', but it was a decadent luxury in a historical moment when the romance of the state—which was inseparable from the science of the state—had to be taught continuously. The lessons pointed in the general direction of a citizenry that was both Enlightened and Romantic:

> Nationalism is being fed by historical and antiquarian researches. Young India is almost repeating in this manner the 'Romantic movement' initiated by Herder and his associates in Germany ... But the compositions, although sometimes rising to poetic levels, are, like Voltaire's ... *La Henriade*, nothing but versified history planned with the avowed object of teaching a political and moral lesson to Young India.[210]

Clearly, the vanguard was not immune to the need for lessons. There is in Sarkar a persistent vacillation: on the one hand he is the Machiavellian who sees justice as secondary even if that is unfortunate, but on the other he is driven by *ressentiment*, in which the perception of injustice is everything and must be taught.

Since postcolonial nationhood is never complete but a process of endless yearning and discrimination, the Romantic and the realistic (not to mention the didactic) must exist simultaneously and continuously within national culture. It is difficult to find a better model for this cultural work than Germany before 1945.[211] Romanticism offered Indian nationalists a way around liberal roadblocks like literacy, world-historical consciousness, rationality, punctuality,[212] whiteness and manhood. But Germany provided a European-pedigreed ideological receptacle for what would otherwise have to be dismissed as backwardness or superstition. Just as importantly, it came with its own exemptions and caveats. The nation-state Sarkar imagined could not be excessively Romantic: the power and instruments that the colonial nationalist sought were also coldly rational, and Sarkar insisted that 'Hindu politics was, as a rule, thoroughly ... Lutheran and Machiavellian'.[213] The combination of Luther and Machiavelli would have to constitute the basic framework of the Indian state in the present and the future. Other icons—Nietzsche, Herder, even Mill— could be delegated to the realm of culture. Culture (and the international theatre of war) was where creative disequilibrium and turmoil was desirable, boundaries were identified only to be transgressed, and where the state did a portion of its work. The state itself, on the other hand, exemplified the arrest and control of turmoil: its crystallisation as the political purpose that defined the race/nation/people.

A dual conception of peoplehood is perceptible here, with the state functioning as an instrument of bifurcation. On the one hand, the people are a body politic, with a political agenda; on the other, they are a culture, with formless and inherent desires (for revenge, conquest, and so on). The former is the rational, organised, unified, restraining level of the state, and the latter is the space of freedom that the state sustains and is sustained by. The separation, however, was particularly fragile, not only because the state was tasked with restraint, and freedom designated as the incubator of fascism (as in Weimar), but also because the political agenda that the state pursued was itself constituted by febrile desires inseparable from Sarkar's understanding of race. Sarkar's construction of nationhood was, in general, premised on similarity and universality: all the world was Romantic, with the possible exception of England.[214] That very dynamic lent a hidden urgency to considerations of 'blood' and Volk. The nation-state was both above race (understood as nothing less than desire itself), and a creature of race. Like Prussia since Frederick, Sarkar's Indian state might or might not be liberal in its rhetoric and institutions, but it had to be consciously self-interested, and it had to be 'militarist'.[215] Simultaneously, it had to be democratic: militarism—the desire for Dreadnoughts and conquest—was vested in 'the people'.[216]

In Germany after 1918, Sarkar saw a quasi-organic community that was cosmopolitan in its political partnerships: racialised but potentially aligned with a wider world of oppressed races, like his own 'Hindu race'. Perceptively but also naively, he wrote:

> Notwithstanding the problem of German irredentas and other minorities, Europe is certainly going to be a far more decent place to live in than before. The nationality principle ... has at length been thoroughly realized. The slogan, 'one language, one state,' may not in all cases turn out to be as convenient in practice as it is mystical and Romantic in theory. But, on

the whole, the anachronism of race-submergence and race-autocracy that prevailed on a large scale between the Jura and the Urals and between the Baltic and the Black Seas has been rung [sic] out once [and] forever.[217]

This is not simply a failure of prescience. It follows from his belief that the state has to acknowledge race and nationhood in order to do its work. The major problem of the pre-war years, he suggests, was that multi-racial, multilingual and multi-national states did nothing to control or mould their human material. Now that races/languages/nations are out in the open domain of statecraft, he expects freedom, which becomes synonymous with not only conflict, but also coercion.

We must ask, at this juncture, how Sarkar could have misread Germany to the extent that he apparently did. He only partially realised the point that Arendt would make about colonialism and totalitarianism: that totalitarianism has its roots in colonialism, which resurfaced as an intra-European dynamic of expansionism.[218] (Peukert has made a similar connection between colonial warfare and Nazi governance.[219]) To recapitulate Arendt's well-known thesis, colonial rule in the late nineteenth century—particularly in Africa—produced a form of deviant statecraft, based on terror and operated by what she called 'the mob': the greedy, racist and power-hungry flotsam and jetsam of liberal-European civilisation. In the interwar period, the mob surfaced within Europe itself, entering into an alliance with capital, overwhelming the weakened nation-states, and opening the door for totalitarianism. This new statecraft subjected Europeans to forms of racism, terror and aggression that hitherto only colonial subjects had experienced.[220]

Arendt's thesis of totalitarianism has drawn its share of criticism, much of it justified.[221] The distinction she made between the rational, liberal nationalism of the Victorian era and the racist, aggressive identity-politics of the interwar years ignored the extent to which reason was implicated in racism, and racist violence normative, not deviant, in nineteenth-century Europe. Greenfeld—and to some extent, Hobsbawm—has made a similar mistake, as have others who distinguish between patriotism (good, Western) and nationalism (bad, Eastern).[222] Also, the 'special' nature of the totalitarian state, which was axiomatic for Arendt, has not held up well. Gellately has implicitly questioned the most basic foundation of Arendt's work, which is the all-obliterating function of terror in the Nazi state. The Third Reich resorted to the widespread use of terror only in its final years,

Gellately has argued, suggesting that until the outbreak of war in 1939, consent and coercion in Germany were so intimately interwoven as to be almost indistinguishable. Terror affected only a small minority who were excluded from the nation.[223]

Since Sarkar did not see democracy as being incompatible with tyranny and regarded it simply as a situation in which the state derived (or claimed to derive) its legitimacy from the popular will, it is not necessary to criticise him for seeing the Third Reich as a further democratisation of the Kaiser's Reich and Weimar. It is more useful to unpack his position for its implications for liberal democracy in a multi-ethnic state. His stances on nationalism and the nation-state can be indistinguishable from Arendt's: both saw nationhood as being primarily a consciousness of shared political interests and historical trajectories. Their nation-state was both limited[224] and inclusive.[225] Sarkar, however, would have disputed the glowing liberal credentials Arendt awarded the European states of the pre-Great-War period: he was too conscious of their colonial depredations, and unwilling to make a convenient separation between 'bad' colonials and 'good' metropolitans.[226] (That, in fact, was a part of his quarrel with Congressmen like Lajpat Rai.[227])

The other misalignment between Sarkar and Arendt is on the subject of terror. Here, personal locations are significant. As a Jewish refugee from Nazi Germany and an activist who worked with Holocaust survivors, Arendt emphasised terror. Terror affected her personally. Sarkar, on the other hand, stood outside the circle of terror. Not only did he leave Germany before 1933, as an Indian bird of passage nesting in the relative safety of the ivory tower, he had been external to the racial politics of Weimar. Moreover, his sense of self was clear: he was an Indian and a Hindu. He walked consistently in the shoes of the majority, even if by default. Not surprisingly, he did not see—or was not overly troubled by—the other side of Gellately's argument: that terror was deployed both systematically and randomly against those defined as external to the nation and the state.[228] The veteran of National Education was unwilling or unable to see the mutually constitutive connections that Peukert has made between education, terror and faith in a future based on the 'scientific temperament'.[229] Likewise, even in 1941, Sarkar did not fully grasp the implications of Fritzsche's point that terror, produced by the violent exclusion of various minorities, underlay the German-majoritarian experience of individuality as well as community.[230]

The selective use of terror in Germany was a basic strategy of constituting insiders and outsiders, and thus, of not only marking the limits of the nation-state, but also travelling continuously towards those limits (without ever arriving).[231] What Sarkar saw, however, was a swirl of political activism followed by the emergence of a regime alive to the need to define those limits. Like most Germans, he saw coercion as remote, and, to use a term pregnant with meaning in German history, as normal. His interwar Germany was a normal nation-state, becoming increasingly democratic and clarifying its boundaries. As Maja Zehfuss and other scholars of modern Germany have pointed out, 'normalcy'—both during and after the war—was a bourgeois strategy of seeing and acknowledging, or rather, not seeing and not acknowledging.[232] Those who saw and acknowledged indiscriminately were relegated to the margins of respectability. For the rest, the terror of those pushed beyond the limits was not so much invisible as beyond the scope of the nationally directed imagination. If we recall the 'state of exception', this is indeed a specific, modern form of normalcy: the 'ordinary' democratic state preserves pockets of extraordinary coercion, in which ordinary expectations of visibility, rights, laws and justice do not apply, and which contain those excluded from normal citizenship.[233] It is important to remember that the state of exception is *not* exceptional: Agamben's point is that it is a norm of the modern state, and that Nazi Germany—with its redundancy of coercive bureaucracies, privileging of the police over the judiciary, obsession with deviance, overlaps of legality and illegality, and empire of camps—was the prototype. (The wider applicability of the prototype can also be glimpsed in Foucault's thoughts on the prison, in spite of Agamben's attempt to distinguish between the prison and the camp: one legal, the other extra-legal.)[234]

With its heavy emphasis on *Realpolitik*, Sarkar's vision of the nation-state, even the democratic, bourgeois nation-state, is pockmarked with 'camps' or states of exception. These are essential to making *matsyanyaya* vanish within the borders of the state, so that the state can appear to be above the struggles of society even as it wades into conflicts, interprets, takes sides, crushes some and enables others. It is here that the managerial state does its most critical managing, continuously defining its borders through race-making and citizen-making, which, for Sarkar, were not only connected (race being largely about political purpose), but also never-ending (since political purposes change historically). He, under the circumstances, could not disavow terror when it came to the functioning of the nation-state: it was normal.

Nazi Germany could then represent a democracy of terror, in which people saw participation in state terror (by informing the police on Jews, communists, homosexuals, and each other) as a normal civic duty and good citizenship. Terror was itself constituted by this participation, since mass participation made terror a highly diffused form of public knowledge.[235] This is a dynamic that Arendt did not fully grasp: she isolated the mob from the public, and terror from civic life. She could not come to terms, therefore, with Reinhard Heydrich's remark that Warsaw-type ghettoes were unnecessary in Germany because Jews marked by the yellow star would be 'under the watchful eye of the entire population'.[236] Sarkar, with his ambivalence about democracy, was better positioned to see this panoptic dynamic, although it might be said that his notion of passive consent is too limited to account fully for the logistics of terror-in-democracy. (Orwell, in *Nineteen Eighty-Four*, came closer than either of them.) Peukert, who also relies on 'passive consent' in his analysis of Nazi Germany, is relatively sensitive to the internal fractures and complexities of passivity/consent, including its interpenetration with both dissent and terror.[237] Terror was not simply obliterative as Arendt argued, but productive, and its major product was race. As Sarkar saw it, however, race was neither definitively connected to terror, nor inherently a problem of modern society. It became a problem when the state failed to manage it effectively at the level of the individual. Hence, 'the sooner... inequalities are accepted as first postulates, the better for human welfare'.[238]

American Examples

Ironically, it was when Sarkar looked at the US that he saw the clearest evidence of the failure, or rather, the partial success, of race-management. He spoke as an indignant Asian observer of anti-Asian discrimination. 'The men, women and children of the Orient have been postulated to be "unassimilable" before anything was attempted in the way of "adopting", naturalizing, assimilating or amalgamating them', he complained after his first visit to America: when it came to Asian immigrants, the American state had failed to respond scientifically, reasonably and responsibly to a standard problem of governance.[239] In an era when the individual (constructed as a deviant or an experiment) had become the primary lens with which the scientist approached the population, the state that was irrational about race failed simultaneously at making individuals and managing populations. (That, indeed, was a criticism that Sarkar's Indian contemporaries often directed at the colonial state.[240])

Referring to eastern- and southern-European immigration to America, Sarkar described the challenges of race-making:

> To America . . . these guests from Europe can contribute their primitive midwifery, agricultural superstition, high birthrate, and rural ignorance. In American cities they make their presence felt by room and clothing that reek with odors of cooking and filth. Like Bohemians in the country towns of Texas they displace old American settlers from their favorite habitations. Jews are shunned by 'Americans' because they eat garlic; Greeks because they are mere barbers and dirty shoe-shiners; Italian fruiterers because they come from Naples, the city of rogues and rascals, or because their women are notorious for cat-like fecundity; and Slavs because . . . of their rows and fights when they get drunk on pay-day or when celebrating a wedding or christening. These are the people that are easily duped by the 'managers' of political parties, and materially help lowering the level of public life. They can be handled without trouble by employers and captains of industry, and are pounced upon by capitalists to be exploited as tools in the breaking of strikes. They spoil the labor market and demoralize the proletariat class. In all respects they represent an enormous drag . . . upon America's advance in civilization, democracy, and efficiency. Such is the raw material that the United States is eager to wash, scrape, chisel and polish, to manufacture 100 percent Americans of.[241]

This is a turning back upon whiteness of a major racist argument against self-government for non-whites. Sarkar borrows wholesale the nativist discourse of immigration in America. This is, at one level, a matter of indifference. He is not interested in being fair to Russian or Italian immigrants; he wants to score polemical points for Asia. At another level, it indicates his alignment with the insider-group within the nation-state: Theodore Roosevelt's WASP-American constituency, with its investment in a particular model of citizenship and statecraft that normalizes *acting upon* those on the margins of the state. It is, essentially, what Partha Chatterjee characterised as the discourse of policy, operating in grimy pockets within the republic constituted by a discourse of rights.[242]

Sarkar liked America.[243] The apparent dynamism of race and republican rhetoric in Progressive-era America—the coexistence of democracy, diversity, and elaborate discourses of exclusion and inclusion, self-congratulation and panic in a *new* global centre—made it an irresistible chemistry-experiment-in-progress. America was more fluid and 'energised' than even Germany, and vitally relevant to races that perceived themselves as ill-managed. In this regard, Sarkar grasped—intuitively and implicitly—the workings of 'internal colonialism', race-making and subject-formation in governmentality. By acting forcefully upon 'misfit' communities, the state effectively dissolves those communities (or renders them purely private), opening up their members to an individuated and unmediated relationship with the state itself. The US had established that relationship with whites but not with Asians, and thus compromised its own modernity:

> On the one hand, the patriotic Americanizers have been trying their best to abolish the 'race lines,' the 'little Italys,' the 'little Hungarys,' etc., from their cities. They are thoroughly convinced, as they should be, that these 'immigrant colonies,' these clan-communities, these towns within towns, present the greatest hindrances to Americanization. On the other hand, American behavior towards Asian immigrants has been the very antithesis of this attitude.[244]

Such a compromise could not fail to appear anomalous to Sarkar. The fear of 'towns within towns' reflects the modern citizen's fear of the ghetto, or, in present-day Indian paranoia, the 'mini-Pakistan' that competes with, diminishes and subverts the nation-state.[245] Sarkar was sympathetic to this fear. He recognised, like Heydrich, that the ghetto is the shadow of the state of exception: a zone apart, signifying of the limits of the state. Unlike the concentration camp or secret prison, the ghetto is a reflection of the weakness of the state, although like camps and black sites, it underlines exclusion from the state.[246] There can be little doubt that between the ghetto and the camp, Sarkar preferred the latter. The eradication of the ghetto was a liberation: as an Asian and a colonised man ghettoised in the world in general and the West in particular, he wanted to break out, *into the state*. It was a remarkable double movement, coming from the right (towards the unitary nation-state) and also from the left (towards racial desegregation). In a related double movement, the modern state that Sarkar saw—either in America or in Germany—acted upon the individual either positively (by 'scraping' him into a proper citizen) or negatively (by enabling or joining the mob). The state normatively broke *into the ghetto*, dissolving it and transforming portions of it into zones of exception.

That, ironically, was inseparable from the inclusion of the individual in the body politic. Sarkar's analysis of anti-Asian discrimination in America reflected his faith in the state as the major political agent of the racial-national community and its individual members. It was the primary source of dignity; it was also the main source of humiliation. As an Indian in the albinocracy, Sarkar was not oblivious to non-state agency in racism: discrimination by private clubs, mob violence, and so on. But it was the forbearance and support of the state that gave mobs and private agencies their power. Without the state, the mob was nothing: power flowed from the state to the mob, rather than from the mob to the state as Arendt argued.[247] An effective state was necessarily discriminating, but unlike the mob, it discriminated intelligently. Sarkar was incensed that American immigration officers treated Indian merchants, scholars and travellers as if they were labourers. Similarly, assaults on 'high-class' Japanese were outrageous, and photographing Chinese students in forced undress was unacceptable not least because they were students, not coolies.[248] Conscious that the technology of governmentality could become an instrument of racial violence, but invested in the basic principles of governmentality, Sarkar compensated by restricting his criticism to situations where the wrong class had been targeted: to errors brought on by racism. His idea of race-management becomes clearer here. He wanted a revision of racial categories based on social-scientific studies of 'assimilability', and the recalibration of the apparatus of race/governance: the suppression of mob violence, the elimination of crude rituals of humiliation, the teaching of individuality to the clannish, the teaching of science and reason to those who wore the uniform of the state.[249]

Colonial rule in India, for Sarkar, was the perpetuation of an untutored and untutoring regime. It was, he wrote (in an attack on Lajpat Rai's failure to react more strongly to the Jallianwallabagh massacre), a 'degrading plight which none but a race that is hastening towards annihilation can tolerate in shame and silence'.[250] Freedom was therapeutic, even clinical. There is here an echo of Gobineau (and Spengler), but Sarkar had mugged Gobineau. He had reinterpreted racial death to mean the death of a *people,* meaning a political community. But this reinterpretation of Gobineau was also deployed by European fascism.[251] Ironically, for all his determination to maintain a world-historical distance from savages, Sarkar slipped into identifying with them; simultaneously, he slipped into identifying with the state that can either assimilate or eradicate the misfits, and that can differentiate 'scientifically' between citizens and aliens, the desirable and the dying.

We are returned to Sarkar's proximity to Agamben's camp-world: the bypassing of formal procedures generates *Homo Sacer,* or 'bare man', produced by the state as an individual through exclusion rather than inclusion.[252] The inmate of the camp, it turns out, is the shadow of the free individual. Both are 'progressive'. The Congress left too had its enthusiasts of eugenics.[253] Sarkar's India needed camps and clinics. Historical 'lag' not only made them necessary, but was constituted by their absence: 'These items of social insurance are entirely unknown as yet throughout India and constitute but another index to her socio-cultural lag in the field of *étatisme* and government compulsion'.[254] Sarkar condemned the 'sterilisation' of widows not only because it destroyed the wholeness of individual women, but also because it displaced on to a backward society—and a backward, ignorant patriarchal family—a legitimate function of the modern state, incidentally lowering birth-rates and depriving the state of an essential resource.[255] (Sarkar admired Ataturk's compulsory-marriage policies.[256]) The imaginary of freedom was inseparable from winning that function—literally, the right to sterilise (or to enforce procreation) and thus 'make' the individual—back from the community.

Conclusion

Regarding Satishchandra Roy, who died in 1904 at the age of 21, leaving behind a small body of writing on the bold, joyful, magnanimous spirit of youth, Sarkar remarked during his Weimar period:

> It is in the school of terror and defiance that the world's youth loves to grow up. Roy's message will be appreciated by the younger representatives of all races and ages and will have a special significance to the leaders of the *Jugend-Bewegung* in present-day Germany.[257]

Sarkar was not praising a uniquely Indian youthfulness; rather, he wanted to claim, for the Indian nation, what was admirable in any modern race. But that universal was actually specific to European Romantic nationalism, with its echoes of Nietzsche on the one hand, and the right-wing youth movements on the other. The youthfulness that Sarkar admired was related to contemporary Indian literary fantasies of children who transcended geography,[258] but it was closer in 'spirit' to what Karl Schenzinger evoked in the 1932 propaganda novel *Der Hitlerjunge Quex*, in which the adolescent Heini, secretly watching a Hitler Youth gathering, is simultaneously terrified, thrilled and awakened to his German identity.[259] Heini's awakening is virtually orgasmic. Sarkar's 'futurism', too, was among other things a deployment of the erotics of youth: the pleasure of the individual becoming self-aware by joining something larger and purposeful. Intended to serve the national state of 'terror and defiance', it was *like* Hitler's conceptualisation of youth as 'the defiant embodiment of masculine strength',[260] but it represented India at a historical moment when modernity was simultaneously exciting, alarming and elusive. The most powerful sign of this modernity was a state that, although 'artificial', might recuperate and recast nature: *Indian* nature. Politics itself became a matter of identifying and reclaiming one's 'blood' and 'ganglionic cells'.[261] It was, however, a blood that the state produced and policed: eugenics and public health were necessary instruments in 'the promotion of human development and national regeneration'.[262] Even home-cooked food became subject to expert regulation.[263] Blood of this nature tied India to Germany not in any crude sense of Aryan kinship, but in the sense of violent transformations, interventions and exclusions surrounding the individual and the body.

Sarkar's vision of individuality as an aspect of freedom that is dangerous, dormant or useless until it is harnessed by the state, and of the state itself as a quasi-individual, leads us inexorably to his fascination with military-authoritarian models of the state. His admiration of German nationalism and the Third Reich should be seen in the light of his desire for a state that could realise the Romantic by scientifically managing its human material. His understanding of the role of the state in a democracy held the door open for spaces of coercion within what was otherwise 'freedom'. In the German case, he indirectly endorsed the racist construction of the Volk with all its exclusions: blood became both Romantic and clinical, and the reification of 'the people' by the state became inseparable from freedom.

Thus, while there is no reason to doubt the sincerity of Sarkar's preference for 'pluralism' and democracy over 'patriot-despots', uncomfortable questions remain about what happens when pluralism and the purposeful nation-state come into conflict. Not only does his adversarial outlook on 'traditional' structures of community and family (reimagined as ghettos) generate issues of dissent and compulsion, there is a persistent tension in his thinking between a nation of 'one people' engaged in the single-minded pursuit of the national interest, and a liberal citizenry that thrives on the absence or overthrow of the despot. It may be suggested that the first preference has to do with policy and the latter with culture and knowledge, but that separation is unsatisfactory, since for Sarkar culture and the state are closely linked phenomena, both being aspects of nationhood. Sarkar's suggestion that culture is a space of unrestrained collaboration, distinct from the space of nationhood and citizenship, becomes untenable when culture must also serve the state.[264] This is, therefore, an area of oscillation, where the liberal is faced with the possibility or necessity of curtailing his liberalism.

One aspect of this tendency to accommodate the illiberal is that freedom is consistently defined in racial terms: to be free means to be free from racial oppression, even if it means being subjected to 'compulsion' or unconstitutional governance. Also, when race is primarily a matter of political purpose within the boundaries of the state, the foreigner (and legitimate partner in cosmopolitanism) is normatively external. Wilful 'internal aliens'—such as separatist minorities—become not foreigners, but racial deviants. Injustice against such deviants has no moral content: it is clinically necessary. It is useful to review Sarkar's rebuke to Sun Yat-Sen for having described Manchus as foreigners in China.[265] Inclusiveness, which is tied to the ability to differentiate correctly between real and false foreignness, is not necessarily benign. It not only allows the state to determine who does not belong, it subsumes various reluctant people within the nation, relegating them to invisible corners. The line between the homeland and the internment camp remains a fine one, especially when external enemies can be identified as a threat that justifies the coercion of internal troublemakers. Racialised freedom goes hand in hand with racialised oppression.

Notes

1 *VT*, p. 483.
2 Sarkar, 'Demo-Despotocracy and Freedom', p. 104.
3 Home Department, Political Branch, 1938, F.79/38, F. 137/38.
4 Flora, 'Benoy Kumar Sarkar', pp. 374–75, 386–88.
5 Flora, *Benoy Kumar Sarkar and Italy*, p. 93.
6 Ibid., pp. 74–88.
7 Hughes, *Consciousness and Society*, pp. 213–29.
8 Flora, *Benoy Kumar Sarkar and Italy*, pp. 88–89.
9 *PB*, pp. 306–7, 322.
10 *PB*, pp. 146–49. On Italy, see J.M. Roberts, *A General History of Europe 1880–1945*. London: Longman, 1970, pp. 427–36.
11 *PB*, pp. 83–87, 102–11.
12 *NBGP*, pp. 79–80; *DIWP*, pp. 161–63.

13 *NBGP*, pp. 222-23. Sarkar's lags could be calculated with remarkable precision: Bengal apparently lagged behind Germany by 12 years in optimising its population. *PPS-1905*, p. 177.
14 *VT*, p. 122.
15 J.S. Mill, 'Considerations on Representative Government', in *Three Essays*. Oxford: Oxford University Press, 1975, p. 15.
16 Bernard Yack, 'Nationalism, Popular Sovereignty and the Liberal Democratic State', in T.V. Paul, G. Ikenberry and John Hall (eds), *The Nation-State in Question*. Princeton: Princeton University Press, 2003, pp. 31-39
17 Gay, *The Cultivation of Hatred*, pp. 211-12; Eric Wolf, *Europe and the People Without History*. Berkeley: University of California Press, 1997, pp. 11-12; *PPS-1905*, pp. 257-76.
18 Benoy Kumar Sarkar, 'Progress Planning as a Scheme of Emancipation on Five Fronts', in Banesvar Dass (ed.), *The Social and Economic Ideas of Benoy Sarkar*. Calcutta: Chuckervertty Chatterjee and Co., 1939, pp. 196-98.
19 *PB*, p. 316.
20 Bayly, *Recovering Liberties*, p. 283.
21 *BSB-II*, p. 802.
22 *VT*, pp. 330-31.
23 Ibid., 218-19.
24 Cohn, *Colonialism and Its Forms of Knowledge*, p. 8; Arjun Appadurai, 'Number in the Colonial Imagination', in Carol Breckenridge and Peter van der Veer (eds), *Orientalism and the Postcolonial Predicament*. Philadelphia: University of Pennsylvania Press, 1993, p. 333.
25 Spengler, *The Decline of the West*, vol. II, pp. 99-103.
26 Gordon, *Brothers Against the Raj*, pp. 96-138; Ravinder Kumar, 'From *Swaraj* to *Purna Swaraj*', in D.A. Low (ed.), *Congress and the Raj*. Delhi: Arnold-Heinemann, 1977, pp. 77-108.
27 *VT*, pp. 117-35.
28 *NBGP*, pp. 192, 257-60.
29 Mark Harrison, *Public Health in British India: Anglo-Indian Preventive Medicine 1859-1914*. Cambridge: Cambridge University Press, 1994, pp. 166-201.
30 *VT*, pp. 432-35, 453-56.
31 Ibid., pp. 120-35, 435, 456-66, 484.
32 Ibid., pp. 450, 537-41.
33 Dipesh Chakrabarty, *Provincializing Europe*, pp. 215-16.
34 Anand Yang (ed.), *Crime and Criminality in British India*. Tucson: University of Arizona Press, 1985, pp. 108-27, 140-63; Dirks, *Castes of Mind*, pp. 43-60; Beteille, *Society and Politics in India*, pp. 4-14.
35 *DIWP*, p. 120.
36 David Arnold, *Colonizing the Body: State Medicine and Epidemic Disease in Nineteenth-Century India*. Delhi: Oxford University Press, 1993, pp. 200-39; James H. Mills, *Madness, Cannabis and Colonialism: The Native-Only Lunatic Asylums of British India*. Houndmills: Macmillan, 2000, pp. 103-28.

37 *VT*, p. 529.
38 *SP*, pp. 58–59; *PPS-1905*, pp. 35–36.
39 *NBGP*, pp. 75–76; Flora, *Benoy Kumar Sarkar and Italy*, p. 73.
40 Smith, *The Ideological Origins of Nazi Imperialism*, pp. 19, 25.
41 *DIWP*, p. 134.
42 Vishvajit Pandya, *In the Forest: Visual and Material Worlds of Andamanese History*. Lanham: University Press of America, 2009, pp. 203–317; Sen, *Savagery and Colonialism in the Indian Ocean*.
43 *VT*, p. 479.
44 *PPS-1905*, p. 323.
45 *DIWP*, pp. 114–15.
46 Ibid., pp. 101, 145, 153.
47 Greenfeld, *Nationalism*, pp. 371–85.
48 Detlev Peukert, *Inside Nazi Germany: Conformity, Opposition and Racism in Everyday Life*. New Haven: Yale University Press, 1982, pp. 67–85, 110.
49 Bandyopadhyay, 'The Political Ideas of Benoy Kumar Sarkar', p. 13.
50 *SHHM*, p. 68.
51 Sanjam Ahluwalia, *Reproductive Restraints: Birth Control in India 1877-1947*. Urbana: University of Illinois Press, 2008, pp. 1–2, 23.
52 Partha Chatterjee, 'The Nationalist Resolution of the Women' Question', in Kumkum Sangari and Sudesh Vaid (eds), *Recasting Women: Essays in Colonial History*. New Brunswick: Rutgers University Press, 1990, pp. 233–53.
53 *NBGP*, p. 436.
54 Sumit Sarkar, *Writing Social History*, p. 181.
55 Home Department, Political Branch, March 1909, 10–11A (23). On colonialist and nationalist patriarchies, see Tanika Sarkar, *Hindu Wife, Hindu Nation*, pp. 191–225.
56 *VT*, pp. 136–60.
57 Ibid., p. 141.
58 *LHL*, pp. i–iv; *BSB-I*, p. 23.
59 *VT*, p. 141; Ferdinand Tönnies, *Community and Civil Society*. Cambridge: Cambridge University Press, 2001, pp. 211–43.
60 Hobsbawm, *The Age of Empire*, pp. 199–200.
61 *VT*, pp. 142, 163–64, 273; *BSB-I*, pp. 243–46.
62 *VT*, pp. 144–45.
63 Tönnies, *Community and Civil Society*, pp. 17–21; *VT*, p. 2.
64 *BSB-II*, pp. 552–54, 598–600.
65 *VT*, pp. 144–45.
66 Bhudeb Mukhopadhyay, *Prabandha Samagra*, pp. 130–34; Hobsbawm, *The Age of Empire*, p. 206.
67 *VT*, p. 448.
68 Ibid., pp. 285–86.
69 Ibid., pp. 310–14.

A Romance of the State 175

70 Ibid., pp. 236–39, 646–64; *BSB-II*, pp. 559–60.
71 See Sen, 'Anarchies of Youth', 'A Juvenile Periphery'.
72 *VT*, p. 255; *PPS-1905*, p. 74; Sen, *Colonial Childhoods*, pp. 76–77.
73 John Springhall, *Youth, Empire and Society: British Youth Movements, 1883-1940*. London: Croom Helm, 1977, pp. 110–20.
74 Peukert, *Inside Nazi Germany*, p. 149.
75 Sen, *Colonial Childhoods*, pp. 72–85, 125–40.
76 *VT*, p. 97.
77 Panchcowri Banerji, 'The Student Community—The Trouble in the Presidency and Bangabasi Colleges', *Nayak*, 14 March 1916.
78 Peter Heehs, *The Bomb in Bengal: The Rise of Revolutionary Terrorism in India 1900-1910*. Delhi: Oxford University Press, 1993, pp. 136–42, 166–69; Sen, 'Anarchies of Youth'.
79 Springhall, *Youth, Empire and Society*, pp. 121–29.
80 See Heinrich Böll, *What's to Become of the Boy, or Something to do with Books*. New York: Alfred Knopf, 1984, pp. 7–49; Peukert, *Inside Nazi Germany*, pp. 145–74.
81 *ISE*, pp. 33–46.
82 Sen, *Colonial Childhoods*, pp. 143–86; Sumitendranath Tagore, *Santiniketan Chena Achena*. Calcutta: Mitra & Ghosh, 2003, pp. 3–15; David Lelyveld, *Aligarh's First Generation: Muslim Solidarity in British India*. Delhi: Oxford University Press, 1996, pp. 13, 262.
83 The instincts were identified as sex, wealth, fame, and creativity. *VT*, pp. 79–81.
84 *PPS-1905*, p. 318.
85 *FYA*, p. 150; Friedrich Nietzsche, 'The Twilight of the Idols', in Walter Kaufmann (ed.), *The Portable Nietzsche*. New York: Penguin, 1976, p. 463.
86 *VT*, p. 158; *BSB-II*, p. 532.
87 Sen, *Traces of Empire*, pp. 19–36.
88 Obeyesekere, *The Apotheosis of Captain Cook*, pp. 8–22.
89 *FYA*, pp. 180–81.
90 *VT*, pp. 636–37; *DIWP*, pp. 99–111.
91 *FYA*, p. 267.
92 Ibid., p. 284.
93 Ibid., p. 268.
94 Ibid., p. 207.
95 See Sarkar's review of Vilfredo Pareto's *Mind and Society* (New York: Harcourt, 1935) in *Calcutta Review*, April 1939.
96 *FYA*, p. 275.
97 Ibid., pp. 296–97.
98 *PB*, p. 22.
99 *FYA*, p. 300.
100 Ibid., pp. 299–300.

176   *A Romance of the State*

101 *PB*, p. vii.
102 M.K., Gandhi, *Hind Swaraj*. Cambridge: Cambridge University Press, 1997.
103 Kaviraj, *The Unhappy Consciousness*, pp. 72–106.
104 *PPS-1905*, pp. 91–92.
105 Minault, *The Khilafat Movement*, pp. 50–60.
106 Bipan Chandra, *India's Struggle for Independence*. Delhi: Penguin, 1989, pp. 323–42.
107 Gordon, *Brothers Against the Raj*, pp. 491–547.
108 *FYA*, pp. 6–7.
109 *SHHM*, pp. 8–12; Bandyopadhyay, 'The Political Ideas of Benoy Kumar Sarkar', pp. 26–27.
110 *PB*, pp. 63–66.
111 Ibid., pp. 92, 98–99.
112 *PPS-1905*, p. 318.
113 *VT*, pp. 610–13; Benoy Kumar Sarkar, *E Kaler Dhan Daulat O Arthashastra* (henceforth, *EKDDA*). Calcutta: N.M. Ray Chowdhury & Co., 1935, pp. 340–41.
114 *DIWP*, pp. 103–4.
115 *PBHS-II*, p. 37.
116 *PPS-1905*, pp. 301–2.
117 Giorgio Agamben, *State of Exception*. Chicago: University of Chicago Press, 2005, p. 2; *Homo Sacer: Sovereign Power and Bare Life*. Stanford: Stanford University Press, 1995, pp. 9, 25.
118 Robert Gellately, *Backing Hitler: Consent and Coercion in Nazi Germany*. Oxford: Oxford University Press, 2002, p. 20.
119 *BSB-I*, pp. 139, 181–203, 210–15; Sumit Sarkar, *The Swadeshi Movement*, p. 131.
120 Hughes, *Consciousness and Society*, pp. 270–71.
121 *PB*, pp. 151, 163, 301.
122 *PB*, pp. 154–55, 166–67; Douglas Peers, *India Under Colonial Rule 1700–1885*. London: Routledge, 2006, p. 78.
123 *PB*, pp. 201–3.
124 *NBGP*, pp. 34–36, 382–83.
125 *PBHS-II*, pp. 43–45.
126 Ibid., p. 49.
127 Sarkar, 'Demo-Despotocracy and Freedom'.
128 *VT*, p. 608.
129 Hughes, *Consciousness and Society*, p. 221.
130 *NBGP*, pp. 121–24.
131 Hobsbawm, *The Age of Empire*, pp. 88, 273–74.
132 *VT*, p. 524.
133 Ibid.
134 *DIWP*, p. 70.
135 Sarkar, 'Demo-Despotocracy and Freedom'.

136 *PPS-1905*, p. 301.
137 Ibid., pp. 21–23; William Hocking, *Man and the State*. New Haven: Yale University Press, 1926.
138 *VT*, pp. 274–78, 444, 451–52.
139 Ibid., pp. 484–85.
140 Foucault, *Discipline and Punish*, p. 170.
141 Sarkar, 'Demo-Despotocracy and Freedom'.
142 Ibid.
143 Benoy Kumar Sarkar, 'The People and the State in Neo-Democracy', *Calcutta Review*, July 1936.
144 See William Leuchtenberg, *The FDR Years: On Roosevelt and his Legacy*. New York: Columbia University Press, 1995, pp. 76–100.
145 Benoy Kumar Sarkar, 'Stalin as the Manager of Leninism' (Part II), *Calcutta Review*, September 1938.
146 Paul Gottfried, *After Liberalism: Mass Democracy in the Managerial State*. Princeton: Princeton University Press, 2001, pp. 49–71.
147 *EKDDA*, pp. 356–57.
148 Benoy Kumar Sarkar, *Italyte Bar Kayek* (henceforth, *IBK*). Calcutta: City Library, 1932, p. 282.
149 Bandyopadhyay, The Political Ideas of Benoy Kumar Sarkar, p. 93.
150 *FYA*, pp. 201–3.
151 *PB*, pp. 22–23.
152 *PPS-1905*, pp. 277–78.
153 *FYA*, p. 300.
154 Sarkar's own anxiety about linguistic federation qualified his endorsement of R.N. Gilchrist's approval of federalism in the colonial administration. Ibid., p. 347.
155 Ibid., p. 316.
156 Benoy Kumar Sarkar, 'The Acceptable and the Unacceptable in Bankim's Social Philosophy', *Calcutta Review*, August 1938, pp. 113–31; *BSB-II*, p. 523.
157 *NBGP*, pp. 50–59.
158 Kris Manjapra, 'Communist Internationalism and Transcolonial Recognition', in Sugata Bose and Kris Manjapra (eds), *Cosmopolitan Thought Zones: South Asia and the Global Circulation of Ideas*. New York: Palgrave, 2010, pp. 166, 171.
159 *PB*, pp. 124–37.
160 Ibid., p. 9.
161 Ida Sarkar, *My Life with Prof. Benoy Kumar Sarkar*. Calcutta: Pramathanath Paul, 1977, p. 21; *NBGP*, pp. 380–81.
162 *PB*, p. 58.
163 Ibid., pp. 25–29, 33.
164 *PB*, pp. 25–29.

165 Sartori, 'Beyond Culture-Contact and Colonial Discourse', pp. 68–84.
166 Chaudhuri, *The Autobiography of an Unknown Indian*, p. 324.
167 Sukumar Ray, *Samagra Shishu-Sahitya*. Calcutta: Ananda Publishers, 1975, p. 3.
168 *BSB-I*, pp. 88–89.
169 Gellately, *Backing Hitler*, pp. 18–19.
170 Ibid., pp. 257–59; Sarkar, 'Demo-Despotocracy and Freedom', p. 104.
171 *SP*, pp. 85, 90, 127.
172 Benoy Kumar Sarkar, 'Winter Relief in Germany', *Calcutta Review*, May 1935; 'German Winter Relief as a Form of Social Relief', *Calcutta Review*, June 1936; 'Winter Relief in Germany', *Calcutta Review*, July 1938.
173 Peukert, *Inside Nazi Germany*, p. 49.
174 Devji has recast Gandhi's position on the Jewish predicament as a coherent moral response to fascism, which Gandhi regarded as unexceptional. Arguably, however, the crisis in Gandhian ideology that Devji identifies with Hiroshima came earlier, with the German application of industrial methods to murder. Neither the nature nor the scale of the problem was evident to Gandhi; it could not have been, given the information available to him. It is debatable whether thinly informed comments and opinions should be counted as ideology, and it is unsurprising that those who looked to Gandhi for a politically *or* morally sustainable response to the Holocaust were disappointed. Faisal Devji, *The Impossible Indian*. Cambridge: Harvard University Press, 2012, pp. 119–50; George Orwell, 'Reflections on Gandhi', in *A Collection of Essays*. Orlando: Harcourt, 1953, pp. 171–79; Dennis Dalton, *Gandhi's Power: Non-Violence in Action*. Delhi: Oxford University Press, 1999, p. 137.
175 Samaren Roy, *M.N. Roy: A Political Biography*. Hyderabad: Orient Longman, 1997, p. 117.
176 Gay, *Weimar Culture*, pp. 1–22.
177 *VT*, pp. 562–63; *NBGP*, pp. 37–38.
178 Gellately, *Backing Hitler*, pp. 40–41.
179 *NBGP*, p. 220.
180 *CP*, p. 59.Ann Stoler, *Race and the Education of Desire*. Durham: Duke University Press, 1995, pp. 19-54.
181 *VT*, p. 479.
182 Gellately, *Backing Hitler*, pp. 90–91.
183 Peukert, *Inside Nazi Germany*, p. 206; Gellately, *Backing Hitler*, pp. 100–106.
184 *VT*, p. 444; *PPS-1905*, pp. 81, 188–90.
185 *VT*, pp. 158, 441; *PPS-1905*, pp. 88–90; See Nancy Ordover, *American Eugenics: Race, Queer Anatomy and the Science of Nationalism*. Minneapolis: University of Minnesota Press, 2003, pp. 3–50; A.M. Stern, *Eugenic Nation: Faults and Frontiers of Better Breeding in Modern America*. Berkeley: University of California Press, 2005, pp. 150–81.
186 *VT*, pp. 442–43.

187 Ibid., p. 436.
188 Benoy Kumar Sarkar, *The Hitler State: A Landmark in the Political, Economic and Social Remaking of the German People* (henceforth, *THS*). Lahore: Civil and Military Gazette, 1934.
189 *NBGP*, pp. 416-17.
190 *BSB-II*, p. 779.
191 *PPS-1905*, pp. 76-77.
192 *VT*, p. 260.
193 Haushofer, *Geopolitics of the Pacific Ocean*, p. vi.
194 Mukhopadhyay, *Samajik Prabandha*, pp. 48-49.
195 *PBHS-II*, pp. 34-39; F.W. Coker, *Organismic Theories of the State*. Charleston: Bibliobazaar, 2009, p. 16.
196 *PB*, pp. 11-15, 18.
197 *FYA*, p. 36.
198 Gay, *The Cultivation of Hatred*, pp. 88-89.
199 On the prosaic and the poetic in Rabindranath, see Amit Chaudhuri, 'Triumphant Eclecticism', *Outlook*, 7 May 2006. http://www.outlookindia.com/article.aspx?231146 (accessed 2 November 2014).
200 *FYA*, pp. 111-13.
201 Ibid., pp. 308-14.
202 Anderson, *Imagined Communities*, p. 6.
203 *FYA*, pp. 308-10.
204 See William Vaughan, *German Romantic Painting*, pp. 7-24.
205 *FYA*, pp. 308-14.
206 Ibid., p. 316.
207 Sarkar, 'The Acceptable and the Unacceptable in Bankim's Social Philosophy'; *PPS-1905*, pp. 95-99, 112.
208 *FYA*, p. 316.
209 Ibid., pp. 308-19.
210 Ibid., pp. 309-10.
211 Greenfeld, *Nationalism*, p. 352.
212 Sumit Sarkar, *Beyond Nationalist Frames*, pp. 10-37.
213 *FYA*, p. 272.
214 'Previous to the advent of the recent phase of civilization', Sarkar wrote, 'East and West ran parallel, nay, identical in the "point of view", in "genius", in "spirit"'. Ibid., pp. 119-20.
215 *FYA*, pp. 15-16, 272. On Prussian/German militarism, see V.R. Berghahn, *Germany and the Approach of War in 1914*. New York: St. Martin's, 1973, pp. 14-17, 25-42; Erich Eyck, *Bismarck and the German Empire*. London: Norton, 1968, pp. 45-52.
216 *FYA*, p. 272.
217 Ibid., p. 30.
218 Arendt, *The Origins of Totalitarianism*, pp. 107, 152, 157; *VT*, pp. 556-57.

219 Peukert, *Inside Nazi Germany*, p. 45.
220 Arendt, *The Origins of Totalitarianism*, pp. 138–39, 157.
221 See Richard King and Dan Stone (eds), *Hannah Arendt and the Uses of History: Imperialism, Nation, Race, and Genocide*. New York: Berghahn, 2007, pp. 1–15.
222 Greenfeld, *Nationalism*, pp. 1–26; Hobsbawm, *The Age of Empire*, pp. 86–111, 143.
223 Gellately, *Backing Hitler*, pp. 2–7.
224 Anderson, *Imagined Communities*, p. 7.
225 Arendt, *The Origins of Totalitarianism*, pp. 50, 125, 226–27, 234–36.
226 *VT*, p. 546.
227 *FYA*, pp. 342–43.
228 Gellately, *Backing Hitler*, pp. 2–3.
229 Peukert, *Inside Nazi Germany*, pp. 247–48.
230 Fritzsche, *Germans into Nazis*, pp. 8–9.
231 Peukert, *Inside Nazi Germany*, p. 245.
232 Peukert, *Inside Nazi Germany*, p. 76; Zehfuss, *Wounds of Memory*, pp. 6, 153; Schissler, *The Miracle Years*, pp. 237–65, 359–75; Sen, *Traces of Empire*, pp. 119–47.
233 Agamben, *State of Exception*, pp. 2–4, 23.
234 Foucault, *Discipline and Punish*, pp. 257–92; Agamben, *Homo Sacer*, pp. 20, 166–67.
235 Gellately, *Backing Hitler*, pp. 136–41.
236 Quoted in Gellately, p. 129.
237 Peukert, *Inside Nazi Germany*, pp. 46, 49–66.
238 *VT*, p. 572.
239 *FYA*, pp. 49–50.
240 Sen, *Colonial Childhoods*, pp. 20–33.
241 *FYA*, p. 57.
242 Chatterjee, *Wages of Freedom*, p. 16.
243 *BSB-II*, pp. 725, 776.
244 *FYA*, p. 59.
245 See Jaffrelot, *Hindu Nationalism*, pp. 233–54.
246 I do not mean specific ghettos, like occupied Warsaw. Warsaw was both a ghetto and a camp. But even Warsaw was sufficiently threatening to the Germans that they felt compelled to invade and eliminate it, hauling off the survivors to places that were more unambiguously camps. Christopher Browning, *Ordinary Men: Reserve Police Battalion 101 and the Final Solution in Poland*. New York: Harper, 1992, pp. 131, 136–37.
247 Arendt, *The Origins of Totalitarianism*, pp. 336–37.
248 *FYA*, pp. 62–63; *PB*, p. 181.
249 *FYA*, p. 58.
250 Ibid., p. 343.

251 Arendt, *The Origins of Totalitarianism*, pp. 172–73.
252 Agamben, *Homo Sacer*, pp. 9, 25.
253 Zachariah, 'Rethinking (the Absence of) Fascism in India', p. 192.
254 VT, p. 480.
255 See Benoy Kumar Sarkar, 'Comparative Birth, Death and Growth Rates', *Journal of the Indian Medical Association*, May 1932.
256 The other side of this coin was his worry about overpopulation in Japan. PB, pp. 209, 313–14.
257 FYA, p. 314.
258 Sen, 'A Juvenile Periphery'.
259 Excerpted in Peukert, *Inside Nazi Germany*, pp. 36–37.
260 The phrase is Hitler's. Quoted in ibid., p. 147.
261 FYA, pp. 168–69.
262 VT, p. 451.
263 BSB-II, p. 536.
264 PB, p. 8.
265 FYA, p. 187.

Conclusion

Sudipta Kaviraj has observed that Indian reactions to the modern state historically fell into two broad patterns: one, associated with Bhudeb Mukhopadhyay and Gandhi, which regarded the state (in its colonial manifestation) as a pathological invasion of a naturally self-governing society, and another, identified with Nehru, which identified the state with the possibility of freedom and justice. The latter has triumphed, Kaviraj argued, even with the subaltern classes beyond the reach of Mill.[1] It is revealing, then, to look at Sarkar's response to the death of the Indian nationalist who was most unlike him: Gandhi. Following the assassination, he tried again to position himself relative to a figure he had long recoiled from but also found irresistible.[2] In an essay in a special issue of the *Calcutta Review*, Sarkar chose to straddle two categories of responses to Gandhi: 'non-Gandhi' and 'anti-Gandhi'.[3] He was clearly distraught; there was no joy or post-mortem vituperation. There was misappropriation, but it was not especially cynical. It was a version of the liberal-nationalist response to Gandhi that has marked the major discourse of independent India, indicating the ideological and political limits of the nation-state that emerged in 1947.

Sarkar's ambivalence towards the Congress-led politics of decolonisation was of long standing.[4] He would attack Gandhi as a peddler of exotica that contributed to the marginalisation of modern India,[5] and Congressmen indiscriminately as effete defenders of the status quo, but never to the extent that he could not turn around and align himself with them.[6] In February of 1948, Gandhi remained a captain of *vishwashakti*. In fact, Sarkar went further and turned Gandhi into the leader of a no-quarter-given race war: 'the General of the Indian War against the whites in South Africa' and beyond, and the formulator of a 'cult of hatred'.[7] Such praise—in which Sarkar drew, astonishingly, upon Anglo-Indian criticism of Gandhi after Pearl Harbor[8]—was a serious distortion of Gandhi's career, but it fit Sarkar's own vision of history as a race war. In this war, Sarkar saw Gandhi as a brilliant strategist who had finally 'surrendered', not so much to his enemies as to his partners. Pointing to Gandhi's apparent acceptance of violence in the 1940s, Sarkar saw either cleverness or capitulation, and responded to both with the satisfaction of having been right all along. He did not feel the tragedy that enveloped Gandhi in his final years, although he was aware of it.[9]

What mattered was incorporating Gandhi partly as friend and partly as foil. When Sarkar summarised the Gandhian agenda, he highlighted the overlaps between Gandhi's vision of a just society and his own modernity, especially the convergences of health, pedagogy and independence. In doing so, he re-exported Gandhi as a universal phenomenon: a globally recognised commodity that connected India to the world. His undeniable stature in world-history compensated for the particulars of his politics. Also, like Joseph Alter, Sarkar grasped that Gandhi was not so much anti-scientific as counter-scientific.[10] That counter-modern vision, Sarkar argued, was compatible with the general run of Indian nationalism since Rammohun Roy. He could piggy-back on Gandhi into histories that were already hegemonic.

Sarkar hijacked Gandhi's economic vision for his own conviction that rapid industrialisation would not happen in India. Since there would be few factories, there might as well be khadi: a Gandhian ideology was rendered as a default position or a 'realistic' imaginary of freedom. In the process, Sarkar buried the ideological problems of mistrification, or the notion that industrial democracy could be founded upon an individuality-of-the-mechanic. The conjunction of 'industrial' and 'democratic' was postponed: like national unity, it would have to await the success of a pedagogical governance that was both ambitious and timid. Sarkar's democracy of the everyman-mechanic was not unlike Gandhi's democracy of the commune, in which 'managers' also knew how to clean latrines, spin cloth and make shoes. Both men were invested in the modern citizen-individual. But their individuals served very different models of the state. The implications of that difference for the dignity of the individual—for freedom from violence and all the rights associated with that freedom—could not be allowed to show too clearly in Sarkar's eulogy.

In spite of his characterisation of ahimsa as race-war, Sarkar remained allergic to any philosophy that separated India from the world of armed statecraft. So he continued to distance himself from Gandhi even as he admired him. His Gandhi was a ruralist, insufficiently alert to the actual sites of historical transformation. He noted Gandhi's social and political work at the local level, but ignored the network of global contacts he had built up. Not being of a state-to-state nature, those were irrelevant to the conviction—shared by Sarkar,

Savarkar, Taraknath Das, Bose, and assorted 'travelling revolutionaries'—that anti-colonial politics required foreign diplomatic support or at least a shadow state with shadow diplomats. Sarkar disingenuously labelled Gandhi a 'stay-at-home': the opposite of the globally engaged cosmopolitan.[11] For him, cosmopolitanism and vanguardism, which were inseparable, involved not just the desire to walk around foreign capitals, but the desire to do so with a nationalist swagger, in military uniform or a diplomat's suit, even if these had to be procured by the imagination. Gandhi seemed reluctant to wear clothes at all. When Sarkar grumbled that Gandhi had reinforced a naked-fakir test that Indian leaders had to pass, he came close to an Orientalist-Churchillian conception of the masses that frustrated any vanguard—colonial or national—and threatened to drag them down to their own level of primitiveness.

The naked-fakir test is one that Sarkar could never hope to pass, and he was transparently bitter about it even as he admired those who had evidently passed.[12] But Gandhi, having 'passed' in two senses of the term, was especially vulnerable to the accusation of fraud, and ironically, of failure. Whenever Sarkar could not deny Gandhi's international engagement, he called it a 'surrender' to 'Non-Gandhi and Anti-Gandhi' or to *vishwashakti* itself. 'Fakir-hood' was a counter-qualification in *vishwashakti*: the wrong kind of renunciation. Ironically, Sarkar and Jinnah were in agreement here. Nehru came closer to the ideal of renunciation, because of that intangible something—empathy—that Sarkar could not conjure up within his expertise. Bose was more troubling: a man whose considerable capacity for empathy and renunciation almost compensated for the fondness for uniforms, but ultimately disintegrated in the horrific murders of INA deserters.[13] Sarkar's commitment to liberal democracy was firmer than that of Bose, who came closer to being a fascist.[14] But it is nevertheless significant that of all contemporary Indian politicians, Sarkar found Bose the most inspiring. It cannot be put down to Bengali parochialism alone. It also has to do with a basic acceptance of the principle of shooting 'deserters' in Takeyama's cave.

In addition to being anti-cosmopolitan, Sarkar's Gandhi had committed four other sins, not all consistent with the first: being a communist fellow-traveller, an Axis-hater, a 'monist' who ignored the plurality of historical forces, and a Bose-hating Bengaliphobe. Sarkar dated the second offence to 1933, a significant year for both Germany and Japan.[15] He was not simply defending Germany and Japan; he was defending them in a particular mode of militarist-authoritarian statecraft. Gandhi, apparently, only belatedly recognised the value of this mode and changed his mind about Japan.[16] By describing Gandhi after 1942 as an undeclared ally of Bose and Japan while being a declared enemy, and a violent man with mystical delusions of non-violence, Sarkar simultaneously condemned Gandhi (as a hypocrite and a loser) and redeemed him (as a pragmatic patriot). He was, of course, right about Gandhi's ambiguous position on non-violence in 1942–43, just as he was right that the Congress under Gandhi was able to use the terrorists as a foil.[17] But his polemic ensured that Sarkar—and Bose— came out as the stronger-willed, clearer-eyed and more consistent leader. Sarkar was willing to see Gandhi as a genius who transcended a historical situation in which the means of violence were unavailable. But he remained unwilling to take non-violence seriously as an ideology in its own right. An unarmed state was a contradiction in terms, and he could not acknowledge that Gandhi may have thought through an alternative.

For all the anxiety that he generated among his Indian observers, Sarkar was not an outlier. His views constitute a determinedly liberal streak within the major channel of Indian nationalism, in which the citizen—contemplating both Ramakrishna and Vivekananda— simultaneously declares 'to each his own', and demands order and organisation.[18] They indicate how capacious that channel was (and remains); they indicate also the limits of that capacity to accommodate. There are two obvious limitations, which are sides of the same coin. The modern, reforming nation-state has had to accommodate its illiberal material: not only the masses, but also the reactionary and incompletely regenerated elites, who articulated anti-modern and 'localist' preferences at every turn. That is a basic aspect of the 'passive revolution', or the compromised and postponed transformation of Indian society.[19] At the same time, it has had to accommodate the liberals who chafed at the constraints within which they were compelled to operate, and whose frustration inevitably took the form of fantasies of violence. It indicates an unresolvable dilemma of the pedagogical state and 'Third-World' nationhood. That unresolvable quality does not mean non-viability. But it does mean living with visible holes in the ideology of the modern Self-in-the-state, which generate in the nationalist a sense of incompleteness and inadequacy: an endless desire for 'conquest', 'virility' and executions, from which Gandhi was arguably free.

Notes

1. Kaviraj, *Trajectories of the Indian State*, pp. 40–77.
2. *FYA*, pp. 175, 301–2, 345.
3. Benoy Kumar Sarkar, 'Gandhi, Non-Gandhi, and Anti-Gandhi in the Pattern of Indian Ideologies', *Calcutta Review* (Special Issue), February 1948.
4. *FYA*, pp. 342, 349–52.
5. *NBGP*, pp. 386–89.
6. *FYA*, pp. 344–45.
7. *DIWP*, pp. 97–98.
8. Arthur Moore, editorial, *The Statesman*, 8 December 1941.
9. Bhashyam Kasturi, *Walking Alone: Gandhi and India's Partition*. Delhi: Vision Books, 1999, pp. 7–19.
10. Alter, *Gandhi's Body*, pp. 3–27.
11. *DIWP*, pp. 99–101.
12. Ibid., pp. 105–06.
13. Peter Fay, *The Forgotten Army*, pp. 345–47 ; Gordon, 515
14. Bose, *India's Struggle*, pp. 312–14; Gordon, *Brothers Against the Raj*, pp. 235, 288, 520–21.
15. *DIWP*, pp. 99–101.
16. Ibid., pp. 97–98.
17. Chandra, *India's Struggle for Independence*, pp. 457–72.
18. *PPS-1905*, p. 237.
19. Chatterjee, *Nationalist Thought and the Colonial World*, pp. 131–66.

Selected Bibliography

Primary Sources: Works by Benoy Kumar Sarkar

Books

Aesthetics of Young India. Calcutta: Kar, Majumder, 1927 (AYI).
The Beginning of Hindu Culture as World Power. Commercial Press: Shanghai, 1916 (BHCWP).
Benoy Sarkarer Baithake, vols I and II (ed. Haridas Mukherjee). Calcutta: Deys Publishing, 2011 (BSB-I and BSB-II).
Chinese Religion through Hindu Eyes. Shanghai: Commercial Press, 1916 (CRTHE).
Creative India from Mohenjodaro to the Age of Ramakrishna-Vivekananda. Lahore: Motilal Banarasidass, 1937 (CI).
Comparative Pedagogics in Relation to Public Finance and National Wealth. Calcutta: N.M. Ray Chowdhury & Co., 1929 (CP).
Dominion India in World Perspectives, Economic and Political. Calcutta: Chuckervertty, Chatterjee & Co., 1949 (DIWP).
E Kaler Dhan Daulat O Arthashastra. Calcutta: N.M. Ray Chowdhury & Co., 1935 (EKDDA).
The Folk Element in Hindu Culture: A Contribution to Socio Religious Studies in Hindu Folk Institutions. London: Longmans, Green and Co., 1917 (FEHC).
The Futurism of Young Asia and Other Essays on the Relations between the East and the West. Berlin: Julius Springer, 1922 (FYA).
Greetings to Young India: Messages of Cultural and Social Reconstruction. Calcutta: N.M. Ray Chowdhury & Co., 1927 (GYI).
The Hitler State: A Landmark in the Political, Economic and Social Remaking of the German People. Lahore: Civil and Military Gazette, 1934 (THS).
Introduction to the Science of Education. London: Longmans, Green and Co., 1913 (ISE).
Italyte Bar Kayek. Calcutta: City Library, 1932 (IBK).
Love in Hindu Literature. Tokyo: Maruzen, 1916 (LHL).
Naveen Asiar Janmadata. Calcutta: Oriental Book Agency, 1927 (NAJ).
Naya Banglar Goda Pattan. Calcutta: Chuckervertty, Chatterjee & Co., 1932 (NBGP).
The Positive Background of Hindu Sociology (Non-Political). Allahabad: Panini Office, 1914 (PBHS).
The Positive Background of Hindu Sociology (Political). New York: AMS, 1974[1921–26] (PBHS-II).
The Political Institutions and Theories of the Hindus. Leipzig: Verlag, 1922 (PITH).

The Politics of Boundaries and Tendencies in International Relations, vol. 1. Calcutta: N.M. Ray Chowdhury & Co., 1926 (PB).
Political Philosophies since 1905. Lahore: Motilal Banarsidass, 1942 (PPS-1905).
Prabuddha Bharat. Calcutta: Ramakrishna Mission, 1936.
Samaj Bigyan. Calcutta: Chuckervertty, Chatterjee & Co., 1940 (SB).
Scheme for Economic Development in India. Calcutta: Oriental Library, 1926 (SEDI).
The Science of History and the Hope of Mankind. London: Longmans, Green & Co., 1912 (SHHM).
The Sociology of Population. Calcutta: N.M. Ray Chowdhury & Co., 1936 (SP).
Villages and Towns as Social Patterns. Calcutta: Chuckervertty, Chatterjee & Co., 1941 (VT).
Vishwashakti. Calcutta: Grihastha Prakashani, 1914.
Yankeestan or Greater Europe. Calcutta: Grihastha Prakashani, 1916 (YT).

Articles

'The Acceptable and the Unacceptable in Bankim's Social Philosophy', *Calcutta Review*, August 1938.
'China, Japan and Young India', *Atmashakti*, 24(2), 1927.
'Comparative Birth, Death and Growth Rates', *Journal of the Indian Medical Association*, May 1932.
'Demo-Despotocracy and Freedom', *Calcutta Review*, January 1939.
'Economic India of Tomorrow', *Calcutta Review*, April 1944.
'Gandhi, Non-Gandhi, and Anti-Gandhi in the Pattern of Indian Ideologies', *Calcutta Review* (Special Issue), February 1948.
'German Winter Relief as a Form of Social Relief', *Calcutta Review*, June 1936.
'The People and the State in Neo-Democracy', *Calcutta Review*, July 1936.
'Progress Planning as a Scheme of Emancipation on Five Fronts', in Banesvar Dass (ed.), *The Social and Economic Ideas of Benoy Sarkar*. Calcutta: Chuckervertty Chatterjee and Co., 1939.
'Review of Vilfredo Pareto, *Mind and Society*', *Calcutta Review*, April 1939.
'Sociology of Creative Disequilibrium in Education', *Calcutta Review*, July 1940.
'Stalin as the Manager of Leninism' (Part II), *Calcutta Review*, September 1938.
'Winter Relief in Germany', *Calcutta Review*, May 1935.
'Winter Relief in Germany', *Calcutta Review*, July 1938.

Archival Sources

Native Newspaper Reports, Bengal (The British Library).
Records of the Home Department, Political and Public Branches, Government of India, 1909, 1929, 1938 (National Archives of India).

Selected Secondary Sources

Agamben, Giorgio. *State of Exception*. Chicago: University of Chicago Press, 2005.
———. *Homo Sacer: Sovereign Power and Bare Life*. Stanford: Stanford University Press, 1995.

Ahluwalia, Sanjam. *Reproductive Restraints: Birth Control in India 1877-1947*. Urbana: University of Illinois Press, 2008.
Alter, Joseph. *Gandhi's Body: Sex, Diet and the Politics of Nationalism*. Philadelphia: University of Pennsylvania Press, 2000.
Amin, Ash (ed.). *Post-Fordism: A Reader*. Oxford: Blackwell, 2000.
Amin, Shahid. 'Gandhi as Mahatma', in Ranajit Guha and Gayatri Spivak (eds), *Selected Subaltern Studies*. Oxford: Oxford University Press, 1988.
Anderson, Benedict. *Imagined Communities*. London: Verso, 1993.
Anderson, Clare. *Legible Bodies: Race, Criminality and Colonialism in South Asia*. Oxford: Berg, 2004.
Appadurai, Arjun. 'Number in the Colonial Imagination', in Carol Breckenridge and Peter van der Veer (eds), *Orientalism and the Postcolonial Predicament*. Philadelphia: University of Pennsylvania Press, 1993.
Appiah, Kwame. *Cosmopolitanism*. London: Norton, 2006.
———. *The Ethics of Identity*. Princeton: Princeton University Press, 2005.
Arendt, Hannah. *The Origins of Totalitarianism*. Orlando: Harcourt, 1976.
Arnold, David. *Colonizing the Body: State Medicine and Epidemic Disease in Nineteenth-Century India*. Delhi: Oxford University Press, 1993.
Austin, Granville. *The Indian Constitution: Cornerstone of a Nation*. Oxford: Clarendon, 1966.
Bailkin, Jordanna. 'The Boot and the Speen: When was Murder Possible in British India?' *Comparative Studies in History and Society*, 48(2): 462-93, 2006.
Bakhle, Janaki. 'Putting Global Intellectual History in Its Place', in Samuel Moyn and Andrew Sartori (eds), *Global Intellectual History*. New York: Columbia University Press, 2008.
Ballhatchet, Kenneth. *Race, Sex and Class under the Raj: Imperial Attitudes and Policies and their Critics 1793-1905*. London: Weidenfeld & Nicholson, 1980.
Bandyopadhyay, Bholanath. *The Political Ideas of Benoy Kumar Sarkar*. Calcutta: K.P. Bagchi, 1984.
Bandyopadhyay, Chandi Charan. *Vidyasagara: The Life of Ishwarchandra Vidyasagara*. Calcutta: n.p., 1895.
Banerji, Panchcowri. 'The Student Community—The Trouble in the Presidency and Bangabasi Colleges', *Nayak*, 14 March 1916.
Baros, Jan. *The First Decade of Batanagar*. Batanagar: Club for the Graduates of Bata School (CGBS), 1945.
Bayly, C.A. *Recovering Liberties: Indian Thought in the Age of Liberalism and Empire*. Cambridge: Cambridge University Press, 2011.
Bayly, Susan. 'Imagining Greater India: French and Indic Visions of Colonialism in the Indic Mode', *Modern Asian Studies*, 38(3): 703-44, 2004.
———. 'Caste and Race in Colonial Ethnography', in Peter Robb (ed.), *The Concept of Race in South Asia*. Delhi: Oxford University Press, 1995.
Beckerlegge, Gwilym. *The Ramakrishna Mission: The Making of a Modern Hindu Movement*. Delhi: Oxford University Press, 2000.
Bell, Andrew. *Mutual Tuition and Moral Discipline*. London: Roake, 1823.

Berghahn, V.R. *Germany and the Approach of War in 1914*. New York: St. Martin's, 1973.
Beteille, Andre. *Society and Politics in India*. Delhi: Oxford University, 1990.
Bhabha, Homi. *The Location of Culture*. New York: Routledge, 1994.
Bhattacharya, Tithi. *The Sentinels of Culture: Class, Education and the Colonial Intellectual in Bengal 1848-85*. Delhi: Oxford University Press, 2005.
Böll, Heinrich. *What's to Become of the Boy, or Something to do with Books*. New York: Alfred Knopf, 1984.
Bose, Phanindranath. *The Indian Colony of Siam*. Lahore: Punjab Sanskrit Book Depot, 1927.
Bose, Subhas Chandra. *The Indian Struggle, 1920-1934*. London: Wishart Co., 1935.
Bose, Sugata and Kris Manjapra (eds). *Cosmopolitan Thought Zones: South Asia and the Global Circulation of Ideas*. New York: Palgrave, 2010.
Breckenridge, Carol and Peter van der Veer (eds). *Orientalism and the Postcolonial Predicament*. Philadelphia: University of Pennsylvania Press, 1993.
Browning, Christopher. *Ordinary Men: Reserve Police Battalion 101 and the Final Solution in Poland*. New York: Harper, 1992.
Burton, Antoinette. *Dwelling in the Archive*. Delhi: Oxford University Press, 2003.
Chakrabarty, Dipesh. *Provincializing Europe: Postcolonial Thought and Historical Difference*. Princeton: Princeton University Press, 2000.
Chakrabarty, Uma. 'Whatever Happened to the Vedic Dasi?' in Kumkum Sangari and Sudesh Vaid (eds), *Recasting Women: Essays in Colonial History*. New Brunswick: Rutgers University Press, 1990.
Chandra, Bipan. *India's Struggle for Independence*. Delhi: Penguin, 1989.
Chatterjee, Partha. *Nationalist Thought and the Colonial World: A Derivative Discourse*. Minneapolis: University of Minnesota Press, 2004.
——. *The Politics of the Governed*. New York: Columbia University Press, 2004.
——. *Wages of Freedom: Fifty Years of the Indian Nation-State*. Delhi: Oxford University Press, 1998.
——. *The Nation and Its Fragments: Colonial and Postcolonial Histories*. Princeton: Princeton University Press, 1993.
——. 'The Nationalist Resolution of the Women's Question', in Kumkum Sangari and Sudesh Vaid (eds), *Recasting Women: Essays in Colonial History*. New Brunswick: Rutgers University Press, 1990.
Chatterji, Joya. *Bengal Divided: Hindu Communalism and Partition, 1932-1947*. Cambridge: Cambridge University Press, 2002.
Chaturvedi, Vinayak. 'Rethinking Knowledge With Action: V.D. Savarkar, the Bhagavad Gita, and Histories of Warfare', *Modern Intellectual History*, 7(2): 417-35, 2010.
Chaudhuri, Amit. 'Triumphant Eclecticism', *Outlook*, 7 May 2006. http://www.outlookindia.com/article.aspx?231146 (accessed 2 November 2014).
Chaudhuri, Nirad. *The Autobiography of an Unknown Indian*. New York: The New York Review of Books (NYRB), 1951.

Selected Bibliography 193

Chaudhuri, Rosinka. 'Three Poets in Search of History', in Michael Dodson and Brian Hatcher (eds), *Trans-Colonial Modernities in South Asia*. London: Routledge, 2012.
Chowdhuri-Sengupta, Indira. 'The Effeminate and the Masculine: Nationalism and the Concept of Race in Colonial Bengal', in Peter Robb (ed.), *The Concept of Race in South Asia*. Delhi: Oxford University Press, 1995.
Cohn, Bernard. *Colonialism and its Forms of Knowledge: The British in India*. Delhi: Oxford University Press, 1997.
Coker, F.W. *Organismic Theories of the State*. Charleston: Bibliobazaar, 2009.
Das, Taraknath. *Foreign Policy in the Far East*. New York: Longmans, Green and Co., 1936.
———. *India in World Politics*. New York: B.W. Huebsch, 1923.
———. *Is Japan a Menace to Asia?* Shanghai: Taraknath Das, 1917.
Dasgupta, Uma. *Science and Modern India: An Institutional History*. Delhi: Pearson, 2011.
Dass, Banesvar (ed.). *The Social and Economic Ideas of Benoy Sarkar*. Calcutta: Chuckervertty Chatterjee and Co., 1939.
de Gobineau, Arthur Comte. *The Inequality of the Human Races*. Burlington: Ostara, 2011.
Dennis Dalton, *Gandhi's Power: Non-Violence in Action*. Delhi: Oxford University Press, 1999.
Devji, Faisal. *The Impossible Indian*. Cambridge: Harvard University Press, 2012.
Dirks, Nicholas. *Castes of Mind: Colonialism and the Making of Modern India*. Princeton: Princeton University Press, 2001.
Dodson, Michael and Brian Hatcher (eds). *Trans-Colonial Modernities in South Asia*. London: Routledge, 2012.
Dower, John. *Ways of Forgetting, Ways of Remembering*. New York: The New Press, 2012.
———. *Embracing Defeat: Japan in the Wake of World War II*. New York: Norton, 1999.
———. *War Without Mercy: Race and Power in the Pacific War*. New York: Pantheon, 1986.
Drinnon, Richard. *Facing West: The Metaphysics of Indian Hating and Empire Building*. New York: Schocken, 1990.
Duara, Prasenjit. 'The Discourse of Civilization and Pan-Asianism', *Journal of World History*, 12(1): 99–130, 2001.
Eaton, Richard. *The Rise of Islam and the Bengal Frontier*. Berkeley: University of California Press, 1993.
Eisenstadt, S.N. 'Multiple Modernities', *Daedalus*, Winter, 129(1): 1–29, 2000.
Ernst, Carl. 'Admiring the Works of the Ancients', in David Gilmartin and Bruce Lawrence (eds), *Beyond Turk and Hindu: Rethinking Religious Identities in Islamicate South Asia*. Delhi: India Research Press, 2002.
Esser, Josef and Joachim Hirsch. 'The Crisis of Fordism', in Ash Amin (ed.), *Post-Fordism: A Reader*. Oxford: Blackwell, 2000.

Eyck, Erich. *Bismarck and the German Empire*. London: Norton, 1968.
Fanon, Frantz. *Black Skin, White Masks*. New York: Grove, 2008.
———. *The Wretched of the Earth*. New York: Grove, 2004.
Fay, Peter Ward. *The Forgotten Army: India's Armed Struggle for Independence 1942-45*. Ann Arbor: University of Michigan Press, 1995.
Fischer-Tiné, Harald. *Low and Licentious Europeans: Race, Class and 'White Subalternity' in Colonial India*. Hyderabad: Orient BlackSwan, 2009.
———. 'National Education, Pulp Fiction and the Contradictions of Colonialism,' in Harald Fischer-Tiné and Michael Mann (eds), *Colonialism as Civilizing Mission: Cultural Ideology in British India*. London: Anthem, 2004.
Fischer-Tiné, Harald and Carolien Stolte. 'Imagining India in Asia: Nationalism and Internationalism 1905–1940', *Comparative Studies in Society and History*, 54(1): 65–92, 2012.
Fischer-Tiné, Harald and Michael Mann (eds). *Colonialism as Civilizing Mission: Cultural Ideology in British India*. London: Anthem, 2004.
Flora, Giuseppe. *Benoy Kumar Sarkar and Italy*. New Delhi: Italian Embassy Cultural Centre, 1994.
———. 'Benoy Kumar Sarkar: An Essay in Intellectual History'. Doctoral Dissertation, Jawaharlal Nehru University, 1993.
Foner, Eric. *Free Soil, Free Labor, Free Men: The Ideology of the Republican Party before the Civil War*. Oxford: Oxford University Press, 1970.
Forbes, Geraldine. *Women in Modern India*. Cambridge: Cambridge University Press, 1996.
Foucault, Michel. *Discipline and Punish: The Birth of the Prison*. New York: Vintage, 1979.
Fritzsche, Peter. *Germans into Nazis*. Cambridge: Harvard University Press, 1998.
Fussell, Paul. *The Great War and Modern Memory*. Oxford: Oxford University Press, 1975.
Gandhi, M.K. *Hind Swaraj*. Cambridge: Cambridge University Press, 1997.
———. *An Autobiography*. New York: Beacon, 1957.
Gay, Peter. *The Cultivation of Hatred: The Bourgeois Experience from Victoria to Freud*. New York: Norton, 1993.
———. *Weimar Culture: The Outsider as Insider*. New York: Harper Row, 1968.
Gellately, Robert. *Backing Hitler: Consent and Coercion in Nazi Germany*. Oxford: Oxford University Press, 2002.
Ghosh, Amitav. *The Shadow Lines*. New York: Viking, 1989.
Gilmartin, David and Bruce Lawrence (eds). *Beyond Turk and Hindu: Rethinking Religious Identities in Islamicate South Asia*. Delhi: India Research Press, 2002.
Gluck, Carol. *Japan's Modern Myths: Ideology in the Late Meiji Period*. Princeton: Princeton University Press, 1985.
Golwalkar, M.S. *We or Our Nationhood Defined*. Nagpur: Bharat Prakashan, 1947.
Gopal, Lallanji. 'The Sukraniti—A Nineteenth Century Text', *Bulletin of the School of Oriental and African Studies*, 25(1/3): 524–56, 1962.

Selected Bibliography 195

Gordon, Leonard, 'Divided Bengal', in Mushirul Hasan (ed.), *India's Partition: Process, Strategy and Mobilization*. Delhi: Oxford University Press, 1993.
———. *Brothers Against the Raj: A Biography of Indian Nationalists Sarat and Subhas Chandra Bose*. New York: Columbia University Press, 1990.
Goswami, Manu. 'Imaginary Futures and Colonial Internationalisms', *American Historical Review*, 117(5): 1461–85, December 2012.
———. *Producing India: From Colonial Economy to National Space*. Chicago: University of Chicago Press, 2004.
Gottfried, Paul. *After Liberalism: Mass Democracy in the Managerial State*. Princeton: Princeton University Press, 2001.
Greenblatt, Stephen. *Marvelous Possessions: The Wonder of the New World*. Chicago: University of Chicago Press, 1991.
Greenfeld, Liah. *Nationalism*. Cambridge: Harvard University Press, 1992.
Guha, Ranajit. *History at the Limit of World-History*. New York: Columbia University Press, 2002.
Guha, Ranajit and Gayatri Spivak (eds). *Selected Subaltern Studies*. Oxford: Oxford University Press, 1988.
Guha-Thakurta, Tapati. *The Making of a New 'Indian' Art: Artists, Aesthetics and Nationalism in Bengal 1850-1930*. Cambridge: Cambridge University Press, 1992.
Harrison, Mark. *Public Health in British India: Anglo-Indian Preventive Medicine 1859-1914*. Cambridge: Cambridge University Press, 1994.
Hasan, Mushirul (ed.). *India's Partition: Process, Strategy and Mobilization*. Delhi: Oxford University Press, 1993.
Hatcher, Brian. *Idioms of Improvement: Vidyasagar and Cultural Encounter in Bengal*. Delhi: Oxford University Press, 1996.
Haushofer, Karl. *Geopolitics of the Pacific Ocean: Studies on the Relationship between Geography and History*. Lewiston: Edwin Mellen, 2002.
Hay, Stephen (ed.). *Sources of Indian Tradition*, vol 2. New York: Columbia University Press, 1988.
Heehs, Peter. *The Bomb in Bengal: The Rise of Revolutionary Terrorism in India 1900-1910*. Delhi: Oxford University Press, 1993.
Hegel, Georg. *The Philosophy of History*. New York: Dover, 1956.
Heisig, James. 'Foreword', in Hajime Tanabe (ed.), *Philosophy as Metanoetics*. Berkeley: University of California Press, 1990.
Herder, Johann. *Reflections on the Philosophy of the History of Mankind*. Chicago: University of Chicago Press, 1968.
Hobsbawm, Eric. *Nations and Nationalism since 1780: Programme, Myth, Reality*. Cambridge: Cambridge University Press, 1992.
———. *The Age of Empire*. New York: Vintage, 1989.
Hocking, William. *Man and the State*. New Haven: Yale University Press, 1926.
Hodges, Sarah (ed.). *Reproductive Health in India*. Hyderabad: Orient Longman, 2006.

Hoff, Derek. *The State and the Stork: The Population Debate and Policy Making in US History.* Chicago: University of Chicago Press, 2012.
Hughes, H. Stuart. *Consciousness and Society: The Reorientation of European Social Thought 1890-1930.* New York: Vintage, 1977.
Inden, Ronald. *Imagining India.* Bloomington: Indiana University Press, 2001.
Iyengar, P.T.S. *Life in Ancient India in the Age of Mantras.* Delhi: Asian Educational Services, 1982.
Jaffrelot, Christophe (ed.). *Hindu Nationalism: A Reader.* Princeton: Princeton University Press, 2007.
Jalal, Ayesha. *The Sole Spokesman: Jinnah, The Muslim League and the Demand for Pakistan.* Cambridge: Cambridge University Press, 1985.
Jünger, Ernst. *Storm of Steel.* New York: Penguin, 2004.
Kapila, Shruti (ed.). *An Intellectual History for India.* Delhi: Cambridge University Press, 2010.
Kasturi, Bhashyam. *Walking Alone: Gandhi and India's Partition.* Delhi: Vision Books, 1999.
Kaufmann, Walter (ed.). *The Portable Nietzsche.* New York: Penguin, 1976.
Kaviraj, Sudipta. *Trajectories of the Indian State.* Delhi: Permanent Black, 2010.
———. *The Unhappy Consciousness: Bankimchandra Chattopadhyay and the Formation of Nationalist Discourse in India.* Delhi: Oxford University Press, 1998.
King, Richard and Dan Stone (eds). *Hannah Arendt and the Uses of History: Imperialism, Nation, Race, and Genocide.* New York: Berghahn, 2007.
Kolsky, Elizabeth. *Colonial Justice in British India: White Violence and the Rule of Law.* Cambridge: Cambridge University Press, 2010.
Kuklick, Henrika. *The Savage Within: The Social History of British Anthropology.* Cambridge: Cambridge University Press, 1993.
Kumar, Ravinder. 'From *Swaraj* to *Purna Swaraj*', in D.A. Low (ed.), *Congress and the Raj.* Delhi: Arnold-Heinemann, 1977.
LaFeber, Walter. *The American Age: United States Foreign Policy at Home and Abroad since 1750.* New York: Norton, 1989.
Lelyveld, David. *Aligarh's First Generation: Muslim Solidarity in British India.* Delhi: Oxford University Press, 1996.
Leuchtenberg, William. *The FDR Years: On Roosevelt and his Legacy.* New York: Columbia University Press, 1995.
Levine, Philippa. 'Rereading the 1890s: Venereal Disease as Constitutional Crisis in Britain and British India', *Journal of Asian Studies*, 55(3): 585–612, 1996.
Lovett, Verney. *A History of the Indian Nationalist Movement.* New York: Frederick Stokes Company, 1920.
Low, D.A. (ed.). *Congress and the Raj.* Delhi: Arnold-Heinemann, 1977.
MacDonald, Ramsay. *The Government of India.* London: Swarthmore Press, 1919.
MacMillan, Margaret. *Paris 1919.* New York: Random House, 2003.
Majeed, Javed. *Autobiography, Travel and Postnational Identity: Gandhi, Nehru and Iqbal.* Houndmills: Palgrave, 2007.

Manjapra, Kris. 'Communist Internationalism and Transcolonial Recognition', in Sugata Bose and Kris Manjapra (eds), *Cosmopolitan Thought Zones: South Asia and the Global Circulation of Ideas*. New York: Palgrave, 2010.
Mauss, Marcel. 'W.H.R. Rivers and the Todas', *Annee Sociologique*, 11: 154–58, 1906–9.
McArthur, Brian. *Penguin Book of Twentieth Century Speeches*. London: Penguin Viking, 1992.
McClintock, Anne. *Imperial Leather: Race, Gender and Sexuality in the Colonial Contest*. London: Routledge, 1995.
Menon, Dilip. 'A Local Cosmopolitanism: "Kesari" Balakrishna Pillai and the Invention of Europe for a Modern Kerala', in Sugata Bose and Kris Manjapra (eds), *Cosmopolitan Thought Zones: South Asia and the Global Circulation of Ideas*. New York: Palgrave, 2010.
Mill, J.S. 'Considerations on Representative Government', in *Three Essays*. Oxford: Oxford University Press, 1975.
———. *Three Essays*. Oxford: Oxford University Press, 1975.
Miller, Harold. *Race Conflict in New Zealand*. Auckland: Blackwood & Paul, 1966.
Mills, James H. *Madness, Cannabis and Colonialism: The Native-Only Lunatic Asylums of British India*. Houndmills: Macmillan, 2000.
Minault, Gail. *The Khilafat Movement: Religious Symbolism and Political Mobilization in India*. New York: Columbia University Press, 1982.
Mishra, Pankaj. *From the Ruins of Empire: The Intellectuals Who Remade Asia*. New York: Farrar, Straus and Giroux, 2012.
Mitter, Partha. *Art and Nationalism in Colonial India, 1850-1922*. Cambridge: Cambridge University Press, 1994.
Mookerji, Radhakumud. *Local Government in Ancient India*. Charleston: Nabu, 2012.
———. *History of Indian Shipping*. London: Longmans Green, 1912.
Moyn, Samuel and Andrew, Sartori (eds). *Global Intellectual History*. New York: Columbia University Press, 2008.
Mukherjee, Haridas. *Benoy Kumar Sarkar: A Study*. Calcutta: Dasgupta, 1953.
Mukherji, U.N. *Hindus: A Dying Race*. Calcutta: Bhaskar Mukerjee, 1929.
Mukhopadhyay, Amal Kumar. 'Benoy Kumar Sarkar: The Theoretical Foundation of Indian Capitalism', in Amal Kumar Mukhopadhyay (ed.), *The Bengali Intellectual Tradition*. Calcutta: K.P. Bagchi, 1979.
Mukhopadhyay, Amal Kumar (ed.). *The Bengali Intellectual Tradition*. Calcutta: K.P. Bagchi, 1979.
Mukhopadhyay, Bhudeb. *Prabandha Samagra*. Calcutta: Charchapada, 2010.
———. *Samajik Prabandha*. Calcutta: Paschimbanga Pustak Parishad, 1981.
Nanda, B.R. *Indian Foreign Policy: The Nehru Years*. Honolulu: University of Hawaii Press, 1976.
Nandy, Ashis. *The Romance of the State and the Face of Dissent in the Tropics*. Delhi: Oxford University Press, 2003.

———. 'The Other Within: The Strange Case of Radhabinod Pal's Judgment on Culpability', *New Literary History*, 23(1): 45–67, 1992.
———. *The Intimate Enemy: Loss and Recovery of Self under Colonialism*. Delhi: Oxford University Press, 1983.
Nehru, Jawaharlal. 'Tryst With Destiny', in Brian McArthur, *Penguin Book of Twentieth Century Speeches*. London: Penguin Viking, 1992.
The New York Times. 'American Idealism Constantly in Evidence Here, Says Hindu Scholar', 11 March 1917.
Nietzsche, Friedrich. *A Nietzsche Reader*. London: Penguin, 1977.
———. 'The Twilight of the Idols', in Walter Kaufmann (ed.), *The Portable Nietzsche*. New York: Penguin, 1976.
———. *The Philosophy of Nietzsche*. New York: Modern Library, 1927.
Noma, Hiroshi. *Zone of Emptiness*. Cleveland: World Publishing Co., 1956.
Obeyesekere, Gananath. *The Apotheosis of Captain Cook*. Princeton: Princeton University Press, 1992.
O'Hanlon, Rosalind. *Caste Conflict and Ideology*. Cambridge: Cambridge University Press, 1985.
Omvedt, Gail. *Dalit Visions*. Hyderabad: Orient Longman, 2006.
Ordover, Nancy. *American Eugenics: Race, Queer Anatomy and the Science of Nationalism*. Minneapolis: University of Minnesota Press, 2003.
Orwell, George. *Burmese Days*. Orlando: Harcourt Brace Jovanovich (HBJ), 1962.
———. *The Lion and the Unicorn*. London: Secker & Warburg, 1962.
———. *A Collection of Essays*. Orlando: Harcourt, 1953.
Pal, Radhabinod. *Crimes in International Relations*. Calcutta, 1955.
———. *The History of the Law of Primogeniture with Special Reference to India, Ancient and Modern*. Calcutta: Oriental Press, 1923.
Pandya, Vishvajit. *In the Forest: Visual and Material Worlds of Andamanese History*. Lanham: University Press of America, 2009.
Pareto, Vilfredo. *Mind and Society*. New York: Harcourt, 1935.
Paul, T.V., Ikenberry G. and John Hall (eds). *The Nation-State in Question*. Princeton: Princeton University Press, 2003.
Peers, Douglas. *India under Colonial Rule 1700–1885*. London: Routledge, 2006.
Peukert, Detlev. *Inside Nazi Germany: Conformity, Opposition and Racism in Everyday Life*. New Haven: Yale University Press, 1982.
Pick, Daniel. *Faces of Degeneration: A European Disorder 1848–1918*. Cambridge: Cambridge University Press, 1989.
Ramaswamy, Sumathi. *Passions of the Tongue: Language Devotion in Tamil India 1891–1970*. Berkeley: University of California Press, 1997.
Ray, Rajat Kanta. *The Felt Community: Commonality and Mentality before the Emergence of Indian Nationalism*. Delhi: Oxford University Press, 2003.
Ray, Sukumar. *Samagra Shishu-Sahitya*. Calcutta: Ananda Publishers, 1975.
Raychaudhuri, Tapan. *Europe Reconsidered: Perceptions of the West in Nineteenth-Century Bengal*. Delhi: Oxford University Press, 2002.

Richards, John. *The Mughal Empire*. Cambridge: Cambridge University Press, 1993.
Robb, Peter (ed.). *The Concept of Race in South Asia*. Delhi: Oxford University Press, 1995.
Roberts, J.M. *A General History of Europe 1880-1945*. London: Longman, 1970.
Roy, Samaren. *M.N. Roy: A Political Biography*. Hyderabad: Orient Longman, 1997.
Said, Edward. *Culture and Imperialism*. New York: Vintage, 1993.
———. *The Question of Palestine*. New York: Vintage, 1992.
Sangari, Kumkum and Sudesh Vaid. *Recasting Women: Essays in Colonial History*. New Brunswick: Rutgers University Press, 1990.
Sarda, Harbilas. *Hindu Superiority: An Attempt to Determine the Position of the Hindu Race in the Scale of Nations*. Ajmer: Rajputana Printing Works, 1906.
Sarkar, Ida. *My Life with Prof. Benoy Kumar Sarkar*. Calcutta: Pramathanath Paul, 1977.
Sarkar, Sumit. *The Swadeshi Movement in Bengal*. Delhi: Permanent Black, 2010.
———. *Beyond Nationalist Frames: Postmodernism, Hindu Fundamentalism, History*. Bloomington: Indiana University Press, 2002.
———. *Writing Social History*. Delhi: Oxford University Press, 1999.
Sarkar, Susobhan. *On the Bengal Renaissance*. Calcutta: Papyrus, 1985.
Sarkar, Tanika. *Hindu Wife, Hindu Nation: Community, Religion, and Cultural Nationalism*. Bloomington: Indiana University Press, 2001.
Sartori, Andrew. 'Beyond Culture-Contact and Colonial Discourse: "Germanism" in Colonial Bengal', in Shruti Kapila (ed.), *An Intellectual History for India*. Delhi: Cambridge University Press, 2010.
———. *Bengal in Global Concept History*. Chicago: University of Chicago Press, 2008.
———. 'Beyond Culture-Contact and Colonial Discourse', *Modern Intellectual History*, 4(1): 77-93, 2007.
Savarkar, V.D. *Hindutva*. Delhi: Hindi Sahitya Sadan, 2003.
———. *My Transportation for Life*. Bombay: Veer Savarkar Prakashan, 1984.
Schissler, Hannah (ed.). *The Miracle Years: A Cultural History of West Germany 1949-1968*. Princeton: Princeton University Press, 2001.
Schneider, Dona and David Lilienfeld (eds). *Public Health: The Development of a Discipline*. New Brunswick: Rutgers University Press, 2008.
Sen, Satadru. *Traces of Empire: India, America and Postcolonial Cultures*. Delhi: Primus, 2013.
———. *Savagery and Colonialism in the Indian Ocean: Power, Pleasure and the Andaman Islanders*. London: Routledge, 2010.
———. 'Anarchies of Youth: The Oaten Affair and Colonial Bengal', *Studies in History*, 23(2): 206-29, 2007.
———. *Colonial Childhoods: The Juvenile Periphery of India 1850-1945*. London: Anthem, 2005.
———. 'A Juvenile Periphery: Geographies of Childhood in Bengali Children's Literature', *Journal of Colonialism and Colonial History*, 5(1), 2004.

Selected Bibliography

———. *Migrant Races: Empire, Identity and K.S. Ranjitsinhji*. Manchester: Manchester University Press, 2004.

———. *Disciplining Punishment: Colonialism and Convict Society in the Andaman Islands*. Delhi: Oxford University Press, 2000.

Shraddhanand, Swami. *Hindu Sangathan: Saviour of the Dying Race*, n.p., 1924.

Smith, Anthony. *The Ethnic Origins of Nations*. Oxford: Blackwell, 1986.

Smith, Woodruff. *The Ideological Origins of Nazi Imperialism*. Oxford: Oxford University Press, 1986.

Smithers, Gregory. *Science, Sexuality and Race in the United States and Australia*. Routledge: New York, 2009.

Sood, Malini. 'Expatriate Nationalism and Ethnic Radicalism: The Ghadar Party in North America, 1910–1920'. PhD Dissertation, State University of New York (SUNY) Stony Brook, 1995.

Sorokin, Pitirim and Carle Zimmerman. *Principles of Rural-Urban Sociology*. New York: Holt, 1929.

Spengler, Oswald. *The Decline of the West*. New York: A. Knopf, 1928.

Springhall, John. *Youth, Empire and Society: British Youth Movements, 1883–1940*. London: Croom Helm, 1977.

Stern, A.M. *Eugenic Nation: Faults and Frontiers of Better Breeding in Modern America*. Berkeley: University of California Press, 2005.

Stoler, Ann. *Race and the Education of Desire*. Durham: Duke University Press, 1995.

Streets, Heather. *Martial Races: The Military, Race and Masculinity in British Imperial Culture 1857–1914*. Manchester: Manchester University Press, 2004.

Tagore, Rabindranath. *Char Adhyay*. Calcutta: Vishwabharati Press, 1938.

———. *Journey to Persia and Iraq*. Calcutta: Viswabharati, 1932.

———. *The Spirit of Japan*. Tokyo: Indo-Japanese Association, 1916.

Tagore, Sumitendranath. *Santiniketan Chena Achena*. Calcutta: Mitra & Ghosh, 2003.

Takeyama, Michio. *Harp of Burma*. Rutland: Tuttle, 1966.

Tambe, Ashwini. *Codes of Misconduct: Regulating Prostitution in Late Colonial Bombay*. Minneapolis: University of Minnesota Press, 2009.

Tanabe, Hajime. *Philosophy as Metanoetics*. Berkeley: University of California Press, 1990.

Thapar, Romila. *The Aryan: Recasting Constructs*. Gurgaon: Three Essays Collective, 2008.

Tönnies, Ferdinand. *Community and Civil Society*. Cambridge: Cambridge University Press, 2001.

Vaidya, C.V. *Epic India*. Bombay: S.A. Sagoon, 1907.

Vaughan, William. *German Romantic Painting*. New Haven: Yale University Press, 1994.

Wattal, P.K. *Population Problem in India: A Census Study*. Bombay: Bennett Coleman, 1934.

Wilson, Kathleen. *The Island Race: Englishness, Empire and Gender in the Eighteenth Century*. London: Routledge, 2003.
Wolf, Eric. *Europe and the People without History*. Berkeley: University of California Press, 1997.
Yack, Bernard. 'Nationalism, Popular Sovereignty and the Liberal Democratic State', in T.V. Paul, G. Ikenberry and John Hall (eds), *The Nation-State in Question*. Princeton: Princeton University Press, 2003.
Yang, Anand (ed.). *Crime and Criminality in British India*. Tucson: University of Arizona Press, 1985.
Zachariah, Benjamin. 'Rethinking (the Absence of) Fascism in India, c. 1922–45', in Sugata Bose and Kris Manjapra (eds), *Cosmopolitan Thought Zones: South Asia and the Global Circulation of Ideas*. New York: Palgrave, 2010.
——. *Developing India*. Delhi: Oxford University Press, 2005.
——. *Nehru*. New York: Routledge, 2004.
Zehfuss, Maja. *Wounds of Memory: The Politics of War in Germany*. Cambridge: Cambridge University Press, 2007.

Index

aboriginality 52, 54, 64–74, 77
Agamben, Giorgio 139, 149, 165, 169–70
'Agastya' (Ordhendu Coomar Gangoly) 16
Ahluwalia, Sanjam 139–40
Alter, Joseph 88n15, 184
amalgamation 15, 35, 166
America (United States) 4, 6, 9, 12, 23, 80, 99–100, 102, 107, 114, 145, 149, 152; New Deal 152, 154; progressivism 27, 61–2, 167; race and immigration 15, 23–4, 27, 55, 68–9, 79, 117, 157, 166–8
American Friends of Freedom for India 102
Andaman Islands 54, 68, 74, 119, 137
Anderson, Benedict 34, 159
Anushilan group 70, 73
Appiah, Kwame Anthony 2, 124
architecture (and housing-morality) 61–2, 141
Arendt, Hannah 57, 89n40, 139, 163–4, 166, 169
Armed Forces Special Powers Act 31
Arya Samaj 52
Aryan (discourse of the) 52, 60, 6, 68–9, 74–5, 158, 171
Ashoka 22, 99, 106
Asia see China; Japan; Pan-Asianism
Ataturk (Kemal Pasha) 84, 148, 170
atomic bombing 34, 117
Aurangzeb 79, 81
Australia 54

Baden-Powell, Robert 54
Bakhle, Janaki 19
Balkh 82

Banarji, Surendra Nath 142
Bandyopadhyay, Bholanath 3, 153
Banerji, Hemchandra 99
Banerji, Panchcowri 142
Bangiya Sahitya Parishad 113–14
Bata, Jan and Tomas 6–7, 31; Batanagar 6
Bayly, C.A. 28, 30
Bayly, Susan 10
Bhartrihari 144
Bismarck, Otto von 100, 153, 154
Boer War 54, 142
Bombay Shops and Establishments Act 142
Bonifica scheme 137
Bose, Jagadish Chunder 105
Bose, Phanindra Nath 16, 42n112, 97
Bose, Subhas Chandra 8, 31, 33, 80, 84, 116, 122, 125n20, 144, 147, 185–6
Brahmanocracy 63
Buddhism 81, 96, 99, 118, 120
Bushido 110, 113–14

caste 29, 30, 49, 52, 57–60, 64, 68–70, 73, 100, 135, 158
Chakrabarty, Dipesh 136
Chanakya (Kautilya) 100, 115; Arthashastra 100
Chatterjee, Bankimchandra 2, 51, 73, 77, 79, 111, 124, 147, 154, 160
Chatterjee, Joya 30, 64
Chatterjee, Kedarnath 99
Chatterjee, Partha 29, 167
Chattopadhyay, Virendra 29
Chaudhuri, Nirad 7, 113, 123
Chaudhuri, Pramathanath 16

204 Index

China 2, 11, 57, 79–80, 95–7, 103, 108, 112–16, 145, 172
Coker, F.W. 158
Comte, August 154
Conrad, Joseph 68
Constituent Assembly of India 123, 150
Cooley, C.H. 27
cosmopolitanism 2, 4, 8, 10, 12–20, 24, 31, 51, 53, 60, 66, 76–7, 80, 95, 104, 111–12, 120, 124, 138, 144, 146, 162, 172, 185
creative disequilibrium 24, 33, 133, 142, 154, 162
criminality 61–4, 69, 135–7, 140–1, 157
Croce, Benedetto 27, 29, 132, 150
Curzon, G.N. (Viceroy) 14, 113

Damodar Valley Corporation 25
Darwin, Charles 2, 3, 21, 117; Social Darwinism 15, 77
Das, Taraknath 6, 107, 125n20, 185
Dawn Society 149
degeneracy 11, 27, 51, 54–64, 73, 76, 87, 89n40, 99, 110, 135, 142, 157
demo-despotocracy 147, 151–2
Derozio, Henry 18
Deutsche Akademie 97, 125n20
Devji, Faisal 156, 178n174
DeVries, Hugo 63
Dirks, Nicholas 69
Dower, John 117, 121
Duara, Prasenjit 2
Durkheim, E. 26, 134
Dutta, Michael Madhusudan 147
dyarchy 58, 142

Eden Hindu Hostel 95
education 1, 6–7, 11–19, 21, 26, 28–31, 33, 37, 41n71, 59, 62, 67, 70, 82–3, 85, 107, 113, 123, 133, 140, 143, 145, 164
Eisenstadt, S.N. 1
Ellis, Havelock 14

energism 101, 109, 145
Engels, Friedrich 24
eugenics 21, 50, 54, 58, 63, 70, 157–8, 170–1

Fanon, Frantz 49–50, 56, 103
fascism 1, 3, 24, 31, 61, 120, 132–4, 139, 143, 149–51, 153, 162, 169, 178n174, 185
federalism 34–7, 177n154
Fischer-Tiné, Harald 2
Flora, Giuseppe 3, 24, 32, 64, 132
folk culture 15, 26, 28, 32, 64–73, 77, 80, 134, 141; Völkisch ideology 2, 15, 51–3, 65, 67, 70, 73–8, 124, 138, 162, 171
Ford, Henry 6
Foucault, Michel 3, 165
Frazer, J.G. 68
Fritzsche, Peter 102, 164
Fussel, Pau 124

Gadkari, R.G. 161
Gajan 66, 70
Galton, Francis 63
Gambhira 66–7, 70–2
Gandhi, M.K. 2, 6, 49, 51, 61, 70, 122, 134, 138, 147, 156, 158, 161, 178n174, 183–6
Gay, Pete 31
Gellately, Robert 139, 149, 155–6, 163–4
Germany 3, 6, 9, 17, 19, 31, 44n173, 54, 59, 96, 100, 107–8, 120–1, 125n20, 136–8, 143, 145, 149, 154–66, 168, 170–1, 173n13, 180n246, 185; Nazi politics 102, 132, 138, 156–8, 163–6; normalcy 156, 165; race 54–5, 97, 156–9, 162–4; Weimar Republic 120, 155–6, 162, 164, 170; Winter Relief schemes 156
Ghadr Party 23
Ghosh, Aurobindo 16

Ghosh, Amitav 85
Ghosh, Barindra (Barin) 16
Gini, Corrado 58, 61, 96, 132
de Gobineau, August Comte 2, 50, 54, 86, 117, 169
Goebbels, Josef 158
Goethe, Johann Wolfgang 16–17, 160
Golwalkar, M.S. 30, 52, 69, 74–5
Goswami, Manu 3, 30, 97
Government of India Act (1935) 58, 152
Great War (World War I) 4, 8, 11, 19–20, 23, 25, 49, 51, 68, 76, 81, 96, 99–100, 102, 108, 114, 123, 133, 135, 148
Greater India 9–10, 34, 82, 107, 114–15, 149
Greenblatt, Stephen 16
Greenfeld, Liah 163
Gumplowicz, Ludwig 104

habituality 6, 56–7
Haeckl, Ernst 115
Harrison, Mark 136
Hatcher, Brian 32
Haushofer, Karl 97, 107, 114, 125n17, 125n20, 158
Hegel, G.W.F. 21, 57
Heisig, James 120–1
Herder, J.G. 36, 47n261, 66–7, 161–2
Hess, Rudolf 97
Heydrich, Reinhard 166, 168
Hindu Mahasabha 85
Hindutva 30, 52, 68, 73–6, 79, 84
Hitler, Adolf 125n17, 125n20, 132, 152, 158, 171
Hobsbawn, Eric 19, 163
Hocking, William 151
Hughes, H. Stuart 96

Indian National Congress 4, 8, 27, 33, 52, 78, 138, 164, 170, 183, 186
individuality 2–4, 6–8, 24, 26–31, 52–3, 61–3, 71, 78, 83, 85, 95, 120–3, 133–48, 151, 153–4, 156–7, 160, 164, 166, 168–71, 184
Italy 27, 31, 45n192, 80, 132, 137–8, 149–50, 153, 155, 167–8
Iyengar, P.T. Srinivas 68

Jadavpur University 7
Jaffrelot, Christophe 74
Japan 4, 8, 18, 55–6, 95–8, 123–5, 125n9, 138, 155, 158, 169, 185; and Indian militarism 113–17; Japanese imperialism 106–13; post-war nationhood 117–23
Japanese Co-Prosperity Sphere 147
Jews, view on 80, 158, 167
Jinnah, M.A. 78, 83, 185

Kabir, Humayun 84
Kalidasa 16, 99
Karve, Irawati 113
Kaviraj, Sudipta 183
Keynes, J.M. 29
Khilafat Movement 25, 27, 76, 83
Khilji, Bakhtyar 79
Kipling, Rudyard 18, 100, 136
Kissinger, Henry 123
knowledge, politics of 11–19
Kramrisch, Stella 16

Lajpat Rai 84–5, 94n216, 164, 169
League of Nations 89n42, 105
Lebensraum 97, 114, 137
liberalism 1–2, 8, 11–12, 19, 26, 28–31, 36–7, 52–3, 59, 63–4, 73, 78–9, 83–6, 97, 133, 138–40, 145–6, 148–9, 152, 156, 161–4, 171–2, 183, 185–6
Lovett, Verney 98–9
Lucknow Pact 83, 147
Ludendorff, Erich 132

Macaulay, T.B. 11, 21
MacDonald, Ramsay 105
Machiavelli 5, 149, 161–2

Mackinder, Halford 107, 158
Mahalanobis, P.C. 61
Majeed, Javed 49, 116
Malaviya, Madan Mohan 70
Malda 1, 66–7, 71, 82, 140
Malthus, Thomas 61
Mancini, P. 5
Mangala-Chandi 72, 77
Manu 2, 101, 144
Martial Races theory 103
Marwaris 37
Marx, Karl (and Marxism) 23, 26, 29, 33, 45n192, 101
Masaryk, Tomas 134
masculinity 33, 69, 95–106, 113–17, 122–4, 140, 171
matsyanyaya 105–6, 115, 122, 153, 158, 165
Matteotti, Giacomo 132
Mauss, Marcel 68
Mayo, Katherine 136
Mazzini, Giuseppe 149–50
Mendel, Gregor 63
Menon, Dilip 19, 53, 116
militarism (and war) 3, 11, 69, 97, 99–101, 104–6, 110, 112, 115, 120, 123–4, 155, 162
Mill, J.S. 2, 11, 29, 133, 162, 183
Minto-Morley reforms 51, 147
miscegenation 50, 55, 60, 69, 86
Mishra, Pankaj 2
mistrification 6–7, 26, 29, 59, 149, 154, 184
Mitra, Baradacharan 72
Mizushima 118–19, 121
Mookerji, Radhakamal 59, 114, 134
Mookerji, Radhakumud 10, 25, 39n36, 42n112, 97, 114, 116, 149
Morgan, L.H. 24, 68
Mueller, Max 81
Mukherjee, Haridas 103
Mukherjee, Satish Chandra 6, 113
Mukherjee, Shyamaprasad 84

Mukherji, Abani 29
Mukherji, U.N. 59
Mukhopadhyay, Amal 101
Mukhopadhyay, Bhudeb 2, 6, 17, 30, 46n218, 59, 95, 100, 141, 158–9, 183
Muslim League 83
Muslims (views on) 30, 51–3, 59, 61, 64, 67, 73–86, 154
Mussolini, Benito 132, 148–9, 153

Namasudra activism 66, 91n101
Nandy, Ashis 4, 30, 46n218, 56–7, 121–2
Napoleon (Bonaparte) 9, 17, 99, 144, 146, 157
National Education 1, 6, 30–2, 59, 66, 82, 107, 143, 149, 164
nature, discourse of 31, 51, 86, 135, 139–47, 160, 171
Nehru, Jawaharlal 5, 8, 10, 25, 27, 29–31, 33, 36–7, 60, 87, 123, 138, 156, 159, 183, 185
New Deal 152, 154
Newton, Isaac 21
Nietzsche, Friedrich 2, 5, 25–6, 31, 56–7, 96, 101–3, 138, 144, 154, 162, 170
Noma, Hiroshi 118
Non-Cooperation Movement *see* Khilafat Movement

Obeyesekere, Gananath 119
Okakura, Kakuzo 115
Orwell, George 7, 40n47, 119, 166

Pal, Radhabinod 98, 121–2
Palit, Haridas 66–7, 77
Pan-Asianism 2, 116
Pareto, Vilfredo 14, 26, 28–9, 33, 42n100, 45n192, 96, 145, 149; theory of circulation of elites 58
parianization 60, 64
Parsons, Talcott 134

Partition of India 79, 83–7
passive consent 151–2, 166
passive revolution 186
Pearson, Karl 63
Perry, Matthew 108
Peukert, Detlev 138–9, 142, 163–4, 166
Phule, Jyotiba 68
Pick, Daniel 63
pluralism 8, 13, 61, 64, 83, 146, 148, 151, 154, 171
political engineering 146, 154
Prasad, Rajendra 35
prerogative state 149
progressivism (American) 27, 61, 167

Quit India Movement 4

Ramakrishna 139, 186
Ramakrishna Mission 12, 51, 143
Rangoon Convention of Religions 139
Ray, Sukumar 111, 155
Redfield, Robert 134
Renan, E. 5
ressentiment 5, 9, 23, 31–4, 97, 101, 103–4, 120, 138–9, 154, 161
Richelieu (Cardinal) 100
Riefenstahl, Leni 158
Rivers, W.H.R. 68
Rizvi, K.N. 62
Robb, Peter 36, 49
Romanticism 1, 3, 23–4, 36, 50, 54, 65–7, 72–3, 82, 85–7, 98, 101, 124, 134, 138, 144, 146, 156, 159–62, 170–1
Roosevelt, F.D. 27, 152
Roosevelt, Theodore 9, 100, 167
Ross, E.A. 27
Roy, Dwijendralal 160
Roy, M.N. 29
Roy, Rammohun 184
Roy, Satishchandra 170
rubble literature 121
rurbanization 57
Russo–Japanese War 106, 109, 116

Sabuj Patra 16
Sadagar, Chand 15
Said, Edward 3, 119
sanitation 61–2, 70, 136
Santals 64
Santiniketan 143
Saraswati, Dayanand 52, 68
Sarda, Harbilas 79
Sarkar, Dhirendra 23
Sarkar, Ida 155, 158
Sarkar, Sumit 30, 52, 66
Sarkar, Susobhan 33
Sartori, Andrew 3, 15, 26, 64, 155
Satya Pir 76
Savarkar, V.D. 2, 10, 30, 52, 60, 74–6, 78, 81–2, 85, 124, 185; *punyabhumi* 74–5, 78–9
Schenzinger, Karl 170
science-world 10–11
Sen, Rajanikanta 65
Sen-Gupta, Narendranath 62
sex 14, 58–62, 64–5, 70, 102, 139–40, 150, 157–8; and urban life 60, 141; and racial boundaries 61–2
Shastri, Haraprasad 114
Shikoh, Dara 76
Shraddhanand (Swami) 52, 59, 89n59
Smith, Anthony 49
Smith, Vincent 80–1
Smith, Woodruff 97
Sorokin, Pitirim 57, 89n47
Soviet Union (USSR) 23, 29, 44n173, 138, 148, 150–1, 154, 156–7
Spengler, Oswald 60, 96, 106, 109, 134–5, 169
Stalin, Joseph 150, 152
state of exception 139, 149, 165, 168
Suhrawardy, A. 76
Sukarno 84
Sukraniti 11, 77, 148, 158
Sun Yat-Sen 79–80, 82, 172
Swadeshi movement 1, 6, 12, 29–30, 64, 66, 70, 73, 76, 140

Index

Swaraj 25, 29, 145
Swaraj Party 83, 147

Tagore, Abanindranath 16
Tagore, Rabindranath 4, 8, 12, 16, 41n90, 82, 98, 109, 116, 134, 159
Takeyama, Michio 117–20, 123, 185
Tanabe, Hajime 120–1, 125
Tewari, Dudhnath 119
Thapar, Romila 68, 99
Tocqueville, A. 23, 150
Tokyo war crimes trials 121–2
Tönnies, Ferdinand 140
Tripathi, G.M. 160
trusteeship 7–8
Two-Nation Theory 80, 83–4

urbanity 27, 32, 57–8, 61–2, 70, 134–6, 142, 147, 151

Vaidya, C.V. 68–9
Varma, Ravi 72
Vedic culture 20, 49, 52, 74
Versailles, Treaty of 155–6, 159
Vidyasagar (Ishwarchandra) 59, 64
Vishwashakti 9, 19–24, 26, 28, 34, 106–7, 113, 123, 139, 143, 183, 185
Vivekananda 12, 20, 101, 116, 136, 186
Völkisch ideology 2, 65, 124

Washington, Booker T. 6, 24
Webb, Sidney 29
whiteness 18, 23, 55–8, 68, 155, 161, 167
women (and society) 2, 14, 20, 58–60, 65, 101–2, 113, 139–41, 144, 170

Yack, Bernard 133
Yellow Peril 24, 103, 109, 114
Young India 5, 8, 12, 18–20, 26, 28, 33, 105, 108, 123, 138, 146, 161
youth (and children), culture and rights of 2, 8, 12, 32, 58, 60–1, 113, 119, 132, 136, 142–3, 154, 166, 170–1

Zachariah, Benjamin 2, 31
zange 120–1
Zehfuss, Maja 165